T0097960

The Kabbalah Experience

By Rav Michael Laitman PhD

The Kabbalah Experience

LAITMAN
KABBALAH PUBLISHERS

By Rav Michael Laitman PhD

Executive Editor: Benzion Giertz
Editors: Clair Gerus, Irena Zolotova
Translation: David Brushin, Chaim Ratz
Proofreading: Susan Morales Kosinec
Layout: Baruch Khovov

Laitman Kabbalah Publishers Website:
www.kabbalah.info
Laitman Kabbalah Publishers E-mail:
info@kabbalah.info

THE KABBALAH EXPERIENCE

Published by Laitman Kabbalah Publishers,
1057 Steeles Avenue West, Suite 532, Toronto, ON, M2R 3X1, Canada.
Printed in Canada.

ISBN: 0-9738268-0-0
FIRST EDITION: DECEMBER 2005

The Kabbalah Experience

TABLE OF CONTENTS

The wisdom of Kabbalah teaches us how to live in the reality that is spread before us. It is a systematic method that has evolved over thousands of years, taught by a handful of unique individuals in every generation. Their task has been to ensure that the truths of Kabbalah would be given to those ready to receive them.

During all that time, Kabbalah was concealed from the public (which was not yet ready to receive it), until the current generation; it was this generation for which this method was specifically developed. That is why the Zohar, the Ari and Baal HaSulam (Rav Yehuda Ashlag, the author of *HaSulam* (The Ladder), a commentary on the Zohar) reveal that from this time forward, the Kabbalah will become a simple and genuine way of life, open to all, with no restrictions. This approach originated in 1995, and we are currently in the midst of this process to expand the reach of Kabbalah.

Why our generation? Because the souls that descend to this world and dress in our bodies evolve from generation to generation. Ultimately, they will arrive at a point of questioning the meaning of their very existence.

The question will form: "What is the meaning of my life?" or "What am I living for?" It will arise not only if we are in constantly intensifying pain, but also if we are filled with peace, fulfillment and pleasure. When the pain of this question suddenly surfaces, it knocks us flat, before we find the solution in drifting in the currents of everyday life.

Indeed, if we contemplate reality, as described in the books of Kabbalists, that speak of "the end of days" ~which we now face~~we become profoundly fearful that, without the wisdom of the Kabbalah, we will not be able to secure safe passage through the challenging times to come.

The wisdom of the Kabbalah allows us to come to know the "Upper World" – the very system that monitors and leads reality. That includes the reality of this world, the whole of humanity and each and every one of us at any given moment. With the help of Kabbalah, we can control the system of the worlds and determine how to conduct our daily lives, which makes this wisdom necessary for everyone.

Until the year 1995, I was busy opening many Kabbalah classes throughout Israel and around the world. As a result, I was presented with an ever-growing number of questions, until I could no longer answer them by ordinary correspondence. Therefore, I decided to set up an Internet site and supply the answers to those requesting them, along with more general knowledge of man and his existence in the world.

The web site quickly developed and expanded, and today over a million people from all corners of the world visit it every month. They download information about the method of Kabbalah and the way to conduct their lives, in addition to submitting numerous questions through email and online discussion forums. They come with private questions and general questions alike.

Still, I often meet new people – in lectures or in more informal discussions – who have not discovered this valuable method, even though the question "What is the meaning of my life?" burns in the heart of every one of them.

All of them seek a clear and scientific answer they can comprehend. Therefore, I have decided to gather all the postings that have accumulated on the forum and publish them. From the multitude of material before me, I have chosen those questions and answers, by which anyone can make their first steps in Kabbalah.

People like you, whose point in the heart (the point that makes us wonder about the meaning of life) has awakened, sent me these questions. This book will give you insights into the path they followed, from the urgent question, "What is the meaning of my life?" "How do I control my destiny?" and "What should I expect of every single act in my daily life?" to the concise answers they received.

These answers are based on a clear and independent vision that evolved in all of them after studying the Upper Forces through the wisdom of Kabbalah. The path each of them took is a personal one, suiting none but them. But through the answers that I provided, based on thousands of years of research and development of the wisdom of Kabbalah, you, too, can discover your personal path.

Be aware that the deeper you go, the more questions will arise, which are answered directly from the Source. That is ultimately what will advance you. Remember, success depends on you alone.

I am with you all the way.

Rav Michael Laitman

CHAPTER 1.
THE THOUGHT OF CREATION

MAN - THE PURPOSE OF CREATION

Q: Many have tried to solve the riddle of the purpose of creation – why we come into this world, why we live and die. What is the purpose of creation according to the Kabbalah and how can one attain it?

A: Man is the center of creation and is its purpose. The Creator created mankind and wishes to raise human beings to the highest possible degree: that of the Creator.

The process of "the attainment of the Creator," meaning getting to know the Creator's attributes, is a means for correction. It is also the very purpose of creation because attaining the Creator, unlike a scientific process, is the gratification and satisfaction given by the Creator. According to the Kabbalah, mankind is the whole of creation (or the First Man). After he was born, he shattered into 600,000 parts. Each part corrects itself independently by equalizing itself with the Creator. Each and every creature must consciously go through that process.

The correction of each part makes it possible to fill it with the Light of the Creator, meaning to feel the Creator. The sensation that the Creator fills you up is a new sensation. It is in that sensation that you will find the spiritual worlds.

Our goal is to be entirely filled up with the Creator. However, as of now, our souls are in a state called "this world," where the Creator is not felt, but is concealed and hidden from them.

When the soul perceives contact with the Creator for the first time, it rises to its first spiritual degree. It then begins to make itself resemble the Creator more and more, and thus feel Him more and more intensively. When all the parts are completely corrected, they will rise to a state defined as "the end of correction."

Q: What will happen if humanity refuses to accept the purpose of creation and objects to its goal? Will the Creator have to destroy and recreate humanity?

A: We have nothing to be afraid of, because even your question comes from the Creator! Man has but the ability to say, "If I am not for me, who is for me?"

This means we must act as though the Creator does not exist, and afterwards, when all is said and done, to ascribe everything to the Creator, from the very first thought to the final act. Everything is planned ahead. Your entire path is set in advance. You are already in your final state; you just cannot feel it yet. All that depends on you is how fast you advance toward the goal. If you read more, the rest will follow. You will see that there is no other way.

Questions of the type you describe arise because we are weak and uncorrected. However, the Creator sees the end and the beginning tied together as one; thus, there is no need for any further action. Everything that happens, happens only inside us, as we eventually sense each occurrence. Outside us, everything is permanent, perfect and eternal.

THE "CORRECTION"

Q: What is the correction, and who must be corrected?

A: The desire to enjoy that was created by the Creator is called a "creature," or the "substance" of creation. However, this desire cannot be fulfilled in its primary form, because as soon as one is filled with pleasure, the joy vanishes. The intent of the Creator from the start was to make the desire complete. However, this only happens when the intent resembles the Creator's attribute of bestowal by one's free choice. Because this attribute is not limited in its use by emotions, man can attain perfection and eternity.

Man, the objective of creation, is obliged to transform the will for self-enjoyment into the will to please the Creator. When one acquires this intent, the desire to enjoy becomes equal to the Creator's desire to give. In conclusion, the creature brings self to perfection by the correct use of its only attribute - the reception of pleasure.

Changing the intent of one's desire involves several phases:

1. Avoiding using desire in its original form.

2. Isolating from one's desire to enjoy only those desires worthy, in quantity and quality, to be used to please the Creator.

3. Spiritually coupling with, and discovering, the Creator. (Possible only through the isolation of the desire, with a corrected aim).

The first two corrections are called "circumcision," and, like all other corrections, are not performed by the creature but by the Creator, meaning a higher spiritual degree than his current one. The creature never has the strength to perform a self-correction. Man's goal is simply to arrive at the desire to be corrected - to send out a prayer, a plea for correction - and the Upper Degree (the Creator) will perform it.

THE EVOLUTION OF HUMANITY

Q: Why did the Kabbalah remain, much like all Jewish thought, in the margins of the development of the cultural world, without influencing the advancement of humanity, as did western philosophy? After all, the Kabbalah sees as its goal the correction of mankind.

A: The purpose of creation is to bring the soul, meaning the whole of mankind, with all of its parts, to a state where its every movement is in harmony with the Creator, who is our criterion for perfection. But first, humanity must go through all the opposite situations in order to realize that, indeed, only the Creator is complete.

Culture and science are only vessels given to us to reveal that we and all around us are destined for adhesion with the Creator. That is our destiny~the highest degree of evolution we must reach.

The Kabbalah, as the whole of the Torah, must still be revealed to mankind. The time has not yet come for this to occur, and only in our time are souls that possess a genuine demand for spiritual development descending to this plane.

INTEREST IN THE PURPOSE OF CREATION

Q: Why are so few people asking themselves questions about creation? How can people be made more interested in learning the purpose of creation?

A: Our world – with its history of torment and its achievements, and the spiritual worlds, with all their substance –- is nothing in comparison to what man is about to discover. The vast magnitude of the design of creation is incomprehensible to a human being.

Billions of people live their lives in our world so that a few dozen will attain the correct concept of the Creator, and from those dozens, only a few will attain Him. But out of those dozens, even those who test themselves in Kabbalah are already chosen ones.

The Kabbalah is revealed from Above; it evolves slowly and will, at some point, burst into everyone's awareness, offering a clear goal for the lives of each of us. Billions of people will actually participate in this process.

THE STATE OF HUMANITY

Q: Relative to the spiritual world, what is humanity's position?

A: Man's place in the Upper World depends solely on the power of the screen that he attained. This, in turn, is determined only by the distance from the state where all of man's desires are in this world, with the aim "for me," and by the nearness to the degree of the Creator, meaning the intent "for Him."

Q: To the best of my understanding, there is always only one man on earth, who is in the Upper World, higher than all other Kabbalists. Who is that man today?

A: It is said: "Israel is not widowed," and also, "There is not a generation when there are no such men as Abraham, Isaac and Jacob."

There are hidden Kabbalists in the world known only to the Kabbalists themselves, and then there are recognized Kabbalists. All of them work in this world and perform their tasks according to the instructions of the Creator.

Their business is only their own and the Creator's. We need not know of their work because we should only deal with what we were born to accomplish: correcting ourselves.

For true correction, we must choose a place that we feel in our hearts is exactly the right place for us. This need not be because of the presence of a great teacher, one who is highly regarded by others, and not because he is eloquent and knowledgeable. One must choose a place where things are spoken that one wishes to know in one's heart.

My advice to you is, search in your heart; be honest with yourself. Agree to nothing, not even the smallest thing, if you do not think it's right, because the soul must find the place where it will be corrected. And when the soul begins to develop from a point into a complete vessel of ten *Sefirot*, then you will feel the Kabbalists.

You will know them, you will be with them, and you will receive the answers to all your questions.

THE PERFECTION OF CREATION

Q: What is perfection and how can it be attained?

A: Perfection is something that cannot be explained, but can be attained! It is possible, however, to explain what characterizes it. There can be only one perfection, never two – either one or both of them are incomplete.

Creation is the state of the Creator because the Creator is unique and supreme. Is it possible to attain the Creator? That is the purpose of the life of each and every one of us. The method by which we can attain perfection is called Kabbalah. If you start to study it, you will feel the most wondrous sensations.

The whole difference between man and beast is that man has the freedom of choice. In the directive, "Therefore, choose life (Deuteronomy 30, 19)" the term, "life," refers to adhesion with the attributes of the Creator.

Q: If, as you say, we have to resemble the Creator, why not aspire to peace?

A: The Creator is in a state of "complete rest" because He is in a perfect situation and does not require any change. You want peace as well, but shame and its other manifestations - vanity, or the quest for knowledge or power–compel you to move on. Your situation is not complete, and therefore, if you do nothing, you are regarded as lazy.

To aspire to your root means to aspire to its perfection. Peace is a result of that perfection.

THE CONCEALMENT OF THE CREATOR

Q: If the Creator is benevolent and wants us to enjoy ourselves, then what is the source of our pain?

A: The Creator is the only source of everything that exists. Where could anything else come from? Because only perfection comes from the Creator, when it encounters man –who holds opposite attributes to those of the Creator – that perfection is felt as the opposite of what it is: imperfection and, in fact, torment. This phenomenon is called "the concealment of the Creator," and herein lies man's problem.

Our task, therefore, is to resemble the Creator by correcting ourselves, so that His influence on us will be felt in its true form, as benevolence. In that state, we should naturally equalize ourselves in every attribute with the Creator, and if one of our attributes is not yet complete, we will naturally feel (to that extent) the influence of the Creator as incomplete.

In order to prevent us from sinning (by accusing and cursing the Creator), so as not to distance us further still from Him (as with impure powers), The Creator hides from us. As long as we feel unhappy, we cannot see that everything comes from the Creator, and only when we begin to feel good, does the Creator reveal Himself as the source of that goodness.

Q: If the torments are a means that aid man, why is it said that the desire to suffer comes from impure forces?

A: I don't understand the term, "means that aid man." It is an expression that praises pain, something which is completely contrary to the purpose of creation. The purpose of creation is to delight us. Pain is an undesirable feeling to the Creator, and its purpose is only to force us to connect to the path of correction.

The sensation of pain distances us from the Creator. It is sent only to shock us, who otherwise desire only rest. By our nature, we operate by the law of maximum pleasure for minimum effort. But when pain forces us to wake up and remember the goal, by searching for the source of the pain, then we should immediately turn to the Creator, as this was the sole purpose for which the pain was sent.

At the end of correction, when we will have used all our powers and desires correctly, there will be no room for even the smallest hint of pain. On the contrary, we will feel wholeness, pleasure and serenity.

THE MEANING OF AGONY

Q: Why does the Creator force His creatures to suffer if He really wants to endow them with "eternal heaven?"

A: Man has asked that question since he was first created and in every generation since. There is no answer to this question.

Rav Yehuda Ashlag writes that it is impossible to understand the outcome of a process or assess it correctly when we are at its beginning, or its middle. Only after we have gone the whole way, and are at the end of the process, can we relate correctly to everything that happened along the way.

There is a good reason for the popular saying, "Do not show a full job half done." Only those who go the whole way will acquire enough wisdom to correctly appreciate everything that has occurred.

Moving forward along the spiritual path creates the sensations we need to help us attain the final result: the sensation of eternity and perfection. It cannot be any other way.

So why didn't the Creator create us complete and eternal to begin with? If He had done so, we would not have been able to feel the perfection and eternity! Along the way, before we come to free choice between our situation and the spiritual situation, we gradually learn to actually appreciate spirituality and make the choice to bring it into our lives.

At that point, spiritual perfection and eternity become desirable and we really do delight in them.

Q: What is the meaning of agony?

A: In answer to this question, I'd like to quote the words of Rav Yehuda Ashlag in his "Introduction to The Study of the Ten Sefirot." Here, he explains why he wrote that book.

"Indeed, if we set our hearts to answer just one famous question, I am sure that all the questions and doubts will vanish from sight and you will look unto their place, and they will be gone. It is the indignant question, asked by all the people in the world, which is: "What is the meaning of our lives?" Meaning, this number of years we have been given, which cost us so heavily, meaning the multitude of pain that we suffer for them, in order to complete them, who is it who enjoys it, or better phrased, whom do I delight?

And it is true that researchers have grown weary of delving over it, and all the more so in our generation, when no one wants to even consider it. Yet, the question still remains as valid and as bitter as ever. And there are times it meets us uninvited, and pokes our mind and throws us to the ground, before we find the old subterfuge to be carried senselessly in the currents of life as always." (Introduction to The Study of the Ten Sefirot, item 2).

After that, the writer explains that only when we learn how to master our own destinies do we receive the answer to that question.

OPEN QUESTIONS

Q: Why does the Creator hide the spiritual world from us?

A: I like your question a lot because it indicates a quest for spirituality. What do you think? Why haven't people found these answers for thousands of years? Or perhaps they have found the answer, but they hid it from us! How is it that so many intelligent people~philosophers, scientists, and researchers~cannot answer man's most important questions?

In fact, why can't we answer it ourselves? Why does the Creator hide these answers from us? Notice that He hides the answers, but He doesn't hide the questions! On the contrary, it is He who makes you ask them, which is why human beings can ask them and taste their bitterness. Read the "Introduction to The Study of the Ten Sefirot" from Item two onward.

THE SPIRITUAL ROOT

Q: Do we influence our position in the spiritual world? Is this the goal of the Correction?

A: In our spiritual root, in *Malchut* of the world, *Ein Sof*, we exist in an eternal, completely corrected situation, which does not change. We have to come to that state by ourselves, through our desire and our consciousness that the root is the single most perfect and desirable situation for us.

We have no influence over the root itself, because the inferior can never influence or change the superior. On the contrary, the inferior is completely dependent on the superior.

How was the connection between the Upper Worlds and the souls formed there? *Malchut* in the world *Ein Sof* (our root) was blended with the first nine *Sefirot* (attributes of the Creator). The Light grew dimmer and finally vanished, and the worlds were created. That part of *Malchut*, which is included in the worlds, is called "*Malchut* of the Worlds."

At the same time, the first nine *Sefirot* influenced *Malchut*. They were mixed in it, and in this way the soul of the first man was created. Thus was contact between the worlds and the souls formed, based on those nine *Sefirot*.

Q: Does creation belong solely to the Creator? Can man have any effect on it?

A: Man has free choice. He comes to a situation where he can freely do anything he wants, but still choose the way of the Creator. This happens when, during man's evolution, he completely agrees with, and recognizes, that the Creator and His actions are perfection. In this way, man resembles the Creator, is equal with Him, and is completely corrected as He is.

Q: I understand that creatures should come to adhesion with the Creator. But that situation is eternal and exists from the very beginning, and time is but a corporeal term. So what has actually changed?

A: Adhesion with the Creator did exist in the world *Ein Sof*, but at the expense of the Creator, who created that situation by Himself. In order for the creature to attain the same situation, he must exert his own efforts, out of his own free will. For that, he needs to disconnect entirely from the Creator, the Light, and to stop feeling Him so as not to be under His influence.

Only then, only out of free choice, will man gradually correct himself through developing the screen, thus attaining equivalence of form with the Creator, to the point of *Ein Sof*, meaning the absolute equivalence with the Creator.

Q: I understand that, just as two hairs cannot grow from the same root, so two objects in this world cannot stem from the same spiritual root. Each creation has its own spiritual root. But I thought that everything came from the same root – Keter?

A: You are right, everything does come from the Creator and then descends to the world of *Atzilut*, where the system of the management and the correction of the soul of the First Man (meaning our souls) is formed.

The three lower worlds to *Atzilut* (*Beria, Yetzira, Assiya*) were created in its image. These worlds are a diminished, yet accurate image of the world of *Atzilut*. Our world was created much like those worlds.

Everything that exists in any of the four worlds descends from the world of *Atzilut*. By the same path, the soul rises from our world to *Atzilut*. We attain the world of *Atzilut* by replacing our attributes, which are called "our world," with attributes called "the world of *Atzilut*." This is our goal in this world, and everyone must follow it.

The degree, the attributes, the place to which we all must rise, is called "our root." The present degree is the place where we are at the given moment, the place where our "I" is, which is called a "branch." Each root has its own branch.

THE SENSATION OF THE RECEIVER

Q: Why did the Creator make His creation feel deficient upon receiving?

A: He did so in order to awaken in us the need to change our intent to receive into intent to give. Only to those whom the Creator wants near Him does He send the sensation that they receive from Him.

In order to feel it, one must first rise to the degree of the revelation of the Creator, to feel Him as the Giver. Man can ask for that revelation because it is for the purpose of correction, not for pleasure.

The host offers his guest food and drink. All the guest actually wants is the food, but along with his desire (vessel) and the future pleasure (the Light), there is yet another sensation – the presence of the host, the giver. Because of that, he feels himself as a receiver, a taker. That sensation is so unpleasant that it overshadows the pleasure of eating the food.

THE FEELING OF SHAME

Q: Why did creation, *Malchut* of the world *Ein Sof,* feel shame, if the Creator doesn't mind which way it receives?

A: You are right. There is indifference on the Creator's part, but not on the creature's part. Creation was formed in such a way that shame is built into it, and the creature must neutralize that feeling. In fact, in our current condition, we are unfamiliar with that sensation; it is not in us, because it can be felt only between the corrupted and corrected attributes of *Malchut.*

We do not have them: they are the sensations of the receiver and the giver. We do not even understand what it means to give or to receive, because in order to feel it, you must possess those two attributes. Everything we feel comes out of comparison with an opposite, but within us are no attributes of the Creator, and thus we can neither feel nor understand the attributes of creation.

THE END OF MATTER

Q: Will the physical world vanish at the end of correction? Is *Malchut* of *Malchut* the material world? Are the souls that do not have a screen always in it?

A: Kabbalah speaks of desires and intents. There is not a single word in Kabbalah that refers to our world, meaning physical bodies.

Creation was made with the desire for pleasure and there are only two participants in it: the soul and the Creator. That is unchangeable!

The intent can be "for me" or "for the Creator." The desire finds the intent "for me" if it does not feel the Creator, and the intent "for the Creator," if it does feel Him.

On the one hand, it is possible to feel the Creator only after you are equipped with an intent for the Creator, but on the other hand, you can only get such an intent through the revelation of the Creator, through the sensation of the Light.

The miracle of the attainment of the screen, the intent for the Creator, hides within that very contradiction. That is why it is said that we must make great efforts in everything we are told to do, such as studying, circulation, teaching others, etc. But we cannot tell in advance which way salvation will come.

Desires in our world are independent of the intent. Our desire for pleasure does not come from the spiritual Light, from the Creator, but from a "Minute Light," which takes the form of this world: sex, wealth, power and knowledge.

The spiritual desire is to delight in the Light, in the Creator. If that desire is self-oriented in its intent, it is considered impure and is called a "shell." If it is a Creator-oriented desire, it is considered pure and is called "holiness."

Therefore, in the beginning, through the influence of proper study and labor, a desire to enjoy spirituality for self develops, and one begins to want the Upper World, the Creator, instead of this world. When that desire reaches its peak, we receive a screen, and only then does our desire become a part of *Malchut* (of the world of *Atzilut*).

Even if we are immersed in impure desires, they are still spiritual because we still want to delight in the spiritual pleasure, the Creator, and not earthly pleasures such as sex, wealth or power.

COMPLETE ADHESION WITH THE CREATOR

Q: When *Malchut* cleaves to the Creator in its final state, does that state last until it is completely nullified within the Creator, or does creation remain separated nonetheless?

A: It is impossible to explain in words the complete adhesion, which is complete in the unity of thoughts and qualities. But the intent of one toward the other is not gone, and herein lies the difference. Creation is not nullified within the Creator, but remains active for Him. It would have been nullified if it had not acquired a screen on the desire.

We see that the Will and the goal of the Creator is for creation to remain independent in its thoughts, and equal to the Creator in strength, will power and intent.

ACHIEVEMENTS OF CIVILIZATION

Q: I understand that my question may sound stupid, but I wish to know: if we imagine that the world starts to improve, will there still be a place for science? Will studying outer space, chemistry, and mathematics be rejected by humanity? Will the world return to the natural economy? Isn't such a world destined to decay and die out?

A: It's a very interesting question. I am also a researcher, a scientist by nature. We each seem to believe that our approach to nature, to the world around us is correct, thus allowing us to exist in it. We can't even imagine that there may be a different and better way of receiving the abundance of nature.

We are constantly worried about how to grab as much as we can from nature and feel upset at the thought that soon we'll run out of natural resources. We are struggling to hold on to the loot.

But everything should be different. If the Upper Light could reach our world, we would be able to receive simply, without struggle, by using our spiritual powers. Now, however, we are forced to receive through the shells, snatching from them tiny sparks of Light for sustenance. That is why all our lives are spent chasing after desired pleasures and not "only good pursued me all the days of my life" (Psalms).

Through blood, we learn the laws of nature in order to use them later in a barbarous manner. But if we could learn them through our resemblance to the spiritual nature, we'd have those laws inside us and could fulfill our desires without the need for physical action.

We wouldn't need billions of unnecessary things, nor would we miss them, as we would be happy without them, and without many other things that will be made by people in the future without making them any happier.

The science of the world would be studied from within, but not by our sketchy experience or by chance discoveries. We would know nature in its perfect harmony and relationships, and learn how to use it wisely.

Today, however, all scientific and technical discoveries bring harm to man, since they only show us how imperfectly we have developed. Hence we can only conclude that all human activity should be strictly determined by its intention for the Creator.

If our intention matches the goal of creation, then we'll develop pleasantly. If not, we will suffer, but only to reveal the evil inside us, to understand and correct it, ultimately achieving the same goal through anguish.

WHY IS RECEIVING FOR MYSELF EVIL?

Q: If "the Creator made a world in order to bestow His abundance to the created beings," then what's wrong with wanting to receive everything "for oneself?" Why is it perceived as evil? Why was it necessary to create a world so imperfect, and a creation so incorrect?

A: The Creator wishes to bestow. Therefore, He created only a desire to enjoy. But in order to enjoy, a desire must not disappear after receiving pleasure.

Pleasure must not destroy desire. Desire must be intact, despite the received pleasure, possibly even growing, searching for new greater pleasures.

Therefore, desire and pleasure must dwell in different objects. For example, consider a mother endlessly caring for her child because her pleasure is in him and not in herself. In contrast, if someone wants to enjoy something, that person receives the pleasure, but doing so immediately extinguishes the desire, and the feeling of pleasure disappears. That is why it is only by living to fulfill another's desires that we can feel never-ending, unlimited (by duration, volume) pleasure.

Therefore, the Creator's Will, which created beings that must bestow upon Him, is simply a precondition for receiving endless, eternal pleasure.

But there's one more result to that action: since we match our actions to those of the Creator, we become like Him and begin to feel what the Creator feels, i.e., we reach His level. And this is not just feeling eternal unlimited pleasure; it is the attainment of a totally different existence.

This existence is called "the goal of creation," because the Creator will never leave us alone until we reach that level - every single one of us, and all of us together.

Why didn't He create us in that state to begin with? Why must man go through so much suffering in order to feel this level? Because we can feel something only out of its opposite. Moreover, the greater the difference between the states, the stronger and more intense the feelings. Hence, reaching the Creator's level compels us to go through states quite opposite to His: humbleness, emptiness, darkness and suffering.

If it's impossible to avoid them, where can we get strength to go through all this? Are tragedies, catastrophes, destruction and pogroms unavoidable? From one generation to another, until the cup of anguish is full to the brink, can't we arrive at tranquility and perfection? Where is the great and perfect Creator?

Our complaints would only be fair if we were not given the instructions for achieving the goal. Kabbalah was given to correct us, to make us like the Creator. By studying how we can change ourselves, we can do so quickly and enter the state of perfection and eternity now, in this world, and in this lifetime.

Kabbalah reveals us to ourselves against the spiritual Light surrounding us, thus forcing us to feel ashamed and humble before the Light (the Creator) prior to physical suffering, and accelerate the emerging desire to get rid of our evil nature, and acquire the perfect properties of the Creator.

By starting to study Kabbalah, we can reach the state of perfection and eternity within three to five years (ideally, and within six to ten years normally). Keep asking those questions.

THE PURPOSE OF CREATION

Q: Are we seeing an incorrect world?

A: The Creator started creation. To be more precise, He created a world of "evil," or corruption. But man finishes creation, meaning man corrects it. Because man has the ability to lead the world, the Creator passes on to him the leadership of creation. The Creator increases the pressure on us to make us take the leadership upon ourselves. That is why the world around us is so bad; the Creator made it so, in order that we begin to correct it.

Q: Can you prove that Kabbalah aims us toward the purpose of creation?

A: Kabbalah is based solely on experimentation, and not on the human mind, or even on philosophy or other rational considerations. It maintains that everything that stems from logic and contemplation lacks any real basis. That is because our minds are a result of our desires, our nature. Therefore, it is impossible for us to discuss anything objectively or impartially.

An ordinary person who is not a Kabbalist can never discuss anything objectively, but only from a personal perspective. Such people cannot exit the boundaries of our world into a wider and more general world.

Those who are endowed with such abilities become Kabbalists. That means they receive higher knowledge about the whole of reality, they see and understand the general laws of nature and where they lead the universe. Those who do not enter the shared space of the universe cannot understand what purpose we are discussing. They are born; they live and beget children who are like them, and then they die, unconscious as ever.

That is why Kabbalah, as a science, refuses to describe the real system of the universe, as well as our purpose, on the basis of man's current false understanding. Rather, Kabbalah takes man out to another space of feeling first, to another outlook on the universe. And those who go by the wisdom of Kabbalah can see that Kabbalah aims at the purpose of creation.

The role of each of us is like the role of the whole universe, because in us are all the components of the universe. Kabbalah teaches this to us when we study the Breaking of the Vessels, which occurred prior to our creation.

As a result of that shattering, all the parts of all the souls got mixed together, so that each soul contains parts of every other soul. This is the source of the mutual responsibility and the reciprocal bond between all mankind that is a major focus of Kabbalah.

A single individual cannot exit to the spiritual world. This would be like one individual beginning to develop the whole of physics or chemistry, and then starting to use these sciences. It would be similar to living like a Neanderthal without using all that humanity has achieved thus far, before attaining that knowledge by one's own resources.

It is for this reason that a beginning student needs a teacher who has already attained the Upper World, and can show the student how to attain each step to develop towards the Upper World. The teacher is a spiritual connection to the student, but the student will understand it only after attaining the Upper World independently.

Unity with the teacher can occur in the preliminary stages because both bodies are on this worldly level. But unity with the Creator is only possible when one goes out to the Upper World. That is why contact with a teacher leads to a contact with the Creator. The teacher is the leader.

Kabbalah explains incarnation as a dressing of souls in new bodies after they have rid themselves of old bodies. That means that the souls of the previous generation dress in new bodies, and thus the new generation appears on earth. Each new generation is made of the same souls robed in newly born physical bodies.

Physical bodies are born, live and die. After their death they go from a stage of animation to a stage of stillness... and that's it. Nothing else happens with those bodies.

Nothing of what the protein body had is re-lived in the new body. A "body" in Kabbalah is a body of a soul – the desire to be filled with Upper Light.

For this reason, we must understand that when the Torah speaks of the soul exiting the body, it refers to the Light leaving the body of the soul. When it says that the soul returns to the body, it means that the Light has returned to fill the soul after its "will to receive" has died, been corrected and became a will to bestow.'

And when it says that a body has been revived, it refers to a will to receive that was once uncorrected, not spiritual; meaning "spiritually dead."

The Kabbalah teaches that the term, "incarnation," refers to the soul, not to the physiological body. The fact that we relate to a corpse with so much respect is because we must relate to everything in this world in accordance with the Upper World. But my teacher would say that he doesn't care where and how his bag of bones will be buried.

There will come a time when the whole of humanity will open its eyes and will see both at the level that it does today, and a greater space, one that Kabbalists call the "spiritual world." That state is called "the coming of the Messiah."

Then, everyone will change their egoistic natures (their bodies) into the nature of the spiritual sphere, a giving nature. Kabbalah calls that process "the revival of the dead."

How can we reach the Creator? We accumulate experience over our cycles in this world and evolve to the level that we are able to begin to develop consciously toward spirituality. In so doing, we learn to oppose unconscious development, as we have been led through by our past cycles. When we attain that certain level, a special desire begins to awaken within us.

All of our desires are to enjoy in this world, but this new desire demands pleasure from a Source of Light, from a spiritual pleasure that cannot be found in our world. That desire pushes us to search for the Source of that pleasure, to seek and find the Creator. The soul is what leads us from that time on.

CONNECTION BETWEEN SUFFERING AND THE GOAL OF CREATION

Q: I can't find an answer to a very important question. How does physical suffering lead to the emerging of spiritual desires and needs? What's the connection?

A: One comes to Kabbalah with the question, "What is the sense of my life?" Then, one begins to study, and draw the surrounding Light that activates the desire for the goal of Creation (and not for some imaginary "spiritual spheres").

There is no difference in various kinds of suffering; the distinction is only external, in their raiment. They all exist due to the lack of Light in the desire. Similarly, all kinds of pleasure come from the Light, regardless of the fact that we feel them in different objects.

OBTAINING LIGHT

Q: How does the Upper Light reach us?

A: The Light that comes to us is so dim, we cannot perceive it. We can only recognize it within the objects we are attracted to, because it is dressed in them. That way, we can receive the Light and enjoy it for our own purposes, but only to that extent, and only at that degree of power.

In order to feel that Light at least as much as those who are in a state of clinical death, we must detach ourselves from our desire to take pleasure. That is exactly what happens to them, and that is why they feel the Upper Light openly.

But even if we completely detach ourselves from our bodies and take on another form, we will feel the Upper One, eternal and perfect, to a lesser degree than we can feel Him in this body in this world. This is because we are in this world and in this body, and can detach from it and rise with our souls to the Highest Degree.

We are able to receive the Light by using a system called, "three lines." The "left line" is the accumulation of all of our desires to please ourselves. The "right line" is the attributes of the Creator. It is clear that a person does not begin by feeling them immediately.

When we study the books of Kabbalah that are written in a special system, we attract a "Surrounding Light." We will be able to feel that Light inside us later on and receive it in the form of pleasure.

However, until we are ready, that Light remains around us, concealed, and waits for us to be ready to receive it. Kabbalists are people who receive that Light openly. Their writing leaves the contact they have with the Light within the text.

Therefore, when we study from a book written by a genuine Kabbalist and in the right system, we can draw in a more effective illumination of surrounding Light, which cleanses the soul and prepares us to receive the Light.

Then, we can be filled with the Upper Light and feel ourselves whole and eternal. But the correction under the influence of the Surrounding Light is done gradually, and in portions.

To the extent that we absorb the attributes of the Light, we correct ourselves, our left line, and become able to receive the Light. Those portions of correction are called the "degrees" or "rungs" of the ladder, the spiritual ladder, which raise a person from the sensation of our world, the sensation of ourselves, to the sensation of the next, the sensation of the Creator.

The middle line is the best possible combination between man's receiving nature and the forces of the Upper Light. It coordinates between them in such a way that a person will self-correct to resemble the Light as much as possible, while still maintaining one's independence.

ON ADAM AND THE WORLD

Q: How should the term *Adam ha Rishon* ("the First Man") be understood – is it a spiritual entity (related to the world of *Adam Kadmon*) or literally a man of flesh and blood in our world? What about all the people before *Adam ha Rishon*?

Also, how does it correlate with the sciences dealing with the origin of man?

I read in your books that all objects and interrelations are ultimately realized in specific people on Earth. So is it literally the first man, or is it the first man to have a screen?

A: The universe and humanity are eternal. There is neither beginning nor end to the development of matter. The formation of the universe is a consequence of the development of the spiritual world. The creation of man stems from the development of spiritual objects, which upon descending in degrees materialize into the lowest forms – the objects of this world.

Of course, we have developed from the more primitive forms, but not by natural (Darwinian) selection. Our development came about by the surfacing *Reshimot* – spiritual genes.

The first manifestation of the point in the heart is *Adam* in this world.

Its first development into sensing the Creator is Abraham.

The first manifestation of the method of uniting with the root is the receiving of the Torah.

I can say only one thing in response to your question: until the point in your heart manifests and forms the first ten *Sefirot*, you will be absolutely unable to understand where you come from and where everything is headed! No explanation will help, since there is no vessel to receive it.

TWO LAWS OF CREATION

Q: Who is the Creator?

A: The wisdom of Kabbalah, which studies the collective law of creation, uses words such as God, Creator, and Emanator, as technical names for forces, lights and degrees. The names, Creator and Emanator, are similar in definition.

For example: each upper degree is called "Creator" when relating to the degree below it, because the upper degree creates, controls, and develops the lower degree.

Creator is also a collective name for everything that exists, besides the souls, which are called "creatures."

The Creator is a collective, special Force that monitors the whole system of creation. That Force is one and unique. In Kabbalah there is but one primary law – the law of creation, which is to delight the creatures in any way the creatures can be delighted. All other laws stem from that one law, and everything that happens does so in the carrying out of that law. Everything that happens at any given moment in creation, its sole purpose is to make people come to the point of utter bliss – to be filled with the Light of the Creator.

The Creator acts much like gravity: in the center of creation is the Creator. The souls were distanced five worlds away from Him. These include AK (*Adam Kadmon*), *Atzilut*, *Beria*, *Yetzira* and *Assiya*, all the way to the farthest point called "our world." From that last point, He pulls us toward Him.

We sense that pull as pain – beginning with disease and ending in painful death. But if we make an effort to approach the Creator by co-operating with that Force, we will not feel the pain. Instead, we will feel that Force as good. If, however, we refuse to go along with that pulling Force, we will feel pain, disease and other troubles to the same extent that we resist it.

The wisdom of Kabbalah enables us to realize ourselves in such a way that we will always, under any condition, be in accordance with that gravity, and thus come to the center of creation. That is the reason that Kabbalah is the most practical science for learning how to live well.

To equalize with the Creator means to be equal to Him in every manifestation. It does not refer to the Upper Force itself, but to how He relates to things, how He appears before us, within us, as a Supreme Power, as Essence, in the way that He wants us to feel Him.

The Creator created us through His wish to give, to bestow. He created our will to receive exactly in the amount that He wanted to give. That is why we must attain everything that He wants to give us – eternity, strength, perfection, total control. This means we must assume all the duties of the Creator.

The primary law of creation is the singularity of the Creator–the one and only power that controls everything. "There is none else beside Him."

The second law of creation is that the Creator is totally benevolent. We cannot settle the contradiction between these two laws as they appear in our conception of reality.

To Kabbalists, this is not an "idea," but a fact they discover within their sensation of the Creator. People cannot begin to understand how there could have been a holocaust if there is a Creator, because they do not feel Him! In fact, the benevolence of the Creator appears only in our corrected desires (vessels). If we are not corrected, then to the extent of the corruption compared to the Light, we will feel the opposite of the goodness of the Creator, feeling torment instead of happiness.

Q: Can you explain the terms *Lishma* and *Lo Lishma*?

A: *Lishma* (for Her name) and *Lo Lishma* (not for Her name): The depth of these terms is immeasurable. The essence of the term, *Lishma*, is found in the words themselves: all the efforts, the aims – only for the Creator. He is the one who receives the results of my efforts.

There is another term: "not in order to be rewarded," which is at an even higher degree, when there seems to be no connection between me and the reward, when all the joy comes not to me, but to the Creator.

I am in the present, below the barrier, below the degree of *Lishma*. That is why I cannot understand the sentence "to work for someone else, without any benefit for myself." After all, regardless of what I think of the reward, I always work for myself.

WHY STUDY?

Q: Why should I study?

A: While we are working *Lo Lishma*, we cannot perceive that our actual purpose can be the opposite of our apparent intentions. That is where the question, "Why study?" comes from. When someone is still unable to see and understand that one must try to go against the mainstream of this world, I say: keep living like everyone else, because you have not yet evolved enough to aim for something higher than this world.

Such doubts about the rightness of the way can also come to advanced students who have already arrived at a certain spiritual level. They must continue to study the wisdom of Kabbalah with perseverance despite the obstacles they encounter, "as an ox for a burden and as a donkey to the burden." Only one who insists on believing can progress, regardless of any reasoning.

DESIRE FOR SPIRITUALITY

Q: What is the "point in the heart" and do we all have it?

A: Every person has a point in the heart, but many people still don't feel it, because they haven't matured enough to feel it. During one's life cycles, one comes to a situation where the point in the heart is revealed. One then begins to feel a desire for spirituality, for the Upper One.

If one currently does not show interest in the spiritual world, then one is still not ready for it, and it would be coercion to try to forcefully awaken that desire.

But if one does feel a need to discover the Upper World, then we must help such a person. There cannot be coercion in either case. Kabbalists always say that only a person who cannot do without Kabbalah can study it.

THE POINT IN THE HEART

Q: Is the development of the point in the heart considered spiritual work with the intent "not for Her name?"

A: Developing the point in the heart consists of several steps:
Working *Lo Lishma*.
Working *Lishma*.
Working "not in order to be rewarded."
We don't know...

The work *Lo Lishma* also contributes to the development of the point in the heart. It develops the point under the influence of the group and the teacher below the barrier. Therefore, *Lo Lishma* is a conscious advancement toward the purpose of creation, as much as one can be aware of it when the Creator is in fact still completely hidden.

There is not a single word in Kabbalah about the situation that precedes the appearance of the point in the heart. In that situation, both the religious and the secular prefer the literal part of the Torah.

When a person's point in the heart is inactive, and there is no desire to develop it, the Torah serves only to assure one of eventual rewards ~ both in this world and in the next.

Such a state is not regarded as *Lishma* or *Lo Lishma*. There isn't even a name for it. It is simply a way of satisfying man's need for self-assurance, justifying his existence.

"Not for Her name" is a situation where one has already discovered the point in the heart, and has begun to develop it. At the beginning of the spiritual work, a person develops the point in the heart, but one's thoughts are still divided between spiritual work and mundane affairs.

Q: Is *Lo Lishma* a kind of correction?

A: *Lo Lishma* means that a person begins to work with the objective of receiving a reward, while still developing the point in the heart. To the extent that one is able to changing one's attributes to resemble those of the Creator, one understands the meaning of the spiritual degree *Lishma*, from its first appearance to the very highest and complete attainment. That percentage constitutes the degrees of spiritual advancement.

Q: Is there a barrier between *Lo Lishma* and *Lishma*?

A: *Lo Lishma* is a spiritual state that precedes the barrier (the entrance to the spiritual world). *Lishma* is the spiritual state one achieves after the crossing of the barrier. Between those two states there is a period when we restrict our intentions and try not to fulfill them. Instead, we want to advance toward the Creator for our own pleasure.

This spiritual situation is like a seed from which a new entity grows. That new entity is called "the crossing of the barrier" and "the beginning of the ascent"

THE PASSAGE - ACQUIRING A SOUL

Q: If we cross the barrier, does it mean we can no longer do something without the right intention, such as in our "ordinary lives?"

A: No one does anything without intention, since nature does not permit doing anything without a reason. When energy is spent, we demand to know what it is spent on. The expending of energy happens subconsciously.

In the process of studying Kabbalah, we gradually start answering these questions more consciously. Crossing the barrier means that all conscious processes will occur with the intent to benefit the Creator, while biological ones will remain as before, since bodies do not change.

THE SENSATION OF SATISFACTION

Q: When people work a lot, they become proud of themselves. Is it right to be proud for the purpose of inner correction?

A: When people invest a lot in their spiritual development, a sense of self-satisfaction develops, and they begin to take pride in their efforts. It is a good idea to be careful of such gratifications.

However, the efforts should continue regardless of one's conclusions about oneself. Naturally, before we cross the barrier between our world and the spiritual one, all our efforts stem from the will to get something for ourselves. But these efforts gradually expose the evil in us, making us feel as though we are growing worse.

For example: I would always drive my neighbor in my car, lend money to friends and help my relatives. These acts gave me satisfaction and made me respect myself, until I suddenly saw that my behavior stemmed from pure selfishness. I wanted to think well of myself, to be highly spoken of, to maintain what I had been taught to do, and thus put my mind at ease. Of course now, when I realize how selfish I was, I get depressed.

Nevertheless, it is a necessary phase.

Q: How do I begin to hate the situation of _Lo Lishma_ so I can perform the restriction?

A: You mean, how can you advance from a spiritual degree of _Lo Lishma_ to the degree _Lishma?_ To do so, you must come to such a high degree of _Lo Lishma,_ that it will be clear to you that _Lo Lishma_ is a false situation, and you will despise that lie.

When you really do begin to hate that situation, and hate that lie of _Lo Lishma_ because you have now discovered the truth, you can compare the two and clearly see where the deceit lies.

If you begin to feel the Light of _Lishma_ within the situation of _Lo Lishma,_ you will see how deep that situation of _Lo Lishma_ is, and you will feel you must get out of it, but can't!

You will already see the evil and despair because you can't escape that situation on your own. At that point, the exodus occurs. The passage from _Lo Lishma_ to _Lishma_ is exactly like a seed that rots and gives life to something new.

Q: Will we be unable to enjoy life in another way after the restriction?! It's as though there is no connection between the spiritual worlds and the material worlds. Before we learn to give, will we be unable to receive any pleasure!

A: If you didn't have a point in your heart that constantly wanted to receive spiritual delight-a pleasure that cannot be given in this world--you would receive pleasure through your five senses. These would bring you a sense of the various phenomena around you; you would satisfy your animate vessel and enjoy life.

But if you have already discovered the point in your heart, the embryo of your soul, the desire to be filled with the Light of the Creator--then you understand that it can only be filled with that Light and not with any substitute. That Light can be given only when your attributes are the same as the One who gives the Light.

The first act toward attaining identical characteristics is the restriction. Just as there is a concealment of the Light from above, from the Creator, so we need to imitate that concealment and infiltrate it into our souls. Only then will we be able to receive Light from Above.

Because the Light is concealed from us, we must change our attributes to be able to receive it. . Then, we will feel the sensation of receiving, and will change our attributes by the same intensity of the sensation of receiving, in order to turn it into giving.

Then, by reason of the law of "equivalence of form," the Light will enter our souls. Those concealed Lights open inside us in accordance with our spiritual progress and the correction of our egoistic attributes.

A vessel that does not feel through its five senses does not belong to this world, but to the next world; it is the vessel of the soul, the point in the heart – a vessel from the other world. If that point ~ the desire for the Upper Light – is in our hearts, we can try to ignore it and just "go with the flow" and try to return to "regular" life, or we can try to break that "regularity" and start studying Kabbalah.

That desire can only be developed with the help of a group.

Leaving the group is not necessarily a physical act. One can remain physically in a group and take part in the activities, but if there is no inner connection or unification of intents with the group, it is just as if one is out of the group.

If a person leaves the group, the point in the heart may be turned off, and there is no telling when it will light up again. By participating in group studies, that point can be developed, and the desire for the Creator intensified. The wisdom of Kabbalah is a method that helps develop that point.

In order to satisfy the desire of that point, the aim should match the pleasure. Matching with the pleasure is called *Lishma*, because the pleasure comes to us in the form of the Creator, and the pleasure can only be received by a special vessel that matches it.

Q: At what phase do we disconnect from the intent _Lo Lishma?_

A: I don't know what it means to give the Creator. But the thought comes by itself. We cannot know what it is, or how it happens. The revelation and the attainment of the spiritual world occurs according to the rule, "Taste and see that the Lord is good." In other words, first one sees a picture, and then one begins to understand it.

CLOSENESS WITH THE CREATOR

Q: Is the circulation of the wisdom of Kabbalah a real spiritual act?

A: It may be unclear how the physical dissemination of the wisdom of Kabbalah can be a spiritual act. However, there are "mediators" who help us advance toward the Creator by realizing the actual motivation behind our actions – to receive. Actions motivated by good aims are called _Mitzvot_. In our world, we carry these out between each other.

Any act should be followed by the intent of wanting to reach the Creator, to contact Him. That should be our motivation with regard to the group. Our connection with the Creator forces us to build a group and create social contacts with our group mates. That is the right use of our ability to act.

Otherwise, if we are incapable of acting "as we should," then, as it says, "Sit and do nothing – is better."

If I work without the intention of coming to the Creator, then what do I work for? If you take action without the intention to approach the Creator, you are doing harm. Such an act is destructive to begin with. Anything that brings us closer to the Creator is preferred to an act that takes us farther from the Creator.

The Creator wants to delight His creatures. He can delight them only to the extent that the attributes of the creatures match His. If you can help people bring their attributes closer to those of the Creator, you are performing the best possible spiritual act in the eyes of the Creator; an act that delights Him most.

How can we try to bring people closer to Him? Through the dissemination of Kabbalah. That is why it is the most effective means to produce spiritual closeness and equivalence of form with the Creator.

It only becomes the most effective means if we do it in order to come closer to the Creator, to please Him. If we seek, we will find the place where we can concentrate our efforts. We need not even search far: a thought about the Creator and the connection with Him will gradually bring us the means, both external and internal.

If the thought of the Creator does not precede the act, it is done on purpose, in order to come to us at the end of the act or during it. There are many reasons for that. But if we do not work systematically according the rule of "think of the end before you begin," if we do not think that this act will intensify our connection with the Creator, we are not trying to draw near Him. Therefore, those actions belong to the "path of pain."

Such actions put us on a dead-end street from which we must turn back and search for another way. They only extend the correction process.

Q: So where is the way out?

A: We have to keep thinking about our contact with the Creator. All our problems in this world indicate that we do not have contact with Him. It is the same problem everywhere – in individuals, in groups, in society and in the whole of mankind.

TO DEMAND FROM THE CREATOR

Q: If even we, who study in a group, keep forgetting about the Creator, how can ordinary people remember Him?

A: The contact does exist. If ordinary people are unable to reach that conclusion, neither will we, as we are all connected. Everything that happens in the general public happens within us, too. It happens in another form, but for the same purpose.

We learned that when a person begins to think about the Creator, it must be understood that if one has found the Creator, it is because the Creator has found this person first and created the desire within that individual to begin thinking about the Creator. Man is but a derivative of the Creator.

We must turn to the Creator to demand to make and afterwards strengthen our contact with Him. But it is we who must demand it. We can't wake up and start thinking about Him by ourselves. When we think of Him, it is actually He who creates and strengthens our desire to think about Him.

The process is entirely in His domain; we must simply demand of the Creator to constantly renew the resources, and ask for His help to strengthen the contact. He is waiting for it. Perhaps it is still without the intent "for Her name," but it doesn't matter – we already depend on Him.

THE REASON FOR PAIN

Q: How do I maintain that awakening and strengthen it?

A: By being aware that the Creator is the one who gives you all the torments, that by putting you in such a state, the Creator asks for your attention. People still can't see the actual reasons for those painful events; they cannot see that it is the Creator who is behind them. They don't understand that the Creator desires to bring us back to Him, to make us advance in the right direction toward the goal.

To avoid pain and suffering, we must ask the Creator to direct our thoughts not toward the pain, but toward its source –Him. We have to ask Him never to detach us from that thought, and to maintain continuous spiritual connection with us through that thought. This prayer is the single most important thing we can do. Here lies the beginning of everyone's way to salvation.

Q: Is there no need for torment in such a case?

A: Pain and suffering are sent to us to awaken our plea for contact with the Creator. We cannot ask for this before we feel our dependency on Him — which emphasizes the significance of that contact. That is precisely why He sends us the pain and suffering.

But it all depends on the amount of pain, its nature, and how we can take that pain and transfer it from the "animate" level to that of human suffering, and use those torments for spiritual progress. Any pain we feel, from the smallest to the greatest, reflects a sensation of the absence of Light, the sensation of the absence of the Creator in the point in the heart, in our souls.

The sensation of the absence of the Creator is torment itself, though we are unaware of it. There is, in fact, nothing but a Light and a vessel, which is the desire for Light.

If I were to turn to Him and beg, "Don't leave me. Stay close to me, stay in my soul," in the simplest of words, it is the most effective means to success.

I am now referring to the beginning of the way. After that, we arrive at the degree of *Lo Lishma* (not for Her name) and *Lishma* (for Her name), meaning "for me and for Him." At that point, I become grateful for the pain! But that will happen later on.

I don't want people to wake up only under the impact of pain and disaster. I want people to awaken through studying and reading books. But they do not bother opening a book until they receive a warning. A person who experiences pain, even the smallest possible pain, can already increase it through the imagination and thus avoid greater pain and suffering in the future.

After finding ourselves in even the smallest of troubles, we should start asking, "What is the meaning of my life, why do I suffer? After all, I was born for pleasure!"

We should help each other advance from that basic question about the meaning of individual pain to a general question about life that would inspire a search to find the answer (the Source of suffering: the Creator).

Everything depends on our efforts, which can help us speed up the process. Our purpose is to speed up the pace, and hasten time.

What, in fact, is pain? If you could see into the spiritual world, you would see that in that place, in those aims (in which you suffer), you lack the desire for the Creator, which is why you feel pain.

Pain is the sensation of the absence of the Upper Light, the Creator. If we fill up that place with the Light of the Creator, we will begin to feel pleasure instead of pain, in those precise places of pain and suffering that degrade us. After the revelation of the Creator, we will feel the greatest pleasure precisely in those situations.

In the meantime, our goal is to regard even the smallest painful event as a major one, intensify its meaning in our eyes and immediately start searching for the actual reason for that suffering. We will begin to search for the reason despite ourselves.

The solution for our problems is in, "Taste and see that the Lord is good." There is no other solution. The pain itself is not the Creator; it is an expression of His absence from our lives. Pleasure means, "Taste and see that the Lord is good." That is the eternal, complete and total pleasure that awaits us.

Q: Some people suffer their entire lives, but still can't feel the point in the heart; it's just not there... why do they suffer?

A: Everyone suffers all the time. Humanity in general has been suffering throughout its history. People lived, died and never understood the actual reasons for their pain. The pain should accumulate and reach a certain level before we can discover the reasons for it, and Who is responsible for it.

Mankind as a whole has already accumulated that critical mass of pain, and we are here to show people the reason for their suffering.

A SINGLE AIM

Q: How do I intensify the sensation of the Creator in order to avoid being disconnected from the thought of Him and His Providence?

A: We cannot always feel the Creator, although that sensation should accompany our every desire. How do we make that aim unceasing? The Creator takes care of that; He guarantees that we always remember Him.

The guidance is to show us how we can make that contact last! Just imagine for a moment that you have lost contact. Think of ways you can make it stronger. Make any effort to maintain it. Gradually, your efforts will accumulate and become a single aim directed at the Creator.

CONTACT THROUGH EVIL

Q: How do we discover evil, and for what purpose?

A: If you remember the idea of creation and its goal, all your calculations will stop being passive. Instead, they will become vessels, or aims with which we contact the Creator and feel Him. Every negative attribute in us becomes a means to an end.

There is no other way to make contact with the Creator–only through our negative attributes, through the evil. The revelation of evil is the beginning of the revelation of good – its opposite. The Creator tells you of your negative attributes to make you want Him when you sense your egoism. We have to try and use the evil to help us make contact with the Creator.

Here, in the midst of my evil, I cleave to Him. Even if it is the opposite side, I still make contact with the Creator. It is here that I ask Him to help me: "Out of the depths have I called Thee, O Lord (Psalms 130, 1)."

Q: Is this what prayer is?

A: Yes, this is prayer. Otherwise, where will you raise your MAN (prayer) from? When you feel that all this is death, and only the Creator has the solution, you ask, you plead and cry. In a moment you'll be dead, like one who stands above the abyss, like the situation in the middle of the exodus from Egypt, standing at the shore before the Red Sea opened.

We needn't hide our negative attributes; only use them creatively in negative situations. We should simply consult the Creator before any action, and only then start acting.

ANGELS

Q: How can I always maintain my aim?

A: Before every thought, every action and every breath you take – think of the purpose!

If a member of my group reminded me of the existence of the Creator, even if quite rudely, by poking me when I fell asleep in class, to me, that person is an angel. It doesn't matter how the creator sends the reminders, but from then on, I can advance. If you think like that, you will see that everyone around you is an angel made to remind you of the existence of the Creator.

We keep getting pushed from Above so we can advance toward the Creator. The problem is that we attempt to find solutions to complex situations with the power of our minds. That pushes us to the path of pain: we begin to get beaten up until we realize that the solution cannot come from our minds.

It is a long process, but it depends on us; we can speed it up only when we are wise enough to understand that we have to search for the solutions above.

But what does this mean? The answer is, whatever the problem, we mustn't lose contact with the Creator! It is written: "Even when a sharp sword is placed upon one's neck – one should not deny oneself of mercy." Even under unbearable pain you can feel perfection, if you only maintain spiritual contact with the Creator despite the pain.

It may appear to others that you are suffering unbearable pain, but you can feel instead completeness and delight if you create a spiritual contact with the Creator, despite the pain.

The body could burn and you would feel nothing. It all depends on the tightness of your connection with the Creator. The stronger it is, the greater the joy; the weaker it is, the lesser the joy.

Pain is given to us only to tighten the contact and attain the spiritual degree where all we feel is pleasure. We must think of it as the most important exercise.

Q: Is it important to do this in a group?

A: It is important to do it inside the group, outside the group, together and alone.

THE SEARCH FOR THE DESIRE

Q: Is the desire for spiritual contact a desire for pleasure?

A: If the desire is there, there is nothing more to work on. It means that the Creator Himself is inviting you to meet Him.

But if there is no desire for contact with the Creator, you must search for that contact. If you already have a sensation of the contact, then you already have a desire for Him. Now, search for the additional desire to unite with Him.

If you are waiting for the desire to come to you, it will not happen by itself. Instead, you will get pain and suffering from Above to make you start asking questions and search for that aim. If you have that aim, Baal HaSulam writes that the Creator Himself gives us the desire for Him, and invites us to draw near. Then comes the time when we must make an effort in order to match the desire of the Creator.

There is only the Creator, the creature, and the contact between them in the world–nothing else! It is precisely when we are in pain that we can turn that suffering, whether individual, national or global into pleasure. The pain is given to us for one purpose only – to contact the Creator through it, thus turning it to pleasure.

If we relate to our pain correctly, we will see that all those torments are simply a reason for us to ascend spiritually, and then the entire world will be at our feet.

WHAT ACTIVATES US?

Q: What is the ego? What is around me, and what should I do with it all?

A: The only thing that was created by the Creator is called *Adam ha Rishon* (the First Man), the collective soul, the creature, *Malchut*. The *Partzuf* of *Adam ha Rishon* was created and then broken in order to correct creation.

This shattering mixed the attribute of the creature—to enjoy– with the attribute of the Creator – to delight. There was, in fact, a kind of blast that caused the attributes of the Creator to penetrate the attributes of the creature.

The parts of Man were shattered and separated. That is why there is a spark of the First Man in each of us. Within that spark exist *Reshimot* (recollections) of all our future situations, from the beginning of the spiritual path to the end of correction. That is because *Adam ha Rishon* fell from the highest state, so the "documentation" of the upper situations and all other states is already within us in a form of *Reshimot* (recorded, programmed data).

That chain of *Reshimot* perpetually evolves within each and every one of us, but we feel only the outermost *Reshimo* (singular of *Reshimot*), the lowest. We feel it as an order to get something, and operate accordingly. In that sense, we are nothing more than robots.

Some people want quiet lives. Others want to grow and search for fame and fortune. Everything that distinguishes one person from another is embedded in the *Reshimot*, like the biological genes.

Everything that happens to us depends on the currently active *Reshimot*. Therefore, it is impossible to demand spirituality of a person if one's outer *Reshimot* give only the desire to rule, for example. Our purpose is to prepare everything that is needed for the implementation of spiritual desires in a person whose *Reshimot* of spiritual development are already active.

The only possibility at our disposal is to speed up the pace of the passage from one *Reshimo* to the next, along the entire chain of *Reshimot*, from beginning to end. We cannot change anything but the pace of the correction.

That is why we should think only about the present moment, and what we must internally correct right now.

WHAT IS THE MEANING OF MY LIFE?

Q: What does it mean to feel "inner necessity?"

A: Inner necessity is when you have a question about the meaning of life and you cannot find the answer to it. In the introduction to the most complex and important book in Kabbalah, *Talmud Eser Sefirot* (The Study of the Ten Sefirot), the author, Rav Yehuda Ashlag, writes for whom this book is intended. It is anyone who is troubled by the question: "What is the meaning of my life?" It is meant precisely for those who wish to know the meaning of the suffering they experience; those who try to understand why things go wrong in their lives.

IMPROVE BY BEGINNING

Q: I'd do anything to improve my life, but how can I before I know anything about Kabbalah?

A: You can improve your life immediately without even knowing a thing about Kabbalah, simply by taking an interest in the wisdom of Kabbalah, wanting to belong to it, and wanting to improve the world. If you continue to study and progress, you will begin to affect the spiritual world voluntarily, consciously, in order to build a better future for yourself.

That means that the study of Kabbalah can be done on several levels, depending on the person himself. Just as in our world, some people live and act passively, doing only one thing throughout their lives, others take initiative and change their lives, influence society, and have an impact on the whole world. The same pyramid exists in our influence on the spiritual world, and, in fact, on the entire reality.

CHAPTER 2.
THE WISDOM OF KABBALAH

KABBALAH AS A SCIENCE

Q: Why is Kabbalah considered a science?

A: Science examines the world with the tools that we have made. The way these tools work is based on our five senses: sight, sound, taste, smell and touch. We cannot invent something new that is unlike what we feel in our senses.

All the information that arrives through these tools and through our senses is analyzed in our brains, creating within us what we think is the image of the world around us. If we could raise the frequency of one of our senses, we would see, for instance, x-rays, or hear sounds that are beyond our current hearing threshold.

In that case, the world around us would appear very different. We would still consider it "our world," but it would change in respect to the world we perceive today.

It's quite possible that there are other parallel worlds to our own, other beings that go "through" us, but we don't feel them because we don't have the appropriate tools for that. How is it possible to study the objective reality around us, when we can only perceive such a small part of it?

All the fields of science deal with what we perceive through our senses, but Kabbalah deals with acquiring knowledge that exceeds their limitations.

For example, when information in the form of sound approaches us, how do we know it is sound? There are waves around us and some of them press our eardrums, which in turn flex an inner mechanism to bring it back to balance. The brain measures the force and the frequency of the return of the eardrum to its original position, and translates that pressure to information about sound. We perceive this data as a combination of sounds ~ a tune, a rustle and other such noises.

In other words, our reaction is only a side-effect of pressure that was first activated on us by our surroundings. We don't know the sounds around us, only those that we feel.

All of our senses are built that way. We never know what's beyond us, and only react to what our senses perceive. The outer world can be infinite in color and sound, but all we can perceive is what goes through our senses.

All sciences are limited by our five senses, whereas the Kabbalah speaks of what can be acquired with the extra sense called "the sixth sense." Through it we can feel the reality beyond our senses. If we compare man to a closed box that gets all its information from the outside, and only within the boundaries of our senses, then Kabbalah speaks of what can be taught, seen and heard outside us, beyond the five senses that limit us.

If we have gone through an ordeal, we can empathize with a person who has gone through a similar experience because we have acquired knowledge of this experience and felt emotions from the same experience. As a matter of fact, we have everything it takes to feel the emotions of our fellow human beings.

A person who has not gone through similar experiences cannot empathize with other people and might be indifferent to a friend's pain. The difference between people and all other parts of nature is only in the ability to sense certain effects from the unfamiliar world outside us.

Our examination of the outer world, which we normally do not attain, is based on the equalization of our inner traits with exterior phenomena. If we develop certain spiritual senses that did not exist in us at birth, we can use them to grasp a higher world–a spiritual, eternal and spacious world that is absent from the conception of ordinary people.

The Kabbalah is a system that develops additional senses through which we begin to feel the spiritual world, as well as our world as we feel it today. In addition to the small portion that we ordinarily perceive, we can move into a completely different field of information. We are born;

we feel ourselves in the biological, "protein" body for some time, and then we vanish.

In this world, in such a state, when we feel phenomena, situations and other incidents, we are completely unaware of where they come from. We are often mentally unprepared for the effects they have on us, which are sometimes unpleasant or even tragic.

These all come to us from outside, but because we can only see a fraction of the world, we think it's sudden or accidental; something unexpected that suddenly comes on stage, but it is only so because we do not see behind the scenes.

How, then, can we properly respond to the incidents that befall us if we cannot see the whole picture? We don't know what the consequences of our actions are, and we cannot see exactly what our actions are causing. Therefore, we cannot grasp the consequences to everything around us.

We are called "the thinking beings"~people think and are "smart," the highest degree of creation. But at the same time, we are completely detached from reality and from the truth. When we take pride in being smart, it only proves that the level of our development is very poor and that we are not even aware of our true state.

The more we get a feel of the spiritual world and a deeper sense of the world of truth, the more we can see the order of cause and consequence. We see what happens with us, understand how we should react to it and begin to be a positive and active part of the universe. That is why the Torah says: "Be a man." We can achieve this by opening our eyes instead of remaining blind.

Of course, if one were "a man," education would not be needed, because education is only needed to complete what we cannot see for ourselves. If we could clearly see the consequences of our actions, we could commit evil, but it would be clear to us what was right and what was wrong. There would be no room for theories and philosophies. Everything would be so obvious that deception would cease to exist because of the full development of our desires and intentions.

Kabbalah describes the way we can acquire that extra sense which enables us to go out to the objective reality instead of the false one. It describes how that sense evolves. Through it, we receive information about how to begin to act correctly, in light of this newly acquired information.

Kabbalists say that this way, we reach beyond the limitations of time and space and life and death. We see our whole lives, even before birth, as well as our future state after leaving this world.

Thus, we can feel the objective reality while being in a physical body, and can rise to a level where past, present and future merge. The whole mechanism of Providence is clear, and we can begin to take an active part in it. By doing so, we are included in the universe and can judge our actions correctly, where before we had failed to do so.

THE METHOD OF THE KABBALAH · ADVANTAGES

Q: You write that the study of the Kabbalah accelerates the advancement of man's soul in its journey toward the spiritual. But that acceleration is certainly accompanied by an over-compression of events. In other words, what man should experience in hundreds of years he'll experience in a few decades. But how strongly?

Moreover, he who studies and attains should contain within him the agony of the whole world, and he should expand his emotional vessels in order to absorb every desire. So what then, is the advantage of Kabbalah?

A: I don't think that I can accurately convey to you the advantages, but:

1. There is no other way to attain the Upper World, but the Kabbalah. It is therefore called "The Path of Kabbalah." You speak of another way - "The Path of Pain." This is not a path, but rather a state where a person temporarily weakens and abandons the vigorous progress of the Kabbalah.

One waits on the side of the road, so to speak, before agony prods further movement to return to the path of Kabbalah and persist with it.

2. The Path of Pain is not another way to advance; it is not even a way, but merely a temporary state until such time as one "gets wiser." It is only called "a path" for purposes of clarity.

3. Through the Kabbalah a person reduces pain and can foresee them. The pain itself is the correction. But a Kabbalist replaces the unnecessary pains, which one gets in order to grow wiser and take the path of Kabbalah, with pains of love for the Creator. Mankind doesn't need the pains of the flesh, but through studying, we can receive only the goal-oriented pains that stem from a most vital need. We don't need to suffer from petty things before we understand what we should actually yearn for.

4. Through a special preparation, we may possibly accelerate our ability to sense, analyze, correct and digest the pains of the desire to enjoy. As a result, these go by so quickly that we immediately use them in the opposite way, meaning we turn desires that were meant to give us pleasure into a basis for desires to please the Creator.

A great part of the Kabbalist's journey is spent in the worlds of *ABYA* (*Atzilut, Beria, Yetzira, Assiya*), where the Kabbalist gradually turns intended and unintended sins into virtues, and thus justifies the works of the Creator and His guidance. In these worlds, the system makes it possible to shorten the process significantly.

REALITY IN THE EYES OF KABBALAH

Q: I read that Kabbalah develops the ability to sense the elements of reality and the spiritual worlds. But I also understand that time and space do not exist; that there are no other worlds and that there is nothing besides the Creator. How then should I properly see reality?

A: Every time people try to understand a new or different reality, they use the attributes and sensations of the world they come from. Through the Kabbalah, they attain a true understanding of the spiritual reality as well as the one they currently sense.

Reality is made of:

1. Matter
2. Form dressed in matter
3. Abstract form (not dressed in matter)
4. Essence

Because we are made of matter, we can only attain the matter and the form dressed in the matter. We will never be able to attain an abstract form, detached from matter.

Yet, despite the fact that we cannot attain two of these four types, they do exist and clothe one another: The essence comes first. The abstract form dresses over the essence, over that comes the form that is dressed in matter, and the matter dresses over all of these.

Kabbalah is a science about the conduct of reality. Man is the subject of the experiment, and thus the science is attained in us. The sensation of the traits of the Creator is the form that is dressed in the matter. The spiritual path is a gradual acquisition of a truer and truer form, and ever-closer traits to those of the Creator. Man can only increase the pace of the acquisition of the Upper traits. That is why Kabbalah was given to us.

Q: What about the lack of sensation of time?

A: You're right; it's hard to understand the lack of the feeling of time. But "time" in spirituality is no more than the changing of emotions. In this world, too, we feel how time "flies" or "stands still," but when we sleep, time still goes by, unlike spirituality.

In spirituality, a "moment" is the passage from one trait to the next in the space of changing traits that grow ever closer to the Creator.

The confusion you feel now is felt by anyone who begins to think and tries to compare the corporeal concepts to the little knowledge they have acquired about spirituality. That time will pass. Don't be afraid of periods of confusion, despair, sensations of failure and so on. They are all necessary so that in the future, you'll be able to feel the exact opposite: you will experience achievement, perfection, completeness and light.

THE ARI AND KABBALAH IN MODERN TIMES

Q: You said that the modern Kabbalah was created by the Ari, and was later renewed by Rav Yehuda Ashlag. How can that be? We know that the Torah was given to us from heaven and that it doesn't change; why then does Kabbalah change, and moreover, how can people change it? Isn't Kabbalah a part of the Torah?

A: The whole of the Torah relates only to the spiritual world. It explains it in the language of pictures, but not a single word of it speaks of our world. It does, however, make use of words to explain the structure of the spiritual world and how it dominates us.

Because the spiritual world is the world of emotions and has no words, we use languages such as the language of the Bible (Pentateuch), the language of legends (*Agada*), the language of the Talmud (Jewish religious laws), and the language of the Kabbalah (*Sefirot*), which is the most precise of all, in order to explain and describe that world. For that reason, most Kabbalists use the language of the Kabbalah.

Within the Kabbalah are several sub-languages as well: the language of the Lights, the language of the vessels, *Gimatria* (use of letters as numerals), matrix, drawings, etc.

Because in each generation new souls descend to this world, each generation needs its own Kabbalah. That is why the Creator sends us a Kabbalist who rewrites the Kabbalah in each generation and fits it to the new generation.

The Torah does not change because it speaks of technical existence. But unsuitable rules were canceled over time. For example, today there is no Temple and therefore none of the rules linked with it or with the holiness of the land apply today.

KABBALAH AND JUDAISM

Q: Is the difference between Judaism and Kabbalah that Judaism is a religion, and Kabbalah is a wisdom based on rationality and understanding?

A: Kabbalah is the wisdom of the revelation of the Creator, the system of the attainment of the Upper revelation, a sublime truth and superior knowledge. Religion does not deal with any of that.

A religious person must know how to follow rules and live within their boundaries. Kabbalah, however, leads to the attainment of the Upper World.

RITUAL

Q: How does Kabbalah relate to customs and rituals of Judaism?

A: Before the soul is revealed, man doesn't feel any inner need for spiritual development. At that stage, man must only obey laws and customs, but does not belong to spirituality. The part that does belong to spirituality is our effort to correct self from the aim "for ourselves" to the aim "for the Creator."

Corrected aims are hidden because no one can see what is corrected in man. These corrections do not bear any external manifestation, but rather change our personal relationship with the Creator. Hence, the concealment.

We perform the acts that concern morality and customs while under the influence of corporeal pleasures, such as sex, money, control, fame, respect, and education, until we develop the aspiration toward the Creator.

When that yearning first appears, the technical acts that belong to the ritual and moral part become less important, and we establish a personal contact with the Creator. That becomes the most important thing in our lives, and we are then changed from an ordinary person into a Kabbalist.

However, even when one becomes a great Kabbalist, the person continues to perform the same mechanical *Mitzvot* as an ordinary believer would. These two are not connected. You can ask great experts in *Mitzvot*, great ravs, and they will tell you that they don't know Kabbalah. You don't have to know Kabbalah in order to keep *Mitzvot*.

TWO SETS OF RULES

Q: Judaism or Kabbalah? That is the question!

A: Judaism is a collection of religious rules that dictate how to conduct ourselves in our world. Other than what we must know, such as how to provide for our livelihood, how to behave, dress, or how to raise a family, Kabbalah teaches something more. The Kabbalah tells what we must do besides providing for the natural needs on the corporeal-human level. A person must observe 613 laws.

Why? There is no rational answer. These laws are not even rational. From a scientific or physiological perspective there is no justification to the prohibition against eating pig's meat, or not driving on *Shabbat* (Saturday).

The wisdom of Kabbalah does not relate to these laws or to anything else that concerns corporeal life. It teaches what is beyond this world, and how to get there. When one begins to inquire into the Upper World and enters it, one discovers that it is comprised of 613 spiritual particles. Their consequences in this world are called the "613 *Mitzvot*," the laws of the Torah.

Q: So if they do not change anything here, why do we still have to keep them?

A: If we observe them in the flesh, we do it unconsciously, and by that we somehow equalize with the 613 Upper Laws, and for that reason we get a certain amount of Light from above. That spiritual Light does not develop us, but guards us, which is why it belongs to the degree of the still, which does not change.

A Kabbalist who attains the Upper World also attains the inner meaning of the 613 laws of the Upper World. Who gave us those laws? Moses. Where did he get them? Not from our world, but from the attainment of the Upper World.

There has always been tension between those who observe the laws solely at the level of this world, and those who want to observe them in the true spiritual form. Those who observe them only at the level of this world assume that mere observance is enough, and regard themselves as dismissed from the upper layer, simply because they do everything "right."

However, those who want to observe them in the Upper World feel that the orthodox way of life does not satisfy them or give them a sense of fulfillment.

TORAH IS KABBALAH

Q: What is the connection between Torah and Kabbalah?

A: Torah is Kabbalah. It speaks only of spiritual laws, of the Creator and the events that take place in the Upper World, while using familiar words from our everyday life. It does not say a single word about our corporeal life, but of man's way to the Creator, and the inner change.

The Torah should lead us to the Upper World, the purpose of our journey here. That is what makes it holy and unique. Moses is considered to be the foremost Kabbalist. Although there were Kabbalistic books before him, he was the first to compose a book of Torah (instructions) about man's path from down to up, from our world to the spiritual world. He described the way in general terms, and for the first time in history, the system of the worlds was described in a literary tongue.

Kabbalists use four languages to describe the Upper World to humanity: the language of the Bible (history), the language of the *Halacha* (Jewish law), the language of *Agada* (legends and tales), and the language of Kabbalah. Without exception, they all speak about the Upper World.

For example, when you open the Zohar, you find an explanation of the text of the Torah, but in a different language--that of the Kabbalah. The Zohar is the interpretation of that Torah (writing the same thing under a different label is called interpretation - *Perush*). So we see that the only difference between the Torah and the Zohar is the language.

Everything that happens in the Upper World, descends - in due time - to our world, and begets its consequences here. The Upper Forces and their consequences, meaning the objects of our world, are linked by "threads," so that from each of the Upper Forces is a consequence that extends to our world, the corporeal object that relates to it, and the thread by which the lower object is manipulated.

Therefore, in order to explain the structure of the Upper World, Kabbalists have chosen to name the Upper Forces by names and appellations from our world. Thus the Upper Object gets its name from the corresponding object in the corporeal world. This language is called "the language of the branches," where the Upper Power is the root, and the physical object is the branch.

If I want to describe what happens in the spiritual world, I speak in terms of this world, and you would think I am talking about this world. But in fact, I mean to speak only of what happens in the spiritual world. This is precisely the way the Upper Worlds are described in our holy books.

Why are they called holy? Because they speak of the Upper Worlds. When we read the Torah we look at it as a "historical novel," but when a Kabbalist reads in it, he sees completely different things.

Q: What is the difference between the study of Torah and the study of Kabbalah?

A: There is no difference. The Torah speaks only of the structure of the Upper World, and says nothing of what happens in our world. It only talks about the structure of the Upper World, but it does it in the language of our world, which is why we think we understand it.

The Torah is called "holy" not because it speaks of the journeys of a primordial nation, or about indecent acts. It is holy because it talks about holy things. The term "holy" (Hebrew: *Kadosh*) means separated, unique, distinct.

Though you do not see the spiritual world behind the stories when you read them, both Kabbalah and the Torah speak of special, spiritual matters, about matters that reach beyond our world. The difference between them is only in the language, but the essence remains the same. Kabbalah speaks of the same issues as the Torah, but uses a technical language of *Sefirot*, worlds, *Partzufim*, ascents and descents.

The difference between the two languages can be compared to the different way we relate to music. Ordinary people listen to music, enjoy it and that's the end of it. When musicians listen to music, they begin to analyze it by notes, tonality, rhythm, etc. A sound technician would examine it for the quality of the sound, filters, frequencies, without any reference to the music and the beauty of it. A mathematician will express it in a formula, in such a way that it would be impossible for anyone else to see the soul behind the dry mathematical facts. Here too, it all depends on which words we use to express what we feel.

The difference between Kabbalah and Torah is precisely in the manner, the language, in which they speak of the spiritual worlds. The Kabbalah speaks of them in technical terms, hence the name "the wisdom of Kabbalah," the "science of Kabbalah," whereas the Torah speaks in a more emotional, yet concealed, language.

The Talmud also speaks about the laws of the spiritual world, but in the language and words of laws of our world, such as: you mustn't eat this or do that. The Talmud speaks only about the laws of the spiritual world, while in our world those descriptions are baseless and the laws don't even apply.

But if we want to live in our world according to the laws of the Upper World, we observe them in the flesh. We observe them because we want to somehow adapt ourselves to them, imitate them in some way. But it is completely untrue that by so doing, we affect the Upper Worlds.

By doing something in our world, with my hands or legs, I change nothing in the Upper World. The Talmud, Gmarah and the Torah speak only of the Upper Worlds. The difference between them and the Kabbalah is only in the language.

THE LANGUAGE OF THE KABBALAH

Q: What language do Kabbalists use among themselves?

A: Kabbalists don't invent their own language. They share the same feelings about the spiritual world. For every feeling about the spiritual world, there is a name. Such a name cannot be changed.

For example, there are twenty-two names, or attributes, involved in the creation of the world. These are marked accordingly as Hebrew letters. Their combinations render a spiritual sensation of an object which can be described by the physical terms of this world.

The description of the spiritual world is the description of man's soul, the description of the degrees of its nearness to the Creator and its feelings of closeness. The more the soul feels the Creator, the nearer it is to Him.

Kabbalah divides the collective soul into parts and gives each part a unique name relating to its traits and describing its operations. Although it is the language of emotions, it is an accurate one.

Kabbalah is the "engineering of the soul." But how can we use such accurate research and descriptions if our language is inaccurate, limited and worldly? For that purpose, Kabbalists established a unique language for their science: "the language of the branches."

Any created being, whether still, vegetative, animate or speaking, as well as anything that has happened, is happening, and will happen, and every object and its guidance, all come from the Creator and go through all the spiritual worlds to a state where He is no longer revealed in our world.

But Providence is renewed perpetually, from Above downward to our world. Anything that exists in our world necessarily begins in the Upper World and gradually descends to ours. Therefore, whatever exists in our world is a result of the world above it. There is a direct link of cause and consequence between the objects of our world and their origin in the Upper World.

Kabbalists accurately discern that link between the Upper Object and this world's object. Anything that exists in our world is an outcome, and is under the guidance of the Upper One. Therefore, Kabbalists can clearly say what is linked with what and call the objects (the roots in the Upper Worlds) by the names of their worldly outcomes: "branches." Hence the name, "the language of the branches."

Furthermore, this link of spiritual root and worldly branches undergoes a continual process of renewal. From the dawn of creation to its end, there is an ongoing process of creation, corrections, and ascents.

This process is run by a program that comes down to our world with its every detail fixed, and determines everything we experience. Each object goes through its own root, although it does mingle with others, but it never disappears and always remains consistent with itself. Of course, as a result, it is impossible to swap one name for another.

In order to find an accurate, yet secret language, we need to use only those words that describe the Upper Spiritual Root, as the Kabbalists have shown us.

The Kabbalists who discovered this language accurately describe for us a spiritual world in words we can understand. There simply cannot be another language. How is it possible to take words from our world and use them to define spiritual concepts? We have to learn to follow the rule that everything we read in the Kabbalah and the Torah are terms that define our spiritual roots, not worldly objects. We must never confuse them!

What stands behind those words are only spiritual objects, or roots, which are in no way connected with our world. The entire Torah is comprised of the names of the Creator; thus, it is called "the work of God."

When the Torah denominates an object or an act, it expresses the spiritual root, which generates that object or action. In our world, we name objects in much the same way. To reiterate, the Torah is a description of the creature's nearing to the sensation of the Creator and how He is found in those emotions.

Kabbalists have used this language to convey and explain information, and put it in writing in the form of words and signs of this world. Just as mathematicians use formulas to communicate ideas, when Kabbalists write or read, they feel what they are talking about, what is implied in these words in the language of the Kabbalah.

To summarize: a word is a sign that expresses a certain spiritual object. This, in turn, expresses a certain feeling. While reading, a Kabbalist can reproduce that feeling, just as a musician reproduces a melody. One does not need words in order to understand the language of music.

ABOUT "THE LANGUAGE OF THE BRANCHES"

Q: You wrote in one of your articles: "There is a singular, reciprocal link between a spiritual root and a corporeal branch." How does that mesh with the fact that there are a great many languages in the world, and only the Hebrew language is the one that creation leans on? Are all other languages an incorrect reflection of the spiritual world?

A: You will be able to find a detailed explanation in The Study of the Ten Sefirot, Part I - Inner Reflection.

A language is only a printout of information that is absorbed in a vessel and felt in it as an action of the Light, the pleasure. In fact, we have no real need for any language because we already have those sensations within us.

However, when we want to convey our feelings to others, we need to present them in a form that would be understood by the person we want to speak to about our feelings. That form is called a "language," and it doesn't matter what language is used. Kabbalists chose Hebrew and through it they conveyed the information desired. They also made use of Aramaic, which was a spoken language in ancient Persia.

The Book of Zohar also uses foreign (Greek) words that were used very freely in Israel, so we, like the Kabbalists, use them as well. I, too, asked my rav that same question, and he said that any language can be modified to convey spiritual information, but since Kabbalists described everything in Hebrew, they built a dictionary~"the link between the root and the branch"~ that today is the basis for this whole science.

The Hebrew language is also called the "holy tongue" because it leads to holiness, to the attributes of the Creator.

Now, there still remains the question why, until today, Kabbalists were either Jews or people who converted to Judaism (proselytes). The reason lies in the uniqueness of their souls. The collective soul of "Adam" consists of 600,000 parts, or 600,000 souls, separated by the intensity of their will.

Before the sin of the first man, every desire was aimed at pleasing the Creator; each was a desire to give to the Creator. But as a result of the sin of the First Man, desires changed from "pleasing the Creator" to pleasing themselves. This is called "a fall" from a spiritual degree to a corporeal one; from an aim to give to an aim to receive.

Before the collective soul was broken, all its parts (souls) were connected by a single intent~"for the Creator." After the breaking, each part that departed from the soul acquired the intent "for itself," and the parts were separated. Now, they cannot understand or feel one another.

The correction of the souls is focused on changing the intent from "for myself" to its former state of "for the Creator." It is a gradual process. Souls are separated from one another by the intensity of their desire. The smaller the desire, the easier it is to change the intent. Therefore, the correction begins with the smallest desires and ends with the greatest.

All desires, in the order of their correction, form a line or a chain: the smallest desires come first, then the greater ones. They are generally divided into two groups: "Galgalta ve Eynaim" (GE) and "Awzen, Hotem, Peh" (AHP). At first, the GE are corrected and then come the AHP. Souls (desires) that are related to GE are called "Jews"; souls (desires) that are related to AHP are called "Nations of the World."

Souls dress in corporeal bodies in our world. Therefore, there are groups of people in our world that connect by the types of their soul and their desires (in fact, this is how nations and peoples are formed). Because the Jews must be the first to correct, there is pressure on them from Above, by the Upper Guidance~the Creator~ in order to bring them to correction. The Creator uses all the means of this world (see Introduction to the Zohar, item 66 through the end).

Because the souls that are called "Jews" must be corrected before all other souls, then in our world, in groups of people with a Jewish type of soul there are Kabbalists. Those are people who came out to the spiritual world and express their impressions and the method of correction in their own mother tongue. That is why Kabbalah is expressed in the language of the Jews.

KABBALAH IS NOT A RELIGION

Q: Is there an equivalent to Kabbalah in other religions?

A: There is no equivalent to Kabbalah in other religions because the wisdom of Kabbalah is not a religion, but a science. It does not relate to religions, beliefs, extrasensory methods, or even Judaism. Any orthodox Jew will answer the question, "Do you know the wisdom of Kabbalah?" by saying that not only do they not know it, but they do not think there is any need to know it. And the response will be correct, as the wisdom of Kabbalah is not necessary for those who are occupied with religious rituals.

Moreover, the wisdom of Kabbalah intensifies both the desire to receive and the desire for knowledge, based on self-awareness and the attainment of the Upper World. Other religions, however, are built on self-restriction and abstemiousness.

THE WORLD, RELIGIONS AND THE SCIENCE OF KABBALAH

Q: Upon multiple readings of your books, I noticed that certain places in the text seemed very familiar. When I tried to analyze them, I became convinced that some Kabbalistic concepts form the basis of various global religions. Though Kabbalah is not a religion, it seems

to have the potential to unite the more progressive representatives of global religions (a topic frequently discussed in the Vatican). Do you foresee such a possibility?

A: Kabbalah is not intended to unite religions, since it has nothing to do with them. Kabbalah is a science studying the essential core of man, the Higher World, the entire universe, and the Creator. The outcome of that study is the discovery that mankind wishes to become like the Creator.

Religions, however, are combinations of rituals designed by humans to support them in their earthly existence. Specifically, it is the "opium for the people," a method of pursuing psychological comfort. That is why Baal HaSulam said that the only optimal religion is "Love thy neighbor as thyself," since it leads to uniting with the Creator.

What we call "religion" is nothing more than a way to create feelings of stability and comfort within our shaky existence.

MEANING OF "KABBALAH"

Q: What are the sources you usually cite regarding the meaning of Kabbalah?

A: The Kabbalist Rav Yehuda Ashlag, author of the Sulam commentary on the Zohar, begins his article, "The Essence of the Wisdom of Kabbalah," with the following definition: "... this wisdom is no more and no less than a concatenation of roots that descend by way of cause and consequence, with fixed, determined rules, that combine to one exalted goal being the 'the revelation of His Godliness to His creatures in this world.'"

GENUINE BOOKS

Q: What do the books of Kabbalah describe?

A: The text in genuine books of Kabbalah describes precisely the way the mechanism that operates reality works. Using charts and formulas, it depicts the "control room of reality" in a form much like a user's manual. These visuals teach us how the laws work in spirituality, and how we can influence them with mind and will, consequently affecting the results that return to affect us.

THE BOOK OF CREATION

Q: Rav Laitman, when you say that *Sefer Yetzira* (The Book of Creation) was written by Abraham the Patriarch, should we imagine one man who reached the spiritual level called, "Abraham," or was it Abraham, the historical figure.

In the second case, if Abraham wrote the book before Moses, then how is the name of the prophet, Yehezkel (Ezekiel), mentioned there (Mishnah 8, p.1)? This prophet lived centuries after Abraham did.

A: The Book of Creation was supposedly written by Abraham. This is the opinion of Judaism, not my own. I actually never say anything on my own and can always provide a reference for my words. That is why my adversaries do not oppose me, they oppose Kabbalah!

Baal HaSulam says in his letters that *Sefer Yetzira* was written by some other Kabbalist. Regarding the time, this is a question only for you and not for Abraham or another Kabbalist. However, nothing will help until you, too, see "from the beginning of the world to its end." The Kabbalist mastering a certain spiritual level sees, feels and bonds with everyone on that level regardless of whether it already happened in our world or is yet to come.

The spiritual world is everlasting; it is timeless. Hence the commentaries on the Torah, even those that are not Kabbalistic, often are written along such lines as, "Abraham said...."

But how could the author have possibly known what Abraham said, if he never wrote it anywhere? The answer is, he knows it from having attained the same spiritual level that Abraham reached when he said it! In fact, the answer to all questions can only exist in one's own attainment of the Higher World.

THE BOOK OF ZOHAR

Q: What is the source of the name - Zohar?

A: Zohar means "splendor," as it says: "The righteous sit with their crowns on their heads, and delight in the splendor of Divinity." The sensation of the Creator (the Light) in the collective soul is called "Divinity," according to the Zohar. In any place where the books of Kabbalah say, "so it was written in the book..." this always refers to the Zohar. All the others are seemingly not considered books because the word "book" (*Sefer* in Hebrew) comes from the word *Sefira*, which comes from the word "sapphire," radiance, a revelation (of the Light, the Creator). This is found only in the Zohar.

Q: There have been many debates about the Zohar over the years. What is the essence of these universal secrets? How can it be written in familiar books, but still remain a mystery? When will I be able to buy the Zohar at a bookstore, read it and discover its secrets for myself?

A: When we speak of spiritual concepts, we must first understand that they are unbounded by time and space, and that there are no words to describe them. This is because everything we feel is bounded by time, space and motion.

Once movement stops, our lives also stop. We cannot picture something motionless, disconnected from time and without volume. For example, the universe exists in a certain space. If we take it out of that space, there will be a void and we will not be able to describe it.

In spirituality, there aren't any bodies, there is no time, there is no distance and therefore spirituality is disconnected from the descriptions and inventions of mankind; spirituality is also disconnected from our structure, our nature and our senses.

Q: Why can't I study Kabbalah directly from the Zohar?

A: The Zohar is an important Kabbalistic book, but it is written in a concealed way, making it impossible to understand until a person is in the spiritual world. Because of that, today we do not start with The Book of Zohar. Instead, there are introductions and books of Baal HaSulam that teach us how to understand what is written in the Zohar.

The Book of Zohar is not a book through which one can attain spirituality; it was written for those who have already attained spirituality. In order to understand it properly, we need to study several other books first, such as: Preface to The Wisdom of Kabbalah, Introduction to The Book of Zohar, Preface to The Book of Zohar and Foreword to The Book of Zohar. Without first acquiring clear and correct knowledge through those introductions, the book will remain completely abstruse to us.

Q: The Zohar was written in the second century BC, but was first discovered in approximately the 13th century. Why did it take so long to be discovered?

A: Baal HaSulam relates to this question in the Introduction to The Book of Zohar (item 61): "We must also ask why was the commentary to the Zohar not revealed before the time of the Ari. Why was it not revealed to his predecessors? And most perplexing of all, why were the words of the Ari and the commentary to the Zohar not revealed until today?"

In order to make it easier to understand, let me explain the words of Baal HaSulam in simpler words.

First, why was the Zohar hidden? The answer is that the world has gone through three phases of development during its 6000 years of existence. The first 2000 are called, Tohu; the middle 2000, Torah; and the last 2000 - the days of the Messiah.

During the first 2000 years the souls, that descended were sublime souls with small Lights. They were not even given the Torah because for these souls, simply existing was enough to correct them.

In the next 2000 years, coarser souls descended that needed a greater Light for their correction, the Light of the Torah. Toward the end of the 6000 years, in the remaining third, the coarsest souls descend. Those need the greatest Lights for their correction - the Light of the Kabbalah. Kabbalah was not needed prior to that, just as the Torah was not needed in the first two thousand years.

During the time of the Ari (end of 16th century), we grew closer to the end of the correction of the main part, the third and last phase of the development of the souls. As a result, the sublime wisdom was revealed through the soul of the Ari. The souls of the first generations were higher than those of the last, but the greater the correction that is needed, the greater the consequent attainment and adhesion.

During the last 2000 years, especially from the time of the Ari, the souls that descend to this world become increasingly coarser and more egotistical. They must therefore study and implement Kabbalah for their correction.

Q: Why does the Zohar have only stories and fables in it, and why is the language so old fashioned if it was intended for us?

A: The Zohar was written like that on purpose, as the book itself will tell you. Only people who have already grasped the spiritual reality can know what is written there and see the text as a cohesive story. They see the pictures and identify the picture and the story as one. We cannot do that because we still don't have the spiritual vision, which is why the Zohar appears to be a bundle of fables and stories.

The writings of the Ari, however, aim at more developed souls from later cycles, and therefore appear different to us. But the most suitable for us are the writings of Baal HaSulam. These are intended for our generation, which is why they appear to us as systematic textbooks, as in any science, much like the ones we study at university.

They offer questions and answers, interpretations of the meaning of the words, and a clear division of issues, which differ by topic. They also show how to perform the relevant topic of discussion. There are special articles that go along with these books that specify how a person should personally relate to one's study.

Thus, our generation has no problem approaching the immediate study of Kabbalah. Unlike all other sciences, this wisdom demands no prior study. It is enough for a person to feel that life is difficult, to have a sense of restlessness, and to see life as meaningless. Then, one can start studying the books and begin to advance.

In his Introduction to The Study of the Ten Sefirot, the most complex text in the study of Kabbalah, in the second item, Baal HaSulam specifies the person to whom he is writing the book. He aims it at only those who feel the burning question, "What is the meaning of my life?"

He adds further in item 155 that by studying, even though the person does not understand the content of the book, it is sufficient to learn simply to escape the pain. Then, the text will open to the student who will begin to see how to behave in order to have a better life.

THE ARI AND THE STUDY OF THE TEN SEFIROT

Q: Rav Laitman, what is your attitude toward the books of the Ari? Is The Study of the Ten Sefirot the only book on Kabbalah that you consider holy?

A: The book, *Sha'ar HaGilgulim*, describes how the Ari at his deathbed forbade all his disciples except Chaim Vital to study Kabbalah. Chaim Vital did not fully attain Kabbalah at that time, and therefore decided not to edit or publish the writings of the Ari.

Three generations later, Rav Tzemach, Rav Paprish and Chaim Vital's son, Shmuel, began to dig out the Ari's writings little by little, sort them out and publish them in book form. However, none of them possessed the entire collection, and therefore could not correctly understand and compile Ari's system of Kabbalah.

Baal HaSulam writes in a letter that due to the above reason, no one (!!!) could understand what the Ari wished to pass on to us until the time of Baal HaSulam. Only in The Study of the Ten Sefirot was the system rendered complete. For that reason, we do not study the other books that Rav Tzemach, Rav Paprish and Shmuel Vital published, although we sometimes take this or that excerpt from them, as was done by Baal HaSulam in The Study of the Ten Sefirot. Besides The Study of the Ten Sefirot, no other books (here I don't mean articles and letters on the spiritual work) contain any systematic compilation of the science of Kabbalah.

THERE ARE NO OTHER WAYS

Q: You can't say there are no other ways except for Kabbalah! It would be more accurate to say that ALL roads lead to the Creator, but Kabbalah is the shortest of them.

A: How can one know that Kabbalah is the shortest way, that it is actually the road leading to the goal?

One travels on the road of Kabbalah relying only on the Kabbalists and on the subconscious sensation of one's heart. There is no other way. No one is able to see it in advance. The point in our hearts, the aspiration for the Higher World, feels that only Kabbalah can provide the expected answer. You may also choose to trust the Kabbalists who discovered it for themselves and described it for you. It is up to you.

CHANGING MY DESTINY

Q: How is the method of Kabbalah different from other methods of attaining spirituality?

A: Except for the Kabbalah, all other methods were developed by man. Humanity has been searching for thousands of years for the way to attain spirituality. Those searches promoted the development of philosophy and other methods for spiritual elevation and enlightenment. But in the end, humanity has found nothing.

Through the Kabbalah, people begin to clearly see what kind of world they live in, and what influences them. They begin to obtain forces with which they can shape nature correctly. They also recognize their own influence, and nature's response to it.

Only the Kabbalah can give us the knowledge of what our future desires will be, how they can be acquired and what knowledge and powers are needed for that. This is all we need to live safely and confidently.

So, is there anything more important to us? If we don't understand the necessity to study Kabbalah, there will be tougher and tougher situations, until we do feel the need to study, because the necessity to study Kabbalah comes when there is no other choice.

Q: What is Spirituality?

A: Although everyone feels as if they know what spirituality is, they have, in fact, no connection with the spiritual world, or any idea of it. They think that the spiritual world can be understood through music, science or popular psychology. But the spiritual world can be understood only through the study of the wisdom of Kabbalah.

This is a clear and concise method that must be taught by a genuine spiritual guide. No music or any dubious psychological experiences can help one attain the spiritual world. You can call what you discover with meditation or special music or exercises a "spiritual world," but that is not the spirituality to which I'm referring.

The spiritual world I am referring to can only be revealed with the wisdom of Kabbalah. The study of the method of Kabbalah is a complex system comprised of man's own work, by which he draws upon himself a special Light.

That Light is a special force that awakens the spiritual desire in us, a desire to get away from the crowd and from the world at large. It is a wish to continue living in this world only physically, in the animate body, whereas everything that has to do with the mind, the desires, should operate on a different frequency altogether, as if one were breaking through an invisible barrier to another world.

Such spiritual attainment cannot be seen, presented, or made apparent to anyone. People who have not experienced it cannot feel or comprehend the explanations. It is a unique feeling and completely intimate, a sensation that is attained through the study of the wisdom of Kabbalah.

The wisdom of Kabbalah is a method to discover and attain the spiritual world, advancing over many spiritual degrees, cycles, and spiritual states. Although music can be Kabbalistic, it is only a byproduct, just as there are byproducts to chemical processes such as a rise in temperature, decrease in pressure, etc. When we strive to attain a certain result, we will receive certain byproducts along the way.

Q: Does that mean there is no Kabbalistic music?

A: A Kabbalist can express emotions in music, in writing, by creating new teaching methods, or by presenting new elements into the process of study. However, music and songs are only supplementary means of expression. Man's real attainment is possible only through a system called "the wisdom of Kabbalah."

THE SIXTH SENSE

Q: Is there such a term as a "sixth sense" in Kabbalah?

A: Only through the system of Kabbalah can one develop the sixth sense. It is because all other methods are based on limitations. A person must lower self to the level of a plant and even to the degree of still (inanimate).

Every other system is based on suppressing the desire to receive: we try to eat as little as possible, breath as little as possible, and think only one thought; close ourselves, isolate ourselves, and live in secluded places.

The wisdom of Kabbalah, however, is completely opposite: it develops the will to receive, intensifies it as much as possible, and makes it even more "egoistic." All other systems aim man toward restrictions and abstemiousness, which is why they cannot be used in order to receive a more comprehensive reality, and work freely in it.

Those who restrict themselves believe they can feel something, but in fact, all they feel is the disappearance of their own egos, nothing more. They may, indeed, feel better because they erase all their desires. It is as though they rise above them, so they feel perfection.

But this does not happen because they rise, but rather because their needs seem to have been reduced. Perhaps this seems more "spiritual," but it is not real development, but in fact, regression. Reduction actually opposes the principal law of nature, which is to develop, expand, and bring about the correction of human nature, inducing a sensation of completion and satisfaction.

MAKE YOUR OWN CHOICES AND BELIEVE NO ONE

Q: Lately, there have begun to appear various study groups for Kabbalah. Is it worthwhile checking them out?

A: It is always worthwhile to explore, at least once, who studies and how they study Kabbalah. It will also help you to get to know yourself. That is why I would advise you to check things out, and afterwards make up your mind.

It is not wise to hide from yourself deductions that you might later on discover. In Kabbalah, you mustn't hide anything from yourself, or you will become used to lying to yourself. This will divert you from your inner struggle with yourself and you could begin to camouflage the drawbacks, ignoring and perhaps even erasing them.

Q: Why are there so many trends in Kabbalah?

A: The time is approaching when the uniqueness of the Kabbalah and the system of Rav Yehuda Ashlag will become widely known. In the meantime, there is room for everyone, for all trends. In fact, all other systems exist only to reveal their futility, thus emphasizing the genuineness of the wisdom of Kabbalah.

The souls that descend to our world are at various stages of development. Some have not acquired a true desire for genuine Kabbalah. There are also people who come to us, and later leave for orthodox religion. I believe we should let people choose their way for themselves.

When I came to my rav, I said, "I have studied with quite a few Kabbalistic teachers. How can I be certain that this is my final stop?" I was thirty-three at the time, and my life stretched ahead of me. My rav was already 75.

He replied, "I have no answer for you, it is something that a person feels in his heart. You should believe no one. And I advise you – what you feel in your heart is the most correct. That will bring you where you should go. But you must never agree with anything. Criticize and doubt everything. The most important objective is to be freed from prejudice, from education and from public opinion. Free yourself from anything extraneous and try to absorb the way your nature tells you. That would be the truest, because any education and any external opinion is coercion."

THE SCIENCE OF REALITY

Q: Isn't Kabbalah another form of mysticism, like many others in the world?

A: No. People want to label Kabbalah as mysticism, blessings, curses, charms, etc. These labels became linked with Kabbalah because it was forbidden to study. But that is really the case. Even the holy Ari writes that it is prohibited to use charms and blessings, because they have nothing to do with Kabbalah.

Kabbalah is a science that teaches the law of reality, of which we are a part. Through this science, we discover those rules and the spiritual world, which is the reason for everything that happens here with us. They are collective rules, which encompass the laws of all the sciences in our world.

Kabbalah is not another belief, or some imaginary view of life unseen; instead, it offers exact, clear laws that depict the structure of the Upper Worlds.

It is when we study Kabbalah that we first acquire knowledge of the world outside our own. We discover the Upper, Spiritual World. Then, we gradually attain the ability to affect it. Through tests and experiments, we learn how to do it, and then we enter the comprehensive reality.

At this point, we begin to work not from within our own bodies, but from our souls, which are our true essence. After all, "man" is not the physical body that is replaced at the beginning of each new life; it is the soul that we, as yet, do not feel.

The purpose of creation is that we will act from within our souls, from the Upper World, and live at the highest degree possible, rather than in the lowest (our world), which is beastliness alone. By discovering our souls, we attain contact with the Upper World, and thus achieve a whole, complete, eternal and blissful life.

Q: Is Kabbalah a mystical experience?

A: It is not a mystical experience. It is something that students learn as rules that they are part of, which they must abide by. These laws are active in all levels of nature – still, vegetative, animate and speaking.

Q: Is Kabbalah just a theory, or has it been tested in practice?

A: It is not a theory. With Kabbalah, a person actually acquires knowledge. You might say that it involves a lot of mathematics and dry rules. It has nothing to do with psychology or other imaginary fantasies. There is a good reason for the name, "The Wisdom of Kabbalah" (the wisdom of receiving): it is a wisdom that teaches one how to receive.

Those who acquire knowledge about the laws of reality begin to use and consequently increase their egos. Unlike other religions and mystical methods, the study of Kabbalah does not require one to nullify one's ego and cancel one's desires. There is no requirement to fast or to mortify self.

One does not have to leave everyday life or abandon family duties. Nor does one float in the air, or practice breathing exercises in order to attain tranquility.

Quite the contrary, students build their egos and turn them into vessels to help them attain the sublime goal. To study Kabbalah, and understand how the Upper World operates, one must be at the center of that world and act from within it.

Therefore, one must perform all one's mundane duties. The attainment of the spiritual reality must be in one's corporeal senses, closely connected with one's normal life.

OPENING A BOOK FOR THE FIRST TIME

Q: Should a person spend one's whole life in a university of Kabbalah and study complex theories?

A: That sounds very nice, but it doesn't work that way. In the study of Kabbalah, we really study our own inner structure, how our emotions are built, and the structure of our souls.

Within us is a key to the understanding of that science; all we must do is study from genuine books of Kabbalah in order to find what is already within us.

Even if we understand nothing of this science, the minute we open a book, our hearts and souls begin to open up. We receive spiritual knowledge about spirituality in a natural way, just as we feel bitterness or sweetness, or heat and cold. There is no need to go to school to feel such things.

The study is only a method that helps us open our souls, our still dormant spiritual senses. Then, when the heart and soul open, we are moved emotionally and naturally to learn about the reality in which we exist.

I am talking about a tangible attainment that does not require any prior wisdom and knowledge, or any philosophizing. It is a method that develops the sensation in the heart, a method for discovering the spiritual world, for receiving impressions with the laws that actually exist in nature, that we still cannot feel, though they continuously act upon us.

I act on the world around me by sitting, speaking, thinking or feeling. All my desires and thoughts go through the entire reality and return to me through the Upper, Spiritual World.

However, because I still haven't made contact with the Spiritual Forces, I don't know how they return to me, and if I harm or benefit myself. In the study of Kabbalah, we learn how to influence reality correctly, to benefit ourselves, and get accurate feedback from reality. That is the science involved, and today it can be revealed to anyone who seeks it.

CHAPTER 3.
THE STUDY OF KABBALAH

INTRODUCTION

Kabbalah has always been taught through books. The first books about Kabbalah were written thousands of years ago. *Adam ha Rishon* (the First Man) wrote the book, "The Angel Raziel," and Abraham the Patriarch wrote the book *Sefer Yetzira* (Book of Creation). The Zohar was written some 1900 years ago.

All of these books are still for sale today. Through them, we can study the wisdom of Kabbalah.

The principal, fundamental book that we study by is called *Talmud Eser HaSefirot* (The Study of the Ten Sefirot). It consists of six volumes and more than 2000 pages that depict the laws of the system of creation in scientific terms. When we study them, we receive a special illumination, a special Providence from Above.

Even if we still do not understand a single word we read, even if we haven't got a clue about the spiritual world, approaching the Creator begins from the very first lesson. But we can only learn by studying from books, or listening to the recorded lessons–there is no other method.

When Kabbalists write books, they have already reached a certain spiritual level. When we read the books, wanting to somehow come in contact with that world from which the Kabbalist wrote, we are enfolded in an illumination from that place. We do not feel it, but it slowly prepares us for the phase when we begin to feel more and more of what the books describe.

This is how one enters the spiritual world. Of course, it is not as simple as I present it – there is a whole system here, involving studying specific articles and lessons and following a specific syllabus.

The system of creation is everything around us, both perceived and imperceived. Our emotions contain what we perceive in our five senses, and what we cannot feel today; however, we will feel in the "sixth sense"-- an additional sense that will be developed in us in the future. We call that information "the system of creation."

Our fathers had a much closer connection with the Upper World than we do. However, once we do go into the spiritual world, we will obtain a stronger and more effective bond because we are more selfish, more evolved and more corrupt. Precisely because of that combination, we have a chance to turn the evil into good, experience deeper feelings in our world, and reach places our fathers never could.

In the beginning, they were closer to spirituality than we are because they were less egoistic. Moreover, we have drifted so much farther from spirituality than they did, that if we did come back to it now, we would have to go that much deeper into the system of creation.

THE GOAL

Q: Why do Kabbalists such as the holy Ari, Rav Kook and Rav Ashlag maintain that it is necessary for any person to study the wisdom of Kabbalah, regardless of age, sex, or nationality?

A: The reason studying Kabbalah is important is that there is a great power in the study of Kabbalah that can be of benefit to everyone.

When we study Kabbalah, even if we do not understand anything we study, but seek only to understand, we awaken within us an influence of the Upper Light.

In one of our lives, we must attain the completion of our souls. If we do not achieve this, through the Upper Light, our torments will gradually increase until they finally make us realize the reason for our pain. It is our souls' need to reclaim the Light that filled it before it came down to our world.

The soul of man starts its existence in the world of *Ein Sof*. It then descends through five higher worlds, before finally clothing our physical bodies. Those worlds are: *Adam Kadmon*, *Atzilut*, *Beria*, *Yetzira*, and *Assiya*. The result of the descent is that we are completely dependent on the components and characteristics of that spiritual system. Thus, we must study that system in order to function according to its laws, instead of roaming blindly through our world, beaten time and again but not knowing why.

The principal law of that system is "altruism." It acts whether we are aware of it or not, and we must follow it whether we like it or not. Disobeying that law produces disasters and tragedies, both individual and collective.

That law is not canceled, although we are stopped as soon as we break it. We will only be able to understand when and how that law works by studying the wisdom of Kabbalah. If we do not use that information, we are headed for disaster.

Q: Who can study Kabbalah?

A: Anyone can study it who relentlessly asks, "What is the meaning of my life?" Kabbalah can be studied only from an inner need, not through coercion. There are ups and downs in one's desire for spirituality. This explains why sometimes one begins to study, and later leaves satiated. It is possible that the same person will return with the same question as before, but this time from another level of development altogether.

Q: How can we know that we are now ready to study Kabbalah?

A: When Rav Kook was asked who was permitted to study Kabbalah, he replied: "Anyone who wants to." If a person really wants to, it is a sign that one is ready. If not, studies should not commence.

We will continue to reincarnate into this world until we decide to study Kabbalah and attain the necessary knowledge to understand and work with the system of creation. This is regarded as the highest degree, the last degree that any person, any soul can and eventually must attain in this life or the next. The method of Kabbalah prepares a person to enter the Upper World with knowledge and powers, without harming self or others. One enters the spiritual world only by the extent of one's correction.

Consequently, there cannot be a situation where a person enters prematurely and inflicts damage. The measure of correction is the measure of the penetration to the Upper World, and the degree of cooperation with Providence.

WHAT TO STUDY AND HOW

Q: What exactly do you learn in Kabbalah? Is it only about the aim, or is it a real "academic study?"

A: Kabbalah is a very real and accurate system, by which a person begins to gradually feel the Creator in mind and heart, to a greater extent than we feel our current environment. The Creator is sensed a lot more clearly, without any self-deception, and through controlled and systematically repeated actions.

Kabbalah is subject to all the requirements that exact sciences are subject to— you can measure emotions and translate them to numbers, you can conduct experiments, repeat them and transfer the acquired knowledge to others. Because of all that, Kabbalah is regarded as a science.

We use everything we're given in this world freely. We do not feel where and from whom it comes. If we were to feel the Giver, even slightly, we would instantly receive a different sensation, a different position, and a different relationship with anything or anyone.

That would immediately place us in a completely different situation. Our whole problem is the absence of the sensation of the Creator. That is why the single most important goal in our world is to feel the existence of the Creator, to establish some sort of contact with Him.

After that, contact will become much easier. When you attain even a little bit of the sensation of the Creator, you hang on to it, and can return again and again to deepen and broaden it.

Once you have achieved the ability to turn to the Creator, you can comprehend the kind of response you will get. This is what is meant by the phrase, "One's soul tutors one." This means that man is led by his own soul, and his own feelings tell him how he should proceed.

But before attaining this, one needs the meticulous guidance of a teacher, a group and books. One also needs to trust others who have already achieved that state.

A WAY OF LIFE

Q: How long is a course in Kabbalah?

A: The wisdom of Kabbalah is a science and a way of life that enables us to live correctly. How long does it take to learn how to live correctly? That depends on the soul. But when we begin to study, we soon feel that we can no longer do without it, because life without it is so strange and narrow that without connecting it to the Upper World, to the soul, and to eternity, life loses its meaning.

When we begin to feel like that, it is no longer possible to detach ourselves from Kabbalah and remain confined to our world.

THE KABBALISTIC APPROACH

Q: How many methods are there for the study of Kabbalah and which is the most efficient for our time?

A: Generally speaking, there were two systems in the study of Kabbalah: one was called the "Kabbalah of the RAMAK" (Rav Moshe Kordoviro); the other is the "Kabbalah of the Ari."

The first was in use until the 16th century, when at the beginning of that century, the Kabbalah of the Ari was established. The Ari described it in his books, and all the Kabbalists after him followed in his footsteps. Baal HaSulam is strictly a Kabbalist of the system of the Ari Known as Lurianic Kabbalah.

The souls that descended to our world before the Ari were from the "old type." But from his time on, there was a drastic change in the souls that descended, and some of them began to demand spiritual elevation.

Q: Is it possible to change the future through Kabbalah?

A: The Kabbalah is meant for precisely that purpose.

STUDY REQUIREMENTS

Q: Can I study Kabbalah by myself?

A: Studying without a teacher is impossible. The teacher should set a spiritual example, explain about the spiritual structure, how it works, how to approach it and how to raise ourselves to it.

Teachers should also explain how we can lift ourselves to a higher spiritual degree and how to control that spiritual level. There has never been a case in history when someone rose without assistance. It was always a case of a rav and a disciple working together.

I myself searched for many years before I found my rav.

Q: How important is it to choose your teacher in Kabbalah?

A: This is a routine question that I hear often. "How will you prove to me that you are the teacher that I need?" This is a very good and just question. It is your life, it was given to you just once and you want to make the most of it. But there is nothing I can tell you. How can I prove to you that I am better than anybody else?

The Kabbalah has a very simple answer: one should study where one's heart desires, where one feels one belongs. It is not a place that you are being persuaded to think is your place, or that you're pushed toward. When you detach yourself from persuasions, from anything external, from your upbringing and from everything that you have heard in your entire life, and feel in your heart that it is the place for you, then you should stay. That is the only test!

Q: How much does group study accelerate the spiritual progress of a person who studies alone?

A: Millions of times. A person who studies alone can only use one's own vessel to receive the Light of the Creator, meaning spirituality. People who study in a group, even if they sometimes argue, create a kind of spiritual vessel that consists of all the participants, and everyone begins to enjoy its illumination. Let us assume that there are ten participants. The illumination that is received is not ten times as much as a single individual can receive, but millions of times stronger.

The reason is the incorporation, meaning the soul of each and every one of the participants consists of 620 parts, with each part joining the others. The mixture of the parts together creates one collective vessel.

Q: What – if any – effect does language have on the study?

A: Kabbalah can be studied in any language. But Hebrew is the natural language because the Jews are the group that should lead humanity to spirituality. They are the descendants of Abraham, the first Jew, the first to have crossed the barrier and entered the land of Israel. This is why he is called a Hebrew (*Ivri*, from the word Over), and his language was Hebrew.

Most Kabbalists wrote in Hebrew because they were the heirs of Abraham, meaning his sons, his children. But in principle, Kabbalah is a study about the creation of the world and can be expressed in any language.

Q: Can Kabbalah be taught in other languages besides Hebrew?

A: If you open the Zohar, you will see that it is written in Aramaic. Aramaic was the spoken language in ancient Persia and the everyday language of Mesopotamia. Therefore, the Zohar was written in the language that was then the most prevalent.

At that time, Israel was under Greek occupation, which is why there are quite a few Greek words in the Zohar, which remained as Kabbalistic terms and names, like Italian words in music.

It makes no difference in what language we study Kabbalah, because when we attain insights about the surrounding world, we attain the emotional form and discover that there are no words, letters or sounds in that form. Even when we feel something in our world, we do not feel it in words and cannot always find the right words to express what we feel.

Words are completely external clothing; their sole purpose is to convey information. This can be done in several ways, which is why language itself has no meaning. Knowledge can be conveyed in English, Russian or any other language, even though the writers of the Kabbalah wrote in Aramaic, Hebrew and some Greek. There are also Kabbalah books in Arabic, and Kabbalists in the middle ages wrote in ancient French.

Again, a language is only an outer dressing to help convey information.

Q: Can a gentile study Kabbalah?

A: Anyone who is interested can study Kabbalah. Kabbalah books have been available for everyone's scrutiny for thousands of years. You can go into any store and purchase any book you want on Kabbalah. No one will ask who you are.

No secrets are taught in Kabbalah. The wisdom of Kabbalah is called "the wisdom of the hidden," not because it is secret in and of itself, but because it reveals things that were hidden before we began to study. It reveals everything that surrounds us.

However, the wisdom of Kabbalah is comprised of two parts: "flavors of the Torah" and "secrets of the Torah." The flavors of the Torah investigate the structure of the spiritual worlds, man's soul, and how one should correct oneself. Everyone is permitted to study that part. This material is written about in books of Kabbalah sold all over the world and translated into English, Russian and other languages. Anyone can learn the flavors of the Torah.

The "secrets of the Torah" is the hidden part of the Torah. Nothing is written about it in any book. That part is taught only after a person has acquired the flavors of the Torah, attained the structure of the spiritual worlds as well as one's own completely, and recognized and partaken of the process of creation.

A person who has attained that level, where physical life and death do not exist, sees the entire process from beginning to end and is above our world. Then the secrets open up like innermost fountains, and we understand the laws that are at the basis of that system. Before that, we will not understand the meaning of those secrets, even if we heard or saw them.

Q: Can you explain Kabbalah to the non-Jews by using general terms, without using the terms of Kabbalah?

A: There's no reason to explain or refrain from explaining anything. Our goal is to make the books of Kabbalah and all the knowledge about it accessible for everyone, all over the world. In principle, non-Jews should come to Kabbalah in masses only after the Jews do, but if there are those among them who've already ripened, they'll follow the same path as Jews. After all, Kabbalah is a method for connecting with the Creator, who is unique. A gentile who walks toward the Creator is called "Jewish," and a Jew who doesn't is called a "gentile."

Q: What is the best age to start studying Kabbalah?

A: There is no age limit for the study of Kabbalah. I have a student who is eighty years old, and I have students who have just finished high school. When you study, there are no differences between age or origin. The soul doesn't make such discriminations.

WOMEN STUDYING KABBALAH

Q: Are women allowed to study Kabbalah?

A: The holy Ari said that everyone could study the wisdom of Kabbalah, provided they have the desire. A desire is when a person feels an inner need to answer the question, "What am I living for?"

If such a desire does not give us peace of mind, then we must study the wisdom of Kabbalah. Kabbalah exists only for that. Rav A.Y. Kook was once asked, "Who could study Kabbalah?" He replied simply: "Anyone who wants to." If there is a real desire, that person will study Kabbalah.

Q: Is there a different curriculum for women?

A: There is no discrimination in spirituality. Women, like men, must attain adhesion with the Creator, the highest degree in creation. But women study differently from men, and so are the ways in which women can approach the Creator.

Q: Can any woman rise to the spiritual world, and if so, to what degree?

A: Yes, any woman can, and no less than a man, provided she has the desire from Above and the devotion from below, the exact same requirements as for men.

Q: Is it the will of the Creator that women will study Kabbalah?

A: Every soul should reach its destiny. All souls should reach equivalence of form with the Creator and become a part of Him, male and female souls alike.

MEN AND WOMEN

Q: Is there a difference in the study of Kabbalah between men and women?

A: No. Man or woman, it doesn't matter. Women must also develop spiritually. The only difference lies in the method. The beginning of the learning process is the same. That is why in our introductory courses there is no difference between the method provided for men and for women.

Later on, if a person goes deeper into the study of the actual Kabbalah, the difference in the method becomes apparent. Men and women begin to feel the world differently, because men and women are indeed two different worlds and have a different perception of creation.

INNER LISTENING

Q: I've begun to take an interest in Kabbalah. I want to start studying, but I'm told it's dangerous. What exactly is the danger in studying Kabbalah?

A: A great many people tried to deter me from Kabbalah: they were religious, secular, Jews and non-Jews alike, and strangers and relatives. I tried to fight the craving to know the purpose of my life, and I couldn't picture a day when I could get up in the morning without asking the same haunting question over and over again. I couldn't imagine a peaceful, thoughtless day, where I could sit down quietly and enjoy my life...

If there's no cure for it, it's like a curse. But the cure exists. If you feel that question burning in your gut, leaving you restless, you might be losing precious time listening to the advice of others and living by their reason, because ultimately you'll go back to what your soul craves.

"A person learns from his soul," so listen to yourself and you'll know what it is you want. If you can rise above the level of those who advise against study, there is nothing that can stop you. Sooner or later you'll come to Kabbalah. I suggest that you read Introduction to The Book of Zohar.

READINESS FOR KABBALAH

Q: Should I rush to study Kabbalah?

A: When a person truly wants something, that person goes out and does it. Therefore, if your soul is ready for ascension, you'll study Kabbalah. And if your soul is not yet ready, you'll remain for awhile on the outskirts of Kabbalah and after some time you'll drift away from it and go on ripening elsewhere.

Keep in mind that you do not find Kabbalah on your own, you are brought here from above...

KABBALAH PROHIBITION

Q: My friends suggested that I don't study Kabbalah. They said it was too soon for me. Why do they think that?

A: Before the 1920s, people did not need to study Kabbalah. Only a chosen few studied in each generation. They received a desire to attain the Upper Reality, the Creator, from above. At the end of the exile, with the reacquisition of the land of Israel after the holocaust, the last era began. It was a return by equivalence of root and branch, a return to the corporeal land of Israel, and at the same time, a return to the spiritual land of Israel. That is why the prohibition of the study of Kabbalah, set up by the Kabbalists themselves, has been completely lifted in our time.

However, people who are completely ignorant of Kabbalah still advocate the old approach, and cannot see that everything has changed in our world. Now there is a comprehensive change in our entire reality. You might say that if, until recently, Providence was dictated from Above, then from our time onward, Providence demands our conscious participation, made by our own choice.

If earlier we were still passive in the process, now we are compelled to partake in the process. The only condition is that we show a desire to partake in the leadership. Otherwise, the Spiritual Force will force us to want it.

There is not a quiet place left on earth. No one will be calm anywhere, especially the Jewish people, because the spiritual law that takes us to the center of creation affects the Jews first.

We are the first who must join in the leadership, and all the peoples will follow us. But it is the other peoples who feel that push, and the Creator urges us through them. It is not to our advantage that we are being struck without understanding why. If we begin to realize the reason for the blows, our situation will improve because then we will know what it is we must do.

Q: Why were we forbidden to study Kabbalah for such a long time?

A: There was no need to study Kabbalah before the return to the land of Israel. The Kabbalists themselves decided on these laws and it was they who hid the books. Rabbi Shimon Bar-Yochai, for example, hid The Book of Zohar and it remained hidden until many centuries later. The same holds true regarding the writings of the Ari. When he died, all his writings were buried along with him. It was not until three generations later that new texts were dug out of his grave and handed over for print.

Kabbalists have hidden the wisdom of Kabbalah since the ruin of the second temple until our days, and passed the information only to a very few.

But now, the exile is over and we have been brought back to Israel. Now we must reacquire the spiritual degree we have lost with the ruin of the second temple. Its loss led to the ruin of the temple and the exile, and only by reacquiring it can we be reestablished here.

PREREQUISITES

Q: Do I have to study the Pentateuch and the other scriptures before I begin to study Kabbalah?

A: You don't have to study anything before you begin to study Kabbalah, because Kabbalah is "contact with the Creator." A person who wants to study Kabbalah is like an infant emerging wet and naked from its mother's womb. What would an infant need to know at that point? When we want to learn about the Upper World, we do not need anything that we learned in this world, because it is the Upper World we wish to enter.

In order to be interested in Kabbalah, you don't need any preconditions other than finding the right sources of information.

ANYONE CAN STUDY KABBALAH

Q: Everyone knows that before you start studying Kabbalah you need very serious preparation. It is said that before one studies Kabbalah one must also be proficient in Torah, forty years old or more, and so on. The Book of Zohar can only be studied with at least one other person, say a disciple and his teacher. Which should I choose?

A: Bans regarding the study of the Kabbalah existed only until the time of the Ari. Kabbalists themselves enforced them because the souls did not yet need the Kabbalah to progress toward the purpose of creation. But since the time of the Ari (end of the 16th century), he himself and other Kabbalists have lifted the ban that they had set up. It was done because souls have reached such a level of development that they've begun to feel within them the need for spiritual, exalted content.

The time of barbarism has ended. Millions of people are beginning to feel the need for the wisdom of the Kabbalah, and those who are worthy will study it. You cannot stop this process. The desire of the entire creation toward the Creator is the very basis of nature, and now it is becoming evident.

Because man's desire is the force that determines his development, if a person wants to study, it indicates readiness mentally and spiritually, and no ban can stop that person from studying.

We should use the very means that we were born with to approach the Creator, and believe that in each given moment, the means that are at our disposal are the very best there are. Despite that, we must never stop searching for better ones.

Kabbalah is an understanding of the Creator, of the purpose of creation, a revelation of the Upper Light (within you, in your emotions), by changing your intentions. It is much like the Torah, in the sense that it, too, is not a historical tale, but a description of the universe and a method to understand the Creator.

In Kabbalah, concepts such as "forbidden" or "impossible" actually mean, "it cannot be done." For example, when it was said that it is forbidden to see the Creator, it means that it is forbidden to receive Light in order to please yourself.

Therefore, the words, "forbidden to study Kabbalah" actually mean, "It cannot be studied because of a lack of will." The statement is still correct today as far as the general public is concerned, but the souls that descend to our world today reach such a level of spiritual development that all their thoughts and earthly desires become aspirations for the Creator.

When that happens, we will say that we are "permitted to study Kabbalah" because we have reached a developed enough desire for it.

Q: Does a person have to be religious in order to study Kabbalah?

A: No, anyone can study. If the Creator gives us the desire, we will begin to feel a new attitude toward life, toward the people around us, toward ourselves.

Our genuine development from matter to spirit should evolve gradually, to the extent that we understand the world we live in. The more we discover the meanness and corruption in our world, the more we will be ready for an inner change. The law of the Upper World defines it in the words: "There is no coercion in spirituality." Only the Creator can change our desires and intentions, so if we study diligently, the change will come.

THE STUDY METHOD

Q: You write that the first phase in the study of Kabbalah is to read as much versatile theoretical material as possible. If during reading questions arise, should I continue reading, or stop until the material has fully "sunk in?" If I feel fatigue or lack of will to continue the study, must I push myself to study the full amount planned? Should I set up a strict schedule and stick by it, or take into consideration the difficulties that arise from time to time?

A: If you're in the initial stages of the study, you should read a lot, but only what you can understand. Read a lot and don't stop. Avoid difficult parts because what you can understand easily now will help you later understand the harder parts.

In fact, it's actually good to study when you feel you're not in the mood for it. At such times, it is best to study the structure of the worlds. There can be great benefits to studying "against yourself," and against your current mood.

For example, if I'm in despair, I should read about yearning for the Creator. We have to experience all the emotions. After all, we are built from combinations of all the feelings and attributes that exist in the world. In Kabbalah you experiment on yourself.

The learning material in Kabbalah is divided in two:

1. A study of the creation of the worlds, the *Partzufim* and the *Sefirot*, the concatenation of the degrees of the concealment of the Creator. That part is crucial to the understanding of the system of creation and its activity. It is studied in the following order: "Preface to the wisdom of the Kabbalah," The Study of the Ten Sefirot," selected sections of the Zohar (*Idra Raba, Idra Zuta, Safra de Tzni'uta*) and The Tree of Life. This material must be studied systematically, regardless of your inner state.

2. The ascent of the soul through the degrees of the spiritual worlds from below upward. Man must read and reread freely the parts that are of most interest. These are studied through the articles and the letters. They were not written in the same language as "The Study of the Ten Sefirot," but in the language of emotion, ethics, analysis of actions and so on. It is not really the wisdom of Kabbalah, but how it is used for the ascent of the soul. You'll read about it in the books of Baal HaSulam, Rabash, as well as in my own books. The study is comprised of an acquaintance with the material, meaning a systematic scan of the material in order to be able to find references, since people who study Kabbalah for the purpose of spiritual ascent are under perpetual changes, and must pick the material they read according to the state they're in at that moment.

CONTEMPORARY STUDY BOOKS

Q: Why do we study only, or mostly, the Zohar, the writings of the Ari and the writings of the Ashlags?

A: Because these are actually one writer, one soul that reincarnated from the first man, through Abraham, Moses, Rabbi Shimon Bar-Yochai, the Ari and finally, Rav Yehuda Ashlag. It is a soul that came down only to show humanity the path for correction. Although there are Kabbalists who know more, they were not given permission to write books meant to teach and correct people, especially not the newcomers to the spiritual path.

Thousands of books have been written throughout the history of Kabbalah, but my rav instructed me to study and teach only through these sources:

- The writings of Rabbi Shimon Bar-Yochai
- The writings of the Ari
- The writings of Baal HaSulam

I advise all of you to start studying these sources. Later on, when you have absorbed the material, you'll be able to understand other writers. This will give you a solid basis from which to examine other sources to see if they suit you as well.

By no means do I devalue other sources. Many of the Kabbalists were at an even higher degree than Rabbi Shimon Bar-Yochai or the Ari. However, they were not permitted to write, or if they were permitted, it was with minor implications that were meant for those who were already in the Upper Worlds.

Q: The articles that we study rely a great deal on the Ladder commentary. What is the Ladder commentary?

A: Rav Yehuda Ashlag (Baal HaSulam) named his commentaries on the Zohar *HaSulam* (The Ladder), because reading it helps one in our world climb the ladder toward the Creator, spanning every degree in between. That is the purpose of creation.

Note that the Zohar commentaries can be understood only after studying all the introductions, the most important of which is the "Preface to the wisdom of Kabbalah."

TOO MUCH STUDY

Q: Can Kabbalah drive someone insane? Can over-exploring Kabbalah have a negative effect on a person with strong emotional responses?

A: No, this is impossible if you study correctly. The learning consists of two parts: reading essays and letters of Kabbalists and the study of the science itself: the structure of the system of creation. Those two must be studied following a certain ratio, in order to sustain their balance in man.

SUPERFLUOUS SOURCES

Q: I feel confused by your principle of restricting alternative sources. If I understand you correctly, all beginners are strongly recommended to use only a number of selected sources. But the book *Al Pi Sod* states that absolutely everything points to the Creator, whether it's the Psalms, *Agadot*, Tanya, the literal Torah, even mathematics and physics, our daily life routine or even Buddhism. Everything is seen in a new way, reminding us of the Creator.

Why is "superfluous material" out of bounds?

A: Although everything in the world does point to the Creator, we are unable to see it. In order to see, we must know the right direction, have a correct approach to reality, and learn the fundamentals of the universal design and the rules of its development, its goal, and the limitations of our perception.

Once this is accomplished, we may "travel" anywhere, though we will lose interest in such travels, since we'll immediately discover the limitations of other approaches to life compared with that of Kabbalah. We will see that everything else is just common psychology devised by ordinary people, not by Kabbalists.

Genuine texts such as the Psalms can be read today, but one should try to interpret them in view of the Kabbalah, since this is what David intended while writing them.

KNOWLEDGE AND ATTAINMENT

Q: It is natural for man to aspire to knowledge. Why, then, has he not satisfied that aspiration over thousands of years?

A: The aspiration to know is wonderful, although it mustn't be an aspiration for knowledge alone, but rather for attainment: in order to attain the studied material from within you, on your own flesh, to discover who my "self" is and where within me lie the matters the books write about. After all, everything that's written there is written from "within," from personal attainment.

Therefore, when we read books about Kabbalah, the authors speak to us from exactly the degree they are describing. There is no "time" in spirituality. As the greatest Kabbalist of our time, Rav Yehuda Ashlag says, "...but out of the great desire and yearning to understand what they are studying, they awaken upon themselves the lights that surround their souls" (Introduction to the Study of the Ten Sefirot, item 155).

Out of a great desire to attain what they are studying, the readers awaken in themselves a surrounding Light from the same spiritual degrees they're reading about.

THE INTENT DURING THE STUDY

Q: You always recommend reading more. But how is a person who simply reads different from another who is interested in philosophy and mysticism, or one who wants the title, "professor of Kabbalah?" Such people do not make even a single step forward in spirituality.

A: Logically speaking, you're right. But the problem is that a person cannot force the right intent on himself. That aim should come from the heart, provided the heart really wants it. This will occur if there is a need to attain something higher, if your soul has developed to the point where it needs the Creator and not the material things in this world.

Only the soul can sense its true desires. We ourselves do not feel it. We may think that a certain desire is burning within, and actually be deluding ourselves.

Yet the soul is what will finally lead us to our goal, as it has led us thus far. It is not through our wisdom or conscious thought that we have come to aspire to the Upper Light.

In order to develop the necessary attributes for growth within, it is advised that "Whatsoever thy hand attaineth to do by thy strength that do." This means, do everything you can to absorb as much material as possible. Read, even if only to enrich your knowledge and brag to your friends about it. In time, the sheer quantity of your studies will bear fruit.

This is also true regarding the first stage of your studies. In order to absorb as much as possible, it is all right to lie to yourself and set goals, specifying self-benefit. But afterwards you will realize that the result depends on the quality of the material, meaning your approach and your intentions. That is why it says, "the Light in it reforms."

Q: I don't have any desire to give, but I know that it's probably within me. How do I awaken it? Do I have to give up something very dear in order to attain it?

A: By no means should you do so! That would only be an egoistic measure from within you. The only way to elevate yourself spiritually is to awaken the influence of spiritual degrees upon you, study with the right aim in mind, and help circulate the Kabbalah. Start, and you'll see how this simple act will change you.

INNER UNDERSTANDING

Q: How do we attain the acts of the Creator? Do we understand in our hearts or in our minds?

A: Anything we attain and speak of is what we attain within ourselves. What we hear, see and feel are not external objects, but our own responses to those objects. When we attain the Creator, we realize that nothing really changes outside us. Only we change inwardly, and we relate to those inner changes as external ones.

Kabbalah is a study of how to sense the Creator. You cannot understand Kabbalah with your mind. It's been said, "Wisdom in the Nations ~ believe; Torah in the Nations ~ do not believe."

Torah is a Light from Above revealed only to those who have corrected their physical desires to enjoy for their own delight and have acquired a screen that can perform *Zivug de Hakaa* (spiritual coupling) with the Upper Light.

People make every effort to absorb everything around them and take in as much as they can with as little effort as possible. In such a state, we experience only our internal responses, as complete egoists. But when we succeed in restricting our intentions to please ourselves, we begin to want to please the Creator, to feel what is outside us without the aim for ourselves. We begin to feel what is outside us because our desire is for something outside us.

Then, to the extent that we want "not for ourselves," we feel the Light of the Creator. To the extent that we get to know the Creator, we feel a desire to give to Him, which results in the buildup of a reciprocal bond between man and the Creator.

The extent of the revelation of the Creator is called a "degree." In man's emotions, these degrees are organized in five groups called "worlds." These are the measurements of the discovery and concealment of the Creator.

SENSES BEYOND REASON AND THOUGHT

Q: Is it enough to use reason and logic in order to understand Godliness?

A: No reason in the world will help us understand spirituality, because it is above our reason and our minds. This is why we can't feel it. Our senses can only examine things they can grasp and analyze, a knowledge that we generally refer to as "this world."

In order to feel the Upper World we must acquire other senses, which we call a "screen." Only with a screen can we feel what is above us, beyond our material sensation, which our natural senses cannot detect.

When we are able to sense the upper World, we also receive a different mind and a different reason. First, we get the wisdom and the reason of the Upper World. Only then do we begin to feel it. The only way to acquire a screen is through the wisdom of Kabbalah.

A GOOD SIGN OF PROGRESS

Q: When I was studying the system of the worlds, I got to the point of the creation of *Malchut* and the first restriction. After that, I stopped understanding and I can't make any more progress.

A: It is actually a good sign if you cannot understand the simplest things. It means that your soul demands to be filled with the sensation of the Creator. This suppresses the need for intellectual understanding. As a result, you do not fill up your brain because your soul will not let you!

However, without a screen, the soul cannot be filled up either. As a result, one tries to learn but can't understand anything. In fact, this is a good sign that shows one's inner demand for spiritual development.

Those whose souls do not motivate them toward inner sensations, but toward knowledge, study well and gain a tremendous amount of knowledge. However, their souls remain empty. At the same time, their knowledge is revealed to be shallow; they don't understand the inner processes because the Creator made a vessel of desire, not a vessel of understanding, so knowledge of Kabbalah can stem only from emotional scrutiny.

DESIRE, NOT TALENT

Q: Can a person with limited talent advance in spiritual degrees by oneself, or does one need additional help?

A: In the Introduction to The Study of the Ten Sefirot ("Breaking the Iron Wall"), Rav Yehuda Ashlag writes that, unlike a business that demands skills, memory, technical abilities, agility, rhythmic sense, and strength, the study of Kabbalah demands no talent, because all the talents are attributes of the body that is in this world. In other words, these attributes pertain to the nature of this world, which are not involved in attaining the Upper One.

There must be an initial desire for the Creator. If it's there, you need nothing more! If you have been endowed with such a desire, the whole process is in your hands from that moment on, because all the forces you need are already in your soul. All it takes is to develop them, and that's your work.

It is in your power to do so because your unique body was created specifically to allow you to attain the purpose of creation. Therefore, no one can say that they were incapable, that circumstances prevented them from attaining the goal for which they were born in this world.

IF YOU STUDY, YOU'LL GET WISER

Q: Will the study of the Kabbalah increase my intelligence?

A: A person's desires are very small at birth. Then they begin to develop to a slight degree. How much these desires develop determines how much the mind develops. The brain can develop only to the extent that it must in order to satisfy our desires.

But when we embark on the study of Kabbalah, our desires grow and we become more and more egotistical, and therefore smarter.

But there is no need to worry: when you study, you will get everything you need for your development from Above. You will actually feel something new within you—a gift from the Creator.

WHEN THE GOAL DISAPPEARS, CONTINUE MOVING FORWARD

Q: Why is it that after years of studying Kabbalah, the goal of life becomes "routine?" Those special thoughts seem to disappear, and it sometimes feels as if there is no movement or attainment. Sometimes the goal itself disappears. Is this a temporary state?

A: Yes, this is temporary. In fact, it is when we feel absolute emptiness, which occurs only when we strive for attainment with all our might, that we make real progress.

Our struggle may be made under the most desperate of situations and after years of disappointments and perpetual reawakening of aspirations for the goal. Then, gradually, it becomes clear that only the Creator can change our situations.

However, such a situation can occur only by total devotion despite the fact that the shells, meaning the egoistic desires to enjoy the Light of the Creator, constantly tell him that he can still do things by himself. Only then, and without any warning, comes the help of the Creator, like a dream come true, at the least expected moment.

Here is what Rav Yehuda Ashlag writes in his book, *Pri Hacham - Igrot Kodesh* (The Fruit of a Wise - Letters), page 161: "... There is no happier moment in a man's life than the moment he finds himself in complete desperation with his own strength, meaning when he has already toiled and done everything he possibly could by himself, but found no remedy.

Because then he is worthy of an honest prayer for His help, for he knows for certain that his own work will bring him nothing, and as long as he feels that he has some strength of his own, his prayer is not complete. That is because the evil inclination always puts itself first and tells him that he must first do anything that is in his power, and only then will the Lord welcome him.

It's been written in that regard: "The Lord is high and the low will see" (Psalms 138, 6). This is because, once man has toiled in all sorts of works to no avail, he becomes truly low. He knows he is the lowest of men; that there is nothing good about his body, and then his prayer is sincere and His generous Hand answers him.

The writing refers to this as follows: "and the children of Israel sighed by reason of the bondage, and they cried, and their cry rose up to God...." (Exodus 2, 23), because at that time, Israel was desperate from the work, as he who draws water from the well in a punctured bucket. He draws water all day long and still has not a drop of water with which to soothe his thirst. So were the sons of Israel in Egypt; everything they built was buried right there in the ground.

So it is with those who have not attained His love. Everything they do for the purification of their souls the day before, is lost entirely today, and each moment and each day they must start anew as though they had never done anything in their life. And then, "The children of Israel sighed by reason of the bondage" because they clearly saw that they were incapable of ever benefiting from their work. That is why their cry was complete, and thus rose up to God. God hears all prayers, but He waits for the sincere one.

In fact, anything, small or large, is attained only through prayer, and we work and toil only to discover our lack of strength and our lowness, that we are worthy of nothing on our own. Only then can we pray an honest prayer to Him.

We cannot simply declare that we are not worthy of anything and therefore should not trouble ourselves with toil. There is a rule in nature that there is none wiser than he who is experienced, and without trying to do what we can, we cannot achieve true lowness in the required measure.

Therefore, we must toil in purification and holiness, as our sages say: "Whatsoever thy hand attaineth to do by thy strength, that do." Understand this, for it is most profound.

I have not revealed that truth to you in order to weaken your heart, and you must not give up on mercy. Although you cannot yet see a thing, when the work is done, then is the time for prayer.

And until that point, believe in our sages who said, "You toiled but haven't found, do not believe." And when the work is done, your prayer will be complete and the Lord will respond generously, as our sages said, "You labored and found, believe." Before this, you are not worthy of the prayer, and the Lord hears only the prayer."

THOUGHTS AND FEELINGS THAT RESULT FROM THE STUDY

Q: You say that the most important thing is to attain the screen. I try to attain it day and night. I've become indifferent to the pain, but still I suffer.

A: Let me relate first to the screen that you're "growing" on your own. The screen is born and develops in us without any intent on our part, because we don't know what it is. All the new things that appear in us are solely the direct result of our studies. We cannot know what should appear in us the next minute. It will always be something new and unfamiliar, so how can we know about it in advance? How can we anticipate it?

"New" means something from a higher degree than my current one. Therefore a screen cannot be cultivated intentionally.

Your lack of joy from your environment is a temporary state. Keep studying and your alienation from society will soon be replaced by the opposite situation: you'll feel that there are more pleasures around you than you ever felt before. Then, you'll discover within you a greater will to receive than before, and it will happen in order to give you something to correct.

My advice to you is to read a lot, and only the material that I suggest you read, those parts that your heart desires. Divide the study between the Preface to the Wisdom of Kabbalah (with the drawings), and articles and letters. Do not prefer one study to the other.

In the morning, before work, study the Preface to the Wisdom of Kabbalah for an hour. Before you go to bed, read the letters and articles that speak of internal work.

Your moods will change many times along the way. It is a natural thing and it shows you're making progress. You have a lot of feeling ahead of you, but you are making an encouraging start. The articles you'll read will show you that your feelings and thoughts are typical of one who is making progress.

RUN BY YOURSELF

Q: You tell us to read our books in order to reach our correction. Is that all we have to do? This way it could take a million years before I reach the Upper World!

A: If you study the material correctly, you'll soon find that many tiny changes happen within you. You'll find you are being led, that there's a soul within you, and that something affects it from the outside.

You'll find that your soul and the Light of the Creator, which affects it, lead you, and not your physical brain. Your mind contains knowledge of the present, whereas the future remains unknown. But even before the future is revealed to you, you want to do more than just fantasize about it; you want to act as if you are in it, as if you have risen to the next degree of awareness.

The surrounding Light that is awakened when man studies Kabbalah correctly, works on the soul and initiates the next spiritual state. That state will then come by itself and replace the present. By making considerable efforts in the study of Kabbalah, a person can accelerate personal changes. That, in fact, is the only freedom of choice we have in this world.

Baal HaSulam writes in the Introduction to The Study of the Ten Sefirot that the Creator rests man's hand on the good fortune and tells him: "Choose this for yourself."

So where, then, is the choice? The choice is, in fact, that either we are pushed from behind, which we will feel as pain, or we run forward by ourselves, ahead of the pain. This is our only freedom of choice.

Anything that happens in our world, anything that people do, is all predetermined, because all the characteristics of man and his environment, both internal and external, are predefined by the Creator. Only for people who crave spirituality and only in their personal efforts is there freedom of choice.

HASTENING TIME

Q: How can I accelerate my spiritual progress and thus spare myself agony?

A: You can do this in the following ways:

- Read the books of Baal HaSulam, Rabash and my own.
- Join a group that aims to discover the objective of creation. Be active and do things for the members of the group and the spiritual leader.
- Begin to write everything you know about spirituality. That way, you can correct your current spiritual degree more quickly and create a need to attain the next degree.
- The most effective means of all is to take an active part in circulating the wisdom of the Kabbalah.

PERSONAL CARE

Q: At first I thought that bad situations came to us so we could try to overcome them. But apparently, there is a specific kind of "bad situation," whose purpose is to show that nothing depends on us, and the final outcome is solely in the hands of the Creator. Can you explain that?

A: There are no "bad situations." The Creator gives us everything for the sole purpose of correcting us. There is the Creator, there is us and there is what we receive from Him. It is said "The Torah makes one weary." It shows man who and what he is, that he's only a tiny egoist.

But the Torah, meaning the Creator, shows man his weakness–his enslavement to his ego–only to the degree that he can bear what he sees. The more we develop and correct, the more obvious it becomes that we are lowly, and far different from the Creator.

We are shown this in order for us to correct ourselves by simply recognizing our own nature and rejecting it.

You are experiencing the beginning of your personal relationship with the Creator. The good and right thoughts came because you felt what you were supposed to feel, but new attainments will come and go every time. Each time you read the right books, you will realize more and more deeply who you are and who the Creator is.

BEYOND PRIVATE PROVIDENCE

Q: Does the collective Providence still influence a person who's begun to study Kabbalah, or is he now only under private Providence?

A: What is the meaning of the study of Kabbalah? When we begin our studies, according to our progress in life, we begin to aim his actions toward the goal, which is to attain a spiritual contact with the Creator. We go under private Providence exactly to that extent, which is the purpose of our search, though it is still unconscious.

If we read only genuine books about the spiritual world, if that is what we find interesting, we are already under the private Providence of the Creator. The Creator guides everyone, but he guides us personally.

Every soul receives the Light from above with growing intensity, and therefore develops in accordance with the purpose of creation. It is called "collective Providence." But when He takes us out of the ranks to promote us faster and pull us toward Him, that is called "private Providence."

In a state of "private Providence," we begin to feel ups and downs. These will be expressed in our sensation of the Creator or its absence, according to our own attributes. We will stop looking at life as others do.

While others say, "Thank God another day went by. I stayed healthy, I did a few things," we, on the other hand, will start evaluating ourselves in greater detail: "Am I closer to the Creator today? Do I have a desire for Him?" Even if our evaluations are negative, they are nonetheless a testimony to our progress.

KABBALAH VS. ASCETICISM

Q: If I understand correctly, the spiritual path begins with the formation of the screen within me, meaning with the restriction on reception of pleasures. Does that not lead to self-oppression? If I have to give up on pleasures, won't that bring me to asceticism, which Judaism forbids?

A: Contrary to all other religions and philosophies, Kabbalah states clearly and unequivocally that spiritual ascent means increased pleasure. The beginning of the path includes the study of the Kabbalah, while the reader maintains a regular way of life without change or limitations. But since our desires influence our acts, if we want to achieve something sublime, we must act accordingly.

Thus, we see that the correction is a process   involving the effect of the Upper Light on man, not of restriction by coercion. That is precisely the difference between Kabbalah and religion: Kabbalah activates the power of the Creator; it is not an oppressing force from the outside. Therefore, when we receive more and more strength from Above, it opens up the channels for greater desires, which can then be corrected and used appropriately.

We cannot live without pleasure. After all, our very essence is the will to receive delight and pleasure, and the purpose of creation is the attainment of perfect pleasure. There's nothing wrong with the pleasure itself; it is only for us to correct its objective, not the desire itself.

PREFERRING SPIRITUALITY

Q: What do I do with my desires? I want a big, beautiful house, though a small one will do just fine. I want a new car, though the old one still runs. As for my job, I'm still interested in one that bears responsibility. Do I have to clear out these desires in order to make room for more study? (My relatives are already unhappy about the whole situation).

A: Anything in our lives–our choices, the steps we take, our preferences, and the way we evaluate our lives—is defined by how necessary we feel these things are. It is said that "All that a man hath will he give for his life" (Job 2, 4).

On the one hand, this quote can be interpreted this way: a person would sacrifice everything for life, health and the possibility to go on living. On the other hand, you can say that one would give everything away (life included) for something without which one's life would be pointless.

We can find examples of this throughout history. Even in our materialistic time, everything depends on our appreciation of material and spiritual values. These values change with our development, making self-coercion unnecessary.

In the Introduction to The Study of the Ten Sefirot, Rav Yehuda Ashlag explains that in the past, at the dawn of history, one who wanted to study Kabbalah and be introduced to spirituality had to restrict self and live on meager bread and water. But today, after corrections have been made in the world by more recent Kabbalists, and due to the development of the souls from generation to generation, all it takes to reach the Upper World is the study of Kabbalah.

Therefore, today asceticism and restrictions that people used to practice are no longer necessary. Kabbalists have drawn the Upper Light toward us, especially since the time of the Ari (16th century), as it says: "the light in it reforms," meaning the study of Kabbalah awakens an invisible illumination of Upper Light that corrects man.

Kabbalists explain that the study of Kabbalah awakens that illumination within the disciple more intensively than any other study. Therefore, they advise anyone who wants to attain spirituality and the purpose of creation to study Kabbalah.

Of course you can go on building houses, buying cars and giving expensive gifts, but it's important to maintain regular studies, read any time you can, and read only the writings of genuine Kabbalists. That study will bring you new internal situations, new values, by which you'll make your decisions.

The primary and the secondary in your life will gradually change, but it must come from within you, not by coercion. There is no coercion in spirituality, and the source of the coercion in our world is the shells.

My advice is to keep studying Kabbalah and be yourself at all times. In time, your soul will guide you and tell you how much energy to put into spirituality and how much to expend on this world.

SPIRITUALITY -- A NEW WAY OF LIFE

Q: I have no desire to do anything anymore. Things that used to give me pleasure - theatre, friends, even vacations – no longer do and I'm losing contact with old friends. What pains me now is my inability to understand the full structure of the world.

My question is: although I feel a lack of excitement, I must still function in this world. How should I utilize the external world for the study of Kabbalah?

A: What you are feeling is the beginning of your receiving new values and your reaction to what is happening to you. This period takes some time; you cannot perform significant changes all at once because your mind, your fundamental and essential systems, your nervous system, and the reciprocal relationships with your environment, make it very difficult for you to do so.

However, the good news is, you have already begun the initial process of inner change. Keep studying and asking questions. You're just like any other person who feels the initial effects of correct study on your inner world. A person who studies Kabbalah does not descend from a previous state, but climbs to a higher one, so there's no reason for despair, much less depression.

Of course, what excited you before now seems unimportant, childish and superficial. Naturally, everything around you changes: you work only for the pay, your contact with the relatives diminishes and exists only to the extent that it's necessary, and your friends are no longer close. These are the external expressions of your inner change.

But externally, you must continue to work and not change a thing! No matter how much your interest drops, you must not follow your desires, but your duty. You must act against your new desires; you must keep working, be with your family, and enjoy sports. All the secondary interests and hobbies are redundant. But you have to maintain contact with your relatives.

Giving up work, even if you have enough money to sustain yourself for the rest of your life, may jeopardize your spiritual progress! And while you must maintain in contact with your relatives, you'll have to gradually detach yourself from your friends. This happens naturally.

There's a law in nature called "the law of equivalence of form." That law makes objects with similar attributes draw nearer, and objects with opposite attributes distance themselves from each other. When signs of spiritual attributes arise, that law begins to act on us to the degree that we have attained these attributes.

HOW DO I CHANGE MY AIM?

Q: I feel that I'm learning for myself, which makes me feel ashamed. There are struggles within me, and I have reached a dead end dealing with them. I feel miserable because I don't know how to change my aim, how to invert it, so that none of the things I do will be for me. What do I do?

A: All those feeling are good at the beginning of the study. They show that you're progressing toward spirituality, toward the barrier, toward the sensations of the Upper World. Each degree, each spiritual situation you experience, must die, or disappear.

In other words, you have to discard the previous degree as unworthy of your new state. As long as the crop does not rot, as long as what remains of it is more than just the knowledge of it, the new stalk will not begin to grow. The same applies to souls: death is the beginning of a new life.

Therefore, the current situation ends when it becomes intolerable. The desire to move on to the next phase is formed out of the intolerable present state, out of shame in the present state. Disagreement with the situation brings with it a new situation. Therefore, the solution lies in focusing solely on the quantity and the quality of the study. You should read a lot (quantity) with the thought that each and every word should bring you new powers and change you from within (quality).

SPIRITUAL FATIGUE

Q: Why do we sometimes reach a state where the Torah wears us out to the point of physical fatigue? Does it mean that we lack desire for spirituality?

A: Only those who learn Kabbalah, who study and work with a teacher and with books in accordance with the principle, "I have created the evil inclination, I have created the Torah as a spice" (I've created the will to enjoy and I've created the Torah - Kabbalah - in order to correct it), are regarded as those who learn Torah. Only then will the Light of Correction (called Torah) shine on them.

But if we study without the aim to be corrected, only to gain knowledge, or to perform some physical acts, it is said that "wisdom in the Nations – believe; Torah in the Nations - do not believe."

Those who do not set before their eyes the correction as a goal are called "Nations of the World" because they do not feel the need for the correction, but only for the benefits that come from the Torah in this world and the next. The Zohar says about such people, "The leech has two daughters that bark like dogs – 'Have, Have.' Let me have this world, and let me have the next world."

Only those who learn the Torah in the Kabbalah find that their strength grows weaker. This is because they study it to receive strength from Above, to be corrected and to resemble the Creator. They do not want to stay at the level of the satisfaction of their corporeal needs. As our sages say, "You are called man, and not those who commit idolatry."

Those who commit idolatry are those who worship their evil inclinations and bow before their egos. You can either bow before the Creator, or before your ego, because only those two possibilities exist.

Bowing before something indicates the desire for it, or for the attribute it symbolizes. Bowing before the ego means a person places the ego above self; there is no desire to suppress it, but to feed on it.

The surrender to the ego is called "bowing before an alien god." In the Kabbalah this is called, "idolatry."

If the disciple studies Torah in order to become a "man," the evil inclination sees that it has nothing to look for here and the natural forces weaken. But at that time, the person still does not have the spiritual powers of bestowal, and therefore is still not attracted to the Creator, as there is not yet the knowledge of who He is.

Being between the two worlds is the state that causes the indifference. It is a necessary phase. After that phase, the Creator gradually appears. Higher spiritual goals appear and the person moves on.

Regarding your question: If your fatigue stems from the lack of genuine desire for spirituality, it is important to understand that there is a work, *Lo Lishma* (not for Her name - not for the Creator) and *Lishma* (for Her name - for the Creator). Working *Lo Lishma* is spiritual work that first entails working with the intent for self.

In order to understand that you're working *Lo Lishma* (and not everyone attains even that), you feel at least slightly~as though from afar~ ~the meaning of working *Lishma*, so that you can compare the two and realize that you're working *Lo Lishma*.

You should be aware that these are only mechanical acts. You must not delude yourself that you have reached anything substantial. Then, gradually, you must ask the Creator to plant in you the power to perform a genuine spiritual act, just for Him.

But all that happens gradually. A temporary physical weakness is a result of the passage from doing things for yourself, to doing them for the Creator. However, you have not yet acquired the strength to do it for the Creator~the aim *Lishma*.

When there's an urge to do something for yourself or for the Creator, nothing is too difficult to achieve. But now, you are right in the middle, in between the situations, and it is a sign of progress toward the goal!

A SPIRITUAL "DROP"

Q: When I first started my studies, I was very excited whenever I went into the classroom, as though I were floating. Now, I feel almost indifferent. Why does it happen and what do other participants feel?

A: Let me remind you that I do not suggest that people who study with me share their emotions~only their knowledge. I do encourage you to share the text that describes the structure of the worlds, the Creator and their activity.

Q: But I still don't feel the line between what I feel and what I know and understand. Does this advice relate to that unique feeling-the prayer, which can only be shared with the Creator?

A: Although you do not understand what is happening to you, if you keep changing, you're making progress! The situation you're describing is a positive one. In general, the more your moods change, the better. This is the only way for man to progress.

If the desire for spirituality hadn't been taken from man, he'd be left with no room for self-work. His will to receive (egoism) would snatch for itself all the fruits of the spiritual work. The majority of our spiritual work should take place during those "drops" when spiritual work is tasteless (like dust).

At that point, we might think that it is our sentence from above, in order to prevent us from working for our egos. Rav Yehuda Ashlag describes it beautifully in the article, "There is None Else Beside Him."

TALKING TO STRANGERS

Q: When I speak of Kabbalah to other people, I suddenly feel very tired, almost ill. Is this a natural reaction of the body?

A: The giving away of knowledge, especially as opposed to discussing personal feelings, can only do good to people with whom you come in contact. You should not talk of your own emotions and experiences, but you can and should speak of your knowledge. When you express your emotions, others seemingly enter your situation, which might harm you. But you can teach others, and that is completely harmless to you.

You are a very sharp and sensitive person, so during the teaching process you feel the enthusiasm, which is hard for you to let go of afterwards. However, this is a psychological response, not a spiritual one.

SHARING THE SPIRITUAL WORK WITH FRIENDS

Q: The other day I felt bad for no apparent reason. Prayer helped for only five minutes. I shared my pain with my friend and everything was okay, but the next morning I felt that he was in torment. Perhaps I should have suffered alone?

A: You should never share you inner sensations and emotions with anyone except the Creator and your rav. That is because other people are not higher *Partzufim* (spiritual entities) than you, and do not lead you. Therefore, even unintentionally, they will project their egos onto you, and you will lose your mental strength for some time.

Although you might feel temporary relief, you will temporarily lose the ability to climb to a higher degree when you share your feelings.

Q: I quote from one of your books: "It is forbidden to discuss inner situations with friends, because it can harm both you and your friend." I remember your saying it can harm me, but what can it do to my friend?

A: The danger is that you impose your feelings on your friend. These include your internal impressions with spirituality and your relationship with the Creator. These are all things that your friend must acquire independently from the Creator and from the books.

Q: I still want to understand what I can and what I cannot tell my friends. The more I try to understand it, the greater is the disorder in my head. It seems that anything a person says contains some portion of emotion toward the Creator. Even if two people speak of the text, they both have thoughts that are similar and that they understand. So how can people who study together be close to one another?

A: It is a very natural thing for us to speak only from ourselves, and in our words, we always include our egos. It doesn't matter if the ego is concealed or revealed~the most important thing is not to talk about spiritual feelings toward the Creator.

You can talk about *Sefirot*, *Partzufim* and about the wisdom of Kabbalah indefinitely, just don't show your feelings, because in doing so, you harm both you and your friend. The same applies for your spouse, children and even complete strangers. Study the books, but never talk about your feelings.

TO DO, OR TO STUDY?

Q: When is a physical act more beneficial than pure study? Is it when a person still does not understand the purpose of the study? How is there progress, if the physical act is "below reason?"

A: Physical actions for the benefit of the group, organizing lectures and Kabbalah study groups, are more beneficial than the study itself. Serving the rav is also more beneficial than studying with him.

In his "Speech for the Completion of the Zohar," Rav Yehuda Ashlag writes the following: "Make for yourself a rav and buy yourself a friend."

In other words, choose a man that you think is important and make a rav of him, meaning your teacher, and try to please him because he is important to you. That way, you'll get used to doing for others, and by the force of habit you'll be able to do for the Creator. By being spiritually close to your rav, you'll receive the degree by which the rav appreciates the Creator, and that will give you a chance to do at least something for the Creator, and enter the spiritual world this way.

At the same time, you will acquire the sensation of the greatness of the Creator and you'll be able to advance to complete adhesion with Him.

Observing the rav's requests with the aim to please him allows you to attain spiritual resemblance with him. You'll be able to receive his thoughts and knowledge, and above all, attain his love and attraction for the Creator, which would give you the ability to develop and progress spiritually.

The study with the rav in itself, however, is always motivated by the desire to attain personal knowledge for yourself. As a result, the study does not bring with it spiritual nearness with the Creator. In other words, by doing things for the rav, you attain his thoughts and through the study you only attain his words.

But this occurs only if the motivation to serve the rav stems from the desire to please the rav, and not the student. In the opposite situation, when the motivation is the will to serve for self-gratification, the study is the goal and becomes more important than serving the rav.

If the environment around a person does not praise the glory of the Creator, as it should, a person will never be able to attain a spiritual degree. Therefore, it is always recommended that the disciple regard self as the lowest (spiritually) compared to one's group. In this way, the student can adopt the state of mind of the collective. The environment is necessary to attain the purpose of creation, which is why you should "buy yourself a friend."

READING WITHOUT UNDERSTANDING

Q: Lately I've been going through a "cooling off period." At first, I was reading your books and I understood everything. Later on, various thoughts began to appear in my mind during my studies. Then, I had to make substantial efforts in order to follow the text. Later still, when I tried to understand what was written, I began to fall asleep over and over while reading the same line.

How do I overcome this obstacle? Should I continue reading without understanding and wait for this to go away, or must I change something?

A: First, I assume that since you've written to me, a lot of things have changed. Even the fact that you could write shows that you are not yet at the bottom of the spiritual drop, or that you have already passed it. You must make an effort to keep reading. That is precisely the effort that will carry you to salvation, to a higher degree. It may be a good idea for you to try listening to audio lessons.

Efforts in circulating Kabbalah help a lot, and will accelerate the changes more than anything. Things will change anyway; the only question is how long the process will take: a day, a month, your entire life? The next degree is right around the corner, and it is in your power to soar to it right now! It depends on you alone and no one else!

It's been said of such situations that "Whatsoever thy hand attaineth to do by thy strength, that do." Therefore, go and search for all sorts of acts relating to Kabbalah.

If you cannot study, translate. If you cannot translate, listen to cassettes or audio lessons, try and explain Kabbalah to someone else, try to start a group, spread books. Those are the most effective things you can do.

CHANGES OUTSIDE OUR SENSES

Q: **Every now and again new insights appear in me, and quite surprisingly. How does it happen?**

A: In the attainment of the Spiritual World, the time factor is of crucial importance, because man has to grow accustomed to spiritual concepts and definitions, and live in them. By "time," we mean that changes occur in us consistently and at a great speed. We don't feel them; in fact, we feel as though nothing is happening. Only afterwards do we suddenly and very profoundly realize the changes that have occurred.

This is a result of those little inner changes that we do not feel. Our sensitivity threshold is very high and only from a certain degree onward do we begin to feel those changes. Everything that goes through you leaves its mark on your soul, and after some time the change suddenly appears. Therefore, the most important thing to do is to read, all the time, no matter how much of the text is absorbed.

THOUGHTS DURING SLEEP

Q: **If I study a lot in the evening and I continue to think about Kabbalah in my sleep, is that part of the spiritual work and progress, too?**

A: What you describe is not a spiritual phenomenon, but a psychological one. The same thing will happen with any text you delve into before you go to sleep. Nonetheless, the fact that you study before you go to sleep and continue to feel the text during sleep is very beneficial. We usually study Kabbalah (the structure of the worlds, the *Sefirot*, phases, light, vessels) between 3:00 AM and 5:30 AM before we go to work in the morning. I recommend that you learn that material one hour in the morning and read the letters and articles "for fun" in the evening.

READING BEFORE SLEEP

Q: What should I read before going to sleep?

A: My teacher read Shamati before sleep. That last night before leaving me he gave it to me, and, falling asleep, said: "Take it and study it." After receiving it, I decided that the time has come to reveal it to all and had it published. Now you, too, have something to read before you go to sleep...

GETTING OVERTIRED

Q: If a person gets very tired and wants only one thing ~ to sleep ~ is there spiritual work in that situation, or should he simply go to sleep?

A: In a situation like that, you should go to sleep. But it's a good idea to read a few lines from Baal HaSulam's *Shamati*.

Q: I'm ashamed to admit it, but sometimes when I read the Kabbalah books that you refer me to, I fall asleep. It is not because I'm not interested; it happens despite my wishes. Even if I don't want to sleep, it's as though I fall under a hypnotic spell. What do I do? Why does this happen to me?

A: First, it is the influence of a Supreme Energy, the surrounding Light. Second, when a student comes to the lesson despite fatigue, it is better than being in a state of simple mental wakefulness when one is well rested. The Light of the Kabbalah is affected by the amount of labor a person puts in, not by the number of pages a person knows.

You can thoroughly explore the whole of The Study of the Ten Sefirot and still have no clue as to what spirituality is. Similarly, you can enter the spiritual world and attain the purpose of creation without knowing The Study of the Ten Sefirot at all.

If you study the right texts and follow my instructions, you'll be more and more convinced that everything goes according to the master plan. When you no longer want to sleep, you'll feel that those times of sleep contributed to your spiritual development. The Creator leads us; all we have to do is open ourselves to Him.

TIME TO FEEL AND TO CONTEMPLATE

Q: In his article, "The Time of Ascent," Baal HaSulam writes that during the spiritual ascent, it is good to read the articles hundreds of times. Is there any indication of how well I absorbed this or that article?

A: There are texts that have to be read and reread according to the general curriculum, and there are texts that one should read only when in the mood, be it letters or articles about the feeling of the spiritual.

It is said that during the ascent, when one feels close to the material, it is good to read just the things that touch one's feelings; i.e., where understanding will come through the heart.

The problem in attaining the spiritual is that we do not have the correct senses. They can be acquired slowly and gradually at just such moments. Thus, there is the time to use the brain, and there is time to use the heart.

SPIRITUAL GAMES

Q: Why is it that each time I hold a book of Kabbalah, I immediately get all sorts of disturbances that "crawl" into my mind, until

I just want to drop it all and leave? But as soon as I'm sent pain from Above, I take a Kabbalah book in my hand and then I have no problem focusing on it?

A: All that the Creator created is a desire to enjoy. In humans, that will is developed more than in all other animals. The goal of the Creator is for man to be like Him: complete and eternal. But that goal can be attained only through the influence of pleasure or pain.

Because we are made to enjoy and to feel pleasure, we cannot *not* feel anything. We feel the scarcity of pleasure as agony. When pleasure comes, we accept it as something natural and take it for granted, thinking, "I deserve it."

When pain comes, we resent it and feel, "I don't deserve this." Again, this stems from the fact that we are born of a substance called "desire to enjoy."

Because the Creator has a desire to bestow upon His creatures, He created us with a desire to enjoy. But if we were influenced by pleasure alone, because we are made solely from a desire to enjoy, we would turn into such egoists that we would become stupid.

Thus, only the search for pleasure forces us to develop. In order to bring us to the complete development, meaning to be like the Creator, there is only one option: bestowal.

When we receive pleasure, we think we deserve it, but as soon as we feel pain, we begin to search for its source. Thus, we gradually come to the Creator, the origin of both the pleasure and the pain.

Pain creates in us a desire to find its source, to know the Creator. Otherwise, we would never know the Creator and would never be able to equalize with Him.

If we are told that studying Kabbalah is good for us, how can we strengthen ourselves on the way? The Creator sends us disturbances so we will learn by overcoming them how to approach Him. And if the disturbances are not enough to give us the strength to overcome them, we are sent more agony to force us to make an extra effort to overcome them.

At that point, the disturbances no longer frighten us because the fear of pain forces us to be on constant alert. And this is the way!

You, after all, want to attain the greatest thing there is, not just in our world, but anywhere! So keep up your efforts, and success is sure to come.

KABBALAH AT WORK

Q: Is it a good idea to study Kabbalah at work? Sometimes there's free time and a possibility to escape to the Internet and read the texts instead of programming. In a way, it is cheating, although the boss will get his work done anyhow. I know that it's important to "come clean" to the study, so what should I do?

A: Let me tell you two stories:

The first: Awhile back, my teacher - Rav Baruch Shalom Ashlag - and Rav Brandywine taught Kabbalah at one of the synagogues in Jerusalem during their break from working as construction workers. Once, when they were about to go to class, a box full of nails fell to the ground and scattered. As a result of staying to pick up the nails, they did not make it to the lesson. When my rav told me about the incident, although it happened more than sixty years ago, he was still upset that the lesson did not take place.

The second story: I once took the rav to a homeopath who happened to be a friend of mine. The practitioner examined him and gave him a prescription. I insisted that the homeopath take money for his service, but when he begun to write the receipt, I said to him, "I get spiritual benefit for paying for my rav, but I don't need a receipt."

The homeopath replied: "When I get money, I write a receipt, because it makes my thoughts honest and that way I don't lie to myself, even unconsciously." I noticed that my rav was very pleased to hear this.

What I want to show through these stories is that you should always try to keep your mind on Kabbalah. If you need to read for five minutes at work, then go ahead and do it, just as others take a few minutes off to smoke. Make a habit of it so that it will always be in you, without it affecting your work.

FREE TIME

Q: I have four hours of leisure a day. Do I utilize the time for spiritual work, or do I do domestic chores? Do I decide according to my mood or by a fixed rule?

A: You have to divide the chores into necessary and unnecessary ones. The division must be set not by mood, but by relevance. Your most important act is to divide the day ahead of time into several parts, regardless of your mood, leaving at least one hour a day for the soul, preferably before you go to sleep. Then, go to sleep early and get up one hour earlier (or two or three) and continue with spiritual reading.

With the rest of the time, you can do what life demands of you, but every now and again, take a break for five or ten minutes and read or listen to something that will help you think later on, while you work.

The best results in correction are attained when a person combines not only the study, but one's whole life, when thinking about the purpose of creation.

A QUESTION IS A VESSEL

Q: Why is it that, as soon as you ask a question, the situation changes? In such a case there is no need for the answer because it always comes too late. Somehow this happens all the time. Why?

A: What matters is the vessel. Once it is completed, the Light (the answer) immediately fills it. If we're ready for the answer, we feel the Upper Light, to the extent of the ripeness of our will. If we're not ready for the answer, we do not feel the Light. The Upper Light is at eternal rest.

It is always in us. When the Light fills the vessel although the vessel has attributes that are completely opposite to the Light ~ they become whole, one. Answers come precisely where there is a question.

The Creator and the creature merge in one attribute, although the creature doesn't feel it. Kabbalists don't hide this merging; on the contrary, they emphasize it. They do it so that others will realize that their efforts are meant to enable them to discover for themselves what is always within, but concealed because of our current corrupted state.

EXPECTING AN ANSWER

Q: Sometimes I feel that the answers are given to me impatiently, perhaps even unwillingly. Doesn't the Creator want me to study?

A: Let's put it this way: there is only one case in which a person should not obey the voice of the Creator ~ if He shows you the way out and says, "Go away." Only in such a case does He invite defiance.

In this way, we indirectly learn of the response of one with a real desire. As a teacher, I can never desert anyone who truly wants to know the Kabbalah, whatever one's character.

CHANGING SITUATIONS

Q: I study Kabbalah and I feel that my whole life is changing: my thoughts, my feelings, my relationships with people, but it all seems strange. You read, and you suddenly begin to understand everything as something uniform. You realize that the Creator created this world so that it would come back to Him. The more the state is exalted, the more you feel your own corruption. Am I studying correctly?

A: Right now, you are going through some of the least pleasant situations:

1. You're drifting from one mood to the next, from high spirits to depression. This way your vessel expands, acquiring the contradictory emotions that are now becoming a part of it. You seemingly acquire the

edges of your vessel. Later on, you'll be able to feel different things in it. When these feelings are in you, they'll be a part of you; they'll be yours.

2. You are also being shown how little you can be yourself, how controlled you are by your moods, how dependent you are on the smallest change in your disposition. This is you and this is your world.

3. You realize that you are easily controlled from Above, that you're not independent, that you're at the hands of an Upper Power that you can't quite feel.

4. Out of these situations you'll begin to reevaluate your previous life, your views, yourself.

5. These states can last many months. In the end, you'll stop seeing them as good or bad and relate them to your own personal feelings. Instead, you will begin to evaluate them as closer or farther from Him. That will be the measurement by which you'll determine whether a situation is good or bad.

6. You'll stop responding to how pleasurable your sensations are, and your feelings about them will "die." You'll stop relating to these situations as pleasurable or painful and you'll be able to define them objectively. Then, you will already be nearing the barrier. About the rest, we'll talk later on...

Keep in mind that you must try to learn a lot, and must study when you are in ascent; you must try not to lose the contact between yourself and the Creator. The minute you move from thinking about the Creator to thinking about yourself, the minute you start to think that you like it here in this situation, instead of thinking about how that situation is near the Creator, which makes it good, is when you'll begin to fall.

But it will take time before you discover that you've fallen, perhaps days. All sins happen during ascents, when you fall from above. When you are in descent, there is nothing one can demand of you because you are weak and detached from spirituality. You are like an animal—depressed and simply enduring life. The habit of systematic study, of participating in a study group, helps accelerate your exit from the fall.

CORRECTION THROUGH STUDY

Q: **I've begun to study Kabbalah and I feel that I've become more irritable and less tolerant.**

A: Those who study Kabbalah constantly correct their will to enjoy, starting from the smallest desires to the strongest ones. That is also the way of mankind: the "will to enjoy" (the will to receive for oneself alone) grows in time and man grows along with it. The greater his will to enjoy, the greater the power that motivates him. If his will to enjoy is small, he aspires for nothing in this world and certainly not in the spiritual world.

As soon as we begin to learn Kabbalah, especially if we are studying not for the knowledge, but for correction, we immediately begin to feel our corrupted desires, our will to receive everything for ourselves at all costs. When we study, these desires continue to grow until we acquire the greatest possible will to enjoy~the will to take pleasure in the Creator.

Each spiritual degree is greater than its former in that it shows us that there is a greater measure of will in us to receive for ourselves. When we correct that will, we find that this is the only way to climb to the next degree.

THE LIGHT REFORMS

Q: **What do I get out of studying Kabbalah, since the Kabbalah has to go into my heart and not to my head?**

A: In the process of the study of the Kabbalah, we attract the surrounding Light, which purifies us and leads us toward the Creator (see item 155 in Introduction to The Study of the Ten Sefirot).

KNOWLEDGE, PLEASURE AND BELONGING

Q: Sometimes I feel like I'm making progress and I know things, but I don't take pleasure in that. In fact, quite the opposite. Sometimes I think I'm paused or even going backwards. Is this normal? Are the sensations of knowledge and progress the pleasure itself?

A: First of all, you can see for yourself that the answers are not what the teacher says, but what you receive from Above ~ within you. Only the answers you have reached by yourself are the true answers. The Light enters the vessel and fills it with Its attributes. The vessel "feels" them as its own and understands that this is the answer.

Furthermore, you can see that definitions have changed somewhat. If mere good feeling was considered pleasure in your eyes before, now the pleasure is the knowledge and the belonging to the purpose of creation. The definitions of pleasure and good feeling will change many times before the end of correction.

At that time, you'll feel the Creator to the fullest, as He really is, instead of feeling Him through filters and screens. Everything we feel, understand, acquire, are all Him, which fills us completely.

To be more precise, we don't attain Him; we attain the feelings that stem from Him, whereas He is within us. But the opposite is also true: our attainments are about Him, and we are within Him.

THE POWER OF IMPRESSION

Q: Why don't the lessons impress me?

A: Because you don't understand what is behind the words. When that becomes revealed to you, you will experience intense feelings.

Q: What is the meaning of the power of impressions in understanding Kabbalah?

A: The power of impressions serves only as energy that attracts one to continue studying the texts. When we study them in order to correct ourselves, to understand and attain the goal, we bring the surrounding

Light to ourselves, which gradually purifies us, thus bringing us closer to the barrier and the adoption of a spiritual nature instead of a corporeal one (to please only ourselves).

CARELESSNESS

Q: What do they mean by carelessness?

A: Kabbalists get together for one purpose only: to attain the purpose of creation. That should be the only reason for any act or thought in anyone's mind and before every gathering. Only then can you speak of the seriousness of the intent. If the mind is distracted, even for a minute, from the purpose of the study, from the purpose of the gathering or from the purpose of creation ~ that is carelessness.

LEARNING WITHOUT A TEACHER

Q: Can people who are interested in Kabbalah, but do not live in Israel, who read the texts on the Internet site, get together and study Kabbalah? Will we make mistakes without a teacher?

A: My dear! Never be afraid of making mistakes. Each step we take always begins with a mistake. As our sages said, "For there is not a just man upon earth, that does good, and sins not" (Ecclesiastes 7, 20), meaning that before a spiritual state of righteousness there is always a state of evilness.

That is because each higher degree is always the complete opposite of the current one, and it is never known exactly how it is opposite. In addition, it will take a long time and many arguments and thoughts before all who wish to understand will formulate a clear opinion about the process of creation and the intentions of the Creator. Once that opinion is conceived, one can begin to mold the newly acquired knowledge.

It would be great if you could meet, read our material and study it together. Even if it speaks of emotions toward the Creator, you can read it together, but without talking about your personal feelings. Texts that teach the structure of the Upper Worlds and their composition are permitted and open for any kind of discussion.

Group study, even without a teacher, promotes the students many times over and accelerates their spiritual development. I, on my part, will help you spiritually as if I were with you, for it is my assignment. Good luck!

VIRTUAL STUDYING

Q: I do not live in Israel, but I very much want to study Kabbalah. Please help me!

A: All the books by Baal HaSulam and Rav Baruch Ashlag are on the site and you can download them for free. After all, circulating the Kabbalah is my life's work. Try to download all the texts and, if you study the material diligently, we'll invite you to a seminar. Then you'll decide if you want to stay.

In this life, we need only one thing ~ a desire for the Creator. If it's there and it's genuine, meaning above all other things, then He will fulfill it.

Q: Can I find an answer to my questions on your site?

A: Many people ask questions and don't even bother to read the material on the site. If you want to understand something in a specific area, you should learn a little bit about the key concepts. I suggest that you read the material on the site, and I'm sure that you'll find there the full answers to your questions.

I'm glad you have questions, but you can acquire knowledge systematically, which will allow you to answer your questions by yourself.

A VIRTUAL GROUP OF KABBALISTS

Q: Do you also attend virtual groups on the Internet?

A: I've established an Internet group of serious students, and through intensive teaching they can attain what I attain with my regular students. Every kind of learning is available today, like real-time video and audio lessons, etc.

Build the group, and we'll start studying. I think that all those who are interested should decide on the matter among themselves first and get to know one another. A group of Kabbalah students is not just another group of people, but people who are going to study and understand the spiritual world together.

I, on my part, promise that you'll get everything my regular students get. We'll begin straight from the most important texts. I will prepare and present them to you along with the drawings and the video and audio lessons.

KABBALAH IN ENGLAND

Q: I'm writing to you from London. Right now, it is impossible for me to study Kabbalah in Israel. Do you know of anyone in London who can help me get started? As I understand it, without a genuine Kabbalist teacher and a group, I cannot make progress.

A: You have all our material on the site, lots of books and direct contact with us. Take the opportunity that you have and go ahead. For the time being, the Creator has given you all you need. It is enough for now, and if you feel an urge to visit us, you're welcome here!

Each person chooses a teacher. Examine, study our material and ask other people questions. If their answers satisfy you, decide whether or not to study with them. It might be a little early for you to learn Kabbalah and correct your soul, and other texts, too, can satisfy you.

Check and see if there are other topics that interest you and, if there are, don't give up on them. But that test is valid only after a few months of study, after you've studied at least the basics of Kabbalah.

IN AND OUT

Q: Can a person learn, leave, learn again and then leave again?

A: It is said, "A thousand go into a room and one comes out to teach." This is very accurate! Thousands of people come to me, but my regular group is no more than a hundred, most between the ages of 25 and 40. The group adds about 15 newcomers every year, out of hundreds who come during the year to lectures in various cities and to the Bnei Baruch center. That shows that anyone can come and go.

Kabbalah does not impose thoughts and it doesn't brainwash you. On the contrary, it is a method that teaches man freedom and independence, because man is born a slave!

TO STUDY, OR NOT TO STUDY? THAT IS THE QUESTION!

Q: Can I study Kabbalah even though I'm not sure how it will affect me?

A: Anyone can begin to study Kabbalah. If the Creator gave you a desire to advance in spirituality, you will develop a unique approach to life, to people around you, and to yourself.

The natural, genuine development of each of us should be gradual, in accordance with our understanding of the world around us. We change to the extent that we discover the other world that exists around us. That is why it is said that there is no coercion in spirituality; it is only a question of will, and only the Creator can change the will.

Therefore, your mission is to absorb the texts diligently and the rest will come in due time, if and when there is a need for it.

A WORTHWHILE EFFORT

Q: It seems that in Kabbalah, just like in any other field, it takes a great effort to make it to the top. But most people are busy with their little everyday problems and their small affairs. The ordinary

person thinks: "Kabbalah relieves us of pain and has a sublime goal. Great! Too bad I'm just an ordinary person, unsuitable for such exalted goals."

Can I progress in spirituality, knowing in advance that I will not be able to give myself entirely to Kabbalah, or is it not worth it for me to even begin?

A: You cannot attain even the smallest spiritual degree without an effort "beyond human ability." That is because it is impossible to change your nature by yourself.

When the sages say that you have to exert yourself "beyond human ability," they mean that by making a great, though not impossible effort, it can evoke the important awareness that nothing can help you but the Creator Himself. You have to be "broken down" to such a point that you reach a true demand of God for help.

The moment you can actually do that, your redemption from your nature will come. You'll be freed from the boundaries of this world and will receive the first Upper Attribute - the first spiritual degree.

"He who walks, defeats the path," and I would add that there is no other path. We do everything by coercion, even chasing money and power. The more we want to escape it, the more the need will push us forward.

I'm sure you remember the story of the prophet Jonah who tried to escape the Creator in order to avoid the correction that was given him to perform. But the city of Nineveh must still be corrected from within.

CHAPTER 4.
SPIRITUAL WORK

THE MEANING OF SPIRITUAL WORK

Q: Are there different ways to attain the spiritual world? What is the meaning of "spiritual work?"

A: Any work starts only after we enter the Higher World in our feelings, since we only then start climbing the 620 steps from the barrier to the end of correction. The period before crossing the barrier is called "the time of preparation for spiritual work."

"SERVING THE CREATOR" MEANS BECOMING LIKE HIM

Q: What does it mean "to serve the Creator?" How can one learn to do that? How can one merit it?

A: This is exactly what the Torah teaches us. It was given for this sole purpose, and it speaks of nothing else. But only Kabbalah presents this work clearly and openly, because it addresses those who have a "point in the heart" (a part of the Creator from Above, the embryo of the soul, through which man starts to feel the Creator) awaken.

The Torah instructs how to expand this point and fill it with the Creator, turning man into a vessel that contains the Creator. It can be made possible only by likening one's properties to those of the Creator, matching one's intentions with His. As He gives to me, so I give to Him. This is the meaning of "serving the Creator."

The greater the resemblance, the more one feels the Creator. It is called "sensing the Higher World." The world is a fragmentary feeling of the Creator and when man ultimately completes his correction, the world disappears and one is tangibly filled with the Creator.

ARE THERE OTHER PATHS TO THE CREATOR?

Q: When I examine the questions in this book, I see that all the answers recommend studying the right Kabbalah books. Is it enough to study, or is there inner work that I should do, and if so, what is it?

A: At birth, there is nothing that ties a person to spirituality. Then, at the right moment, symbolically named in Kabbalah, "thirteen years," the Creator sends a message to a person to come to Him.

From this moment on, a person must respond to that call. How? And how do you develop your own desire? For that purpose, Kabbalists wrote their books. There is no other way to develop except by them, under the guidance of a teacher who helps reading the books correctly, in a group, where the will grows as a result of the mutual group activity.

AT THE KING'S TABLE

Q: How does a person who feels attracted to spirituality begin to learn?

A: The attraction toward spirituality begins when a person begins to feel the Creator. But as soon as one begins to feel spirituality and the Creator, one also feels Him as the Giver, and herein lies the problem. The presence of the Giver makes us feel that we are only taking and think only of how to take from this world for our own pleasure.

Rav Yehuda Ashlag used to tell a story about this situation, called "The Host and the Guest." It is an authentic Kabbalistic story that all Kabbalists tell. Let's assume that you are a host and I'm a visitor at your house. You know me perfectly well, as the Creator knows man.

This means that you, as the homeowner, know all the things I like, all my secret desires, with which you set the table. I, the guest, come to your house and see that the table is indeed set exactly the way I like. Naturally, I want everything I see before me.

The host warmheartedly invites me in. "Please come in, I have prepared your favorite delicacies." I sit at the table. What am I supposed to feel? I understand that the homeowner wants me to enjoy with all his heart, but that, unfortunately, does not put my mind at rest, because his very presence prevents me from enjoying. If I hadn't seen him and if the table had been mine, I could enjoy the delicacies and, would eat them without a second thought!

Similarly, the Creator has set a table for us. Then, he retreated – that is our present feeling. As soon as the Creator (the host) reveals himself, the problem arises because I see Him, the Giver, and I begin to feel like the 'taker.' That sensation of charity eradicates any pleasure I might receive.

Q: Isn't it important that the homeowner prepared everything out of the kindness of his heart?

A: It's not important. Even if the homeowner wants to give us everything, we would still remain the receiver and the Creator, the Giver. We cannot compensate for that difference. Only if we study the doctrine introduced by Kabbalah will our problem be solved.

The essence of the doctrine is that there is the Creator, the homeowner, who has a desire to give. As we see, He, too, has a need: He hungers for our joy. He suffers if we are not happy, just as the guest suffers when the feeling of shame stops him from eating the delicacies. At that point, everything depends on the guest.

Can he enjoy a complete and endless pleasure? On the one hand, if he eats the delicacies on the table, he will merely enjoy the food and that will be the end of it. On the other hand, he can rise to a higher degree of pleasure, to more sublime sensations, and by that equalize with the host.

How? By deciding to refrain from taking anything from the host! However, the result of the guest's refusal is to throw the host into torment. He tries to persuade the guest to taste some of the food, and that opens up a possibility of doing something for the host, to give to him, instead of receiving from him.

How? By receiving from him, but only with the intent in mind to please him. Simply put, the guest does him a favor. By enjoying himself, the guest gives the host pleasure, thus moving from receiver to giver.

The guest uses his own hunger along with the fact that the host has prepared the food for him, that he wants to please him. He also uses the shame, without which the guest could never have stopped himself. The guest needs all those things in order to enjoy, and at the same time to give the host joy.

When the guest tastes the delicacies, he feels his host's joy at his pleasure. This way, both become equal and mutually dependent!

That is the essence of the connection with the Creator. Man must gradually prepare himself, even before he begins to feel the Creator, and as soon as he's ready, the Creator opens up to him and there evolves a process where man becomes the giver to the Creator ~ just as the Creator gives to him.

Let's assume that the Creator wants to give man a hundred kilograms of pleasure, but man is only capable of receiving twenty, and the other eighty kilograms cannot be accepted, because if he receives them, it'll be only for his own pleasure and that would reawaken the shame.

When we visit someone's house, we feel the same sensations. "I can take this, but I cannot take that. I don't feel comfortable taking this, but I do feel comfortable taking that," etc. It is an automatic behavioral response that occurs every time we cannot escape feeling like the receiver.

Man equalizes with the Creator to the extent that he can receive, in order to please the Creator. If, for example, I can receive twenty percent of the food from you, then it would be correct to say that in that twenty percent I have equalized with you.

In the spiritual world, equalizing with something means sensing it to the fullest ~ its spiritual state, its thoughts, and its sensitivities. In other words, man receives the delicacies at the king's table as much as he is equal to the King, the Creator.

The ladder of the spiritual world is built according to that very principle: man receives more and more for the pleasure of the Creator, thus rising on the ladder until he can receive the entire one hundred percent. At that point, he can give to the Creator one hundred percent, just as the Creator gives him one hundred percent. Both are interdependent, taking and giving one another pleasure.

That is called a *Zivug de Hakaa* (spiritual mating) of man and Maker. That state is also called "the end of correction." This is the state that we should strive to achieve.

It is an astonishing situation. Even the smallest connection with the Creator opens before man unlimited possibilities to attain perfection second to none, compared to the things we know in our present condition.

There is a constant standoff between the host and the guest, because the host wants the guest to receive the full one hundred percent, whereas the guest feels that he must overcome a dreadful feeling of shame stemming from the very presence of the host. This makes it impossible for the guest to enjoy the delights that the host had prepared for him.

This situation also exists in our world. The more spiritually evolved one is, the greater is the shame one feels, to the point that one might be willing to die if only to avoid the sensation of self-degradation.

Most of the time, we are afraid of contacting the Creator. The entire method of preparing man using Kabbalah is based on building that contact with the Creator, as well as man's expectation that the contact will be pleasurable.

Q: We talked about feeling the greatness of the Creator. What is the meaning of the presence of the host for you, if you're the visitor?

A: I feel him as the giver in every course, in every bite I take. What, for example, has changed in the salad, if the host is or is not next to you? The only thing that has changed is its inner content. The salad becomes more than a source of pleasure; it becomes a vessel by which I can make spiritual contact with something higher than myself.

Then, the nature, the will to receive all the delights becomes a means to attain something completely different, and a person sets sail into the spiritual sphere.

THE FIRST SPIRITUAL DEGREE

Q: How does a person cross the barrier for the first time?

A: When we change our aim from "for me" to "for the Creator," we begin to feel within (or around) us that which was previously hidden from us due to our nature of reception for ourselves alone. That new sensation is called the Upper World, or the Creator.

One feels the Creator according to how much of that aim is at one's disposal. That amount is one's first spiritual degree. In fact, anything lower than that degree does not exist. One can only rise from that basic step.

After the first degree, we get an additional desire aimed "for ourselves." This makes us think we have fallen from the previous degree. However, that feeling comes because we have been given a new, corrupted will.

The "fall" is the sensation of the next degree in its corrupted state. Thus, each time a person corrects the corporeal aim from "for myself" to the spiritual aim of "for the Creator," the fall is mended and one ascends to the next degree. (In fact, a person must crave this correction, but the Creator is the one who actually fixes it.)

Q: If a person has already felt the Creator, can that feeling disappear forever?

A: When we have moved on to the Upper World, we carry on upwards. Everything develops according to our efforts, where the degree of our efforts determines the rate of our development. But if we have not yet moved into the Upper World, and can only feel the surrounding Light, then this feeling stems from our will to receive for ourselves. Therefore, it cannot be guaranteed that future sensations will necessarily be spiritual.

Q: Can a person make such a terrible mistake and do something so wrong when "touching" the Upper One, as to make that door close and never open again?

A: It is impossible to think of anything that does not belong to one's current degree. When a person reaches a certain level, it determines one's every wish, thought, plan and mistake. It works like internal software.

It is said, "Sanctity only increases, never decreases." Generally speaking, nature moves ever forward. The drop should be accepted as a situation where one receives a new vessel, a new desire.

DECIDING TO RESTRICT

Q: Is it possible to delight the Creator without giving something up, without restricting myself, without performing the first restriction, but only changing the aim from "for me" to "for the Creator?"

A: When you begin to delve deep inside and feel your own nature in all its lowness, you'll understand why it is natural to be fooled by it. Our nature always puts on forms that are "real," "genuine," "useful," and "desirable." It is impossible to grasp that all our actions are performed *only* to please ourselves.

Therefore, we must cut off any contact with the desire and the pleasure. That is our "restriction" ~ the decision to not follow our own corporeal nature. Later on, we will reach such a level of correction that we become completely indifferent to the outcome.

Only after that phase, and according to the measure of correction, can we begin to contemplate how to act, not for ourselves, but for the Creator. Now we can see that correction is made of several consecutive steps, which necessarily begin with the restriction.

ANALYZING DESIRES

Q: How do Kabbalists determine which desires can be corrected and which can not? Are there considerations in Kabbalah or does everything come with attainment and experience?

A: The Creator created the will to enjoy because His attribute ~ to delight ~ and His desire ~ to bestow ~ are total and complete. But the will to enjoy needs to be corrected, perfected, and made complete. A person does not possess an independent will. Without feeling that the will comes from within, a person cannot truly enjoy anything.

The will to enjoy originates in the Creator, but in order to feel pleasure, you must feel His absence. What is the pleasure that stems from the Creator? It is the pleasure we receive when recognizing the perfection of the Creator and His stature. These alone are worthy of being received as pleasure, because that is the most sublime state.

Therefore, the creature should be together *with* the Creator, and be *as* the Creator. Being with someone and being as someone is only possible when we equalize our attributes, desires and thoughts.

But how can we creatures, with our will to enjoy, want to delight in the Creator, in His perfection and His stature, and make that will stem from within ourselves?

For that purpose, the Creator hides Himself. By gradually descending from Above, He slowly distances Himself and creates five worlds (in Hebrew the word, "world," also means "concealment"): *Adam Kadmon, Atzilut, Beria, Yetzira, Assiya.*

Each degree, or each world, is another degree of concealment of the Creator. Below these worlds is our world, where the Creator is not felt at all. The will to enjoy is five worlds apart from the Creator, until the Light reaches our world, which is why we only feel ourselves in this world. But that can only be felt through the concealment that the worlds create. Thus, if the Creator is completely hidden, we creatures are left alone.

The whole of nature in our world is in exactly that state. The still, vegetative, and the animate only feel themselves, and remain with that feeling, whereas the speaking creature, man apart from feeling himself and his will to enjoy, begins to feel a longing for something higher, too.

While the Creator is in a state of total concealment, the creature cannot feel that the Creator is hiding from him. Yet, the very sensation of distress, originating from the absence of the Creator, indicates His existence and the possibility that one can feel Him.

The prospect of aspiring for the Creator arises in us because there is a spark from Above within our will to receive. That spark is placed in us in order to let us choose which is best: the perfection of the Creator, or our own situation.

In order for that to happen, the desire to feel the Creator's nature and His attribute of bestowal is implanted within our egotistical desires. This implantation is accomplished by a spiritual process called "the breaking of the vessels" (a "vessel" is a desire or aim).

That process mixes the attribute of the creature - to take pleasure - with the attribute of the Creator - to render pleasure. Thus, man gets to choose which of the two is better and more complete.

The process of choice is called "the correction of the breaking." It is a process that spreads over many life cycles under the providence of a special system designed to manage the correction, called "the world of *Atzilut*."

At the end of the correction, the creature (the soul) wants to resemble the Creator in everything. Once it has gone through all the states of equivalence of form with the Creator, and through the comparison that the creature renders between itself and the Creator, the creature justifies the Creator entirely.

Equalizing the attributes (the equivalence of form) brings adhesion with the Creator, and, in this way, we grasp His thought. That, in short, is the whole story. The rest, you'll just have to discover by yourself.

THE ABILITY TO DECIDE

Q: I still want to better understand the term, "analysis." You say that scrutiny should be at the beginning of any learning process. Yet, since a true analysis cannot come at the beginning of the learning process, I wonder what efforts we can make in our desires to change ourselves? Can a prayer for this change come by itself?

A: We can never force ourselves to change. We can only change if we are changed from Above. If we are not granted new attributes from Above, nothing will help; not my words and not your will. Therefore, all we need do is make an effort. The change will come from Above, but it may not be as we would want it to be, but quite the contrary. Up Above, they know better...

Therefore, the first stages in the study and the advancement are the regular reading of all the texts. Read the books of Baal HaSulam, Rav Baruch Ashlag and mine, especially the parts you are attracted to. There is an Upper Light in the text that works to gradually change you. Just filling yourself with what is written in those books will enable you to analyze your condition from a point of view that is not corporeal or physical.

Then, the texts will begin to act within you, and the Light will gradually penetrate you and begin to change you gradually, though at first you will not be aware of it. As a result, you will acquire an inner knowledge, an ability to sort out which is closer to spirituality and which is farther.

CORRECTING SURROUNDING LIGHT

Q: Where does the correcting force come from, and how exactly does it do it?

A: In order to help climb to the next degree, the superior degree lowers down its bottom part, called *AHP* (*Awzen, Hotem, Peh*), to the degree below it. As result, we realize how we should change, how we can be corrected and where to receive the strength for it.

The correction is performed through the Surrounding Light, since in the lower vessel there is still no screen in which to take the Light. Just think about it: if it could take in the Light, it wouldn't need to be corrected, would it? The correction always comes from the superior degree, to which the vessel should rise when it is not yet corrected. That is why the correction is always induced from the outside, through an Upper Force that works as a Surrounding Light.

THE SCREEN: A SPIRITUAL DECISION

Q: The screen enables the soul to make decisions in the spiritual world. Do people in our world have a similar instrument they can rely on?

A: People in our world do not know anything yet, because they are blind and groping in the dark. They should only do what it takes to get them into the Upper World, meaning, they should attain a screen. We cannot appreciate a situation ahead of time and make decisions because we have not received the screen, the force of the Creator. We receive the screen as a result of the effect of the Light on the desire.

Q: How can we attain a screen if we have no Light?

A: There is a hidden effect to the Light; its influence can be aroused only by reading genuine Kabbalah texts. The screen is acquired through study, absorbing the texts, and connecting with the Rav. Therefore, it is important to read genuine texts, because even without understanding them we advance forward in the right direction. The hidden Light does influence!

As for the time a person is in our world, it is said in the Introduction to The Study of the Ten Sefirot that "Whatsoever thy hand attaineth to do by thy strength, that do (Ecclesiastes 9, 10)."

This is so because only after tremendous efforts can a person attain the effect of the hidden Upper Light. This will give one the power to be redelivered, enter the Upper World, and experience the reality of the sensation of the Creator. Then, the person will receive the very first screen, and behave in such as way as to please the Creator, as opposed to receiving for self alone.

Q: Why is the Creator called "Existence from Absence?"

A: In the beginning of creation, *Malchut* is called a point, a black point over the face of the white Light. After that, it spreads and covers the whole of the white Light and corrects itself in such a way that it shines like that Light, along with it. That *Malchut* is called "Existence from Absence," because the "will to receive pleasure" did not exist prior to creation, and hence was not felt. When we begin to feel that our whole nature is actually a desire to delight in the Light of the Creator, we are then considered a creation.

THE IRON WALL AROUND US

Q: From the Introduction to The Study of the Ten Sefirot (item 1): "First, I find it necessary to destroy an iron wall that has separated us from the wisdom of Kabbalah, since the ruin of the Temple and up to our current generation..." I have three questions for you on this issue:

1. Of what is this wall built?

2. Under what conditions was it erected?

3. Why is this wall standing between Israel and Kabbalah?

A: 1. The iron wall is inside our hearts, between its egotistical intention "for ourselves" and the point in the heart, the screen, and the altruistic intention "for the Creator."

2. The disciples of Rav Akiva (who taught, "Love thy fellow man as thy self"), experienced a downfall. They descended to the level of unfounded hatred, and with them, the entire Jewish people fell. There were earlier declines in spiritual level, such as the destruction of the First Temple, and from then on, such downfalls have continued to the present day. However, in our time begins the process of realizing the need for correction, and along with this, the rise of souls to the barrier and beyond it.

3. The barrier is an iron wall that separates us from the spiritual, from Kabbalah. By definition, Kabbalah is not a science of entering the higher world - that is only a part of it. Kabbalah is a method that teaches how to unite with the Creator and achieve the goal of creation, meaning Kabbalah actually starts beyond the barrier.

4. The barrier stands between Israel and Kabbalah because the desire called "Israel" (with the aim "for the Creator") is under the power of egoism (Egypt), surrounded by this wall. Today, this desire feels the need to escape from "Egypt."

CROSSING THE BARRIER

Q: Please answer my question: Do people feel when they actually cross the barrier? If so, is this feeling lasting or temporary? I mean, can a person know certainty that he is already THERE?

A: We go through all processes both before and after crossing the barrier in full consciousness, but the crossing itself is impossible to predict in advance. Crossing the barrier is a one-way climb to the spiritual world, but never back to ours. We are aiming to achieve *Lishma*, the intention "to please the Creator," complete unity with Him, like a fetus inside its mother's womb. Hence once filled with such a sensation, we will realize that we are THERE.

Q: In "The Attainment of the Worlds Beyond" there is a line: The lowest spiritual level is the level at which the spiritual becomes more important than the material. Do I have it right – when a person values the spiritual more than the material he steps into the spiritual?

A: Yes, but it cannot be achieved coercively. It can only be achieved under the influence of the Higher Light, as must all changes we go through.

Q: Does a person who is in the spiritual need a rav, a group, and books?

A: The answer is yes, and more than before. However, at this point the student already understands how much they are needed!

Q: Is it right to say that ... one who is not in the spiritual evaluates everything through egoism?

A: Yes.

Q: Therefore, would you say that a person who is in the spiritual evaluates everything through altruism, since egoism has been corrected?

A: Yes, to the extent that it really has been corrected.

MITZVOT IN KABBALAH

Q: What is a precept (**Mitzva**) and what is a prayer in Kabbalah?

A: A prayer in Kabbalah is a precise and written instruction that was written in a Kabbalistic prayer book from instructions given by Kabbalists. It is the management of the system of creation.

Observing *Mitzvot* means observing spiritual laws. The *Mitzvot*, in and of themselves, don't have any rational basis, because a *Mitzva* (singular for *Mitzvot*) is an action and law in the Upper World. Those are (altruistic) rules of bestowal, of giving; therefore, their reflection in an egoistic world, such as our own, appears strange and irrational.

There isn't any natural reason to observe *Mitzvot*. They can be observed or not observed. You will not break any of the rules of our world if you do not observe them. However, a person who wants to become equal with the upper laws on an external level does observe them.

One should want to observe the *Mitzvot* in our world, too, according to one's level of spiritual development, and not because of some fear or some anticipated reward. They should only be observed from a desire to equalize with the Creator in as many parameters as possible.

Q: How do Kabbalists relate to observing *Mitzvot*?

A: Many people think that, for some reason, Kabbalah slights *Mitzvot*. But Kabbalists refer to observing *Mitzvot* as any other religious person does. Kabbalah even praises *Mitzvot* and gives them a higher, spiritual meaning. This is because, according to Kabbalah, a "*Mitzva*" is a term that relates to the spiritual world and not to ours.

An ordinary person thinks that *Mitzvot* represent the Creator's desire for people to observe them when they are in this world. But the wisdom of Kabbalah explains that *Mitzvot* denote a spiritual nature, laws of the Upper World, by which the souls and the operations of the Creator live.

Just as there are natural laws in our world (gravity, electricity, chemical laws etc.) so there are laws in the spiritual world, and they are called *Mitzvot*, as simple as that. We must observe the rules of the world we live in because we exist in them and cannot refrain from obeying them. By studying them, we can utilize them as efficiently as possible, because we cannot act against nature.

The natural laws of the spiritual world are sharp and crystal clear to the extent that a person can be in them, meaning in the Upper World.

If a person does not observe them, that individual only feels and exists in our world.

But we can only observe Mitzvot, meaning the laws of the Upper World, if we have a "screen," the aim "for the Creator," by having a desire opposite to our natural one, and detachment from our egos.

Consequently, the Mitzvot can be observed to the extent that we retire from our egos, and the level of our submission to the Upper World.

Is it possible to retain the attribute of receiving for self (egoistic) in our world, while observing the laws of bestowal, of giving (altruism), of the Upper World, the spiritual Mitzvot?

No, it is impossible. The laws can only be acted out mechanically, in substance, according to how they reflect their roots.

That is why, by performing what the Torah writes about, with our attributes in this world, we are observing Mitzvot, the existence of their symbols in this world, although not observing in the spiritual sense.

Q: What is the origin of observing Mitzvot?

A: Mitzvot in our world are a replica of actions performed in the spiritual world. Those actions, which are also called Mitzvot, are performed in the spiritual world using the screen, which is the aim "for the Creator." Only actions with the screen constitute the essence of spiritual laws.

When we rise to the spiritual world, we do not become just another resident, but our presence there stems from our observance of the laws of the degree that we belong to. For example, we can exist, walk, move, and fly, only because we learned to use the law of gravity correctly. The same principle applies to a person in the spiritual world. By observing the spiritual laws (called "observing Mitzvot"), we enter it and become a resident. When all 613 Mitzvot are observed, it means that we will follow all the laws and observe them to the fullest.

Q: What is the place of *Mitzvot* in Kabbalah?

A: *Mitzvot* are, in fact, spiritual laws and their place is above our world. In order to really observe them, one must first rise to the spiritual, Upper World. We observe the *Mitzvot* in our world only because we want to somehow equalize with the Upper One.

We do not affect anything by observing *Mitzvot* only in our world. This, however, does not negate the observance of *Mitzvot* in our world by those who still cannot observe them in the Upper World. All Kabbalists were as religious as everyone else, in the sense that they observed *Mitzvot* in our world, with their corporeal body.

We have to understand that observing *Mitzvot* in our world only demonstrates a desire to observe them in the Upper World, nothing more. For example: on Passover (*Pessach*) and on *Sukkot*, Kabbalists are particularly meticulous about observing *Mitzvot* that relate to these holidays, and even more so than others. Passover symbolizes the rejection of leavened food (will to receive), or egoism.

On Sukkoth, the thatch symbolizes the screen, the increase of the power of faith above reason. The rejection of the will to receive and the screen are the foundations of any spiritual ascent, which is why Kabbalists especially cherish those holidays and stress their importance by observing their actions in this world.

Q: Does a person who studies Kabbalah have to observe *Mitzvot*?

A: No. You can begin to study without any preparation. No one will ask you anything. Afterwards, you will decide for yourself whether to observe *Mitzvot* or not.

Q: Can one attain spirituality simply by observing *Mitzvot*?

A: No one has ever attained the revelation of the Creator by merely observing physical *Mitzvot*. This is because one who takes the path of *Pshat* (literal Torah), cannot feel the necessity for spirituality. One comes to Kabbalah because of a different need.

I have already said that in our main textbook, The Study of the Ten Sefirot, which is a complex and profound composition, Rav Yehuda Ashlag asks: "What is the meaning of my life?" Did he have to write more than two thousand pages of completely mathematical text to answer it?

Without understanding what happens in the spiritual worlds, you cannot understand what happens in our own, or answer the question, "What is the meaning of my life?"

KABBALISTIC MEANING OF MITZVOT

Q: In your last book, you wrote about **Mitzvot** (commandments). It's very difficult to observe something without any understanding of its meaning or the corresponding laws in the Upper World. Where can I find materials on the Kabbalistic meaning of **Mitzvot**?

A: Read the answer to the question, "Can I change the world?" The meaning of Mitzvot is that when you observe them in their true sense, not by your hand and legs, but with the aim directed toward the Creator, then you can grasp Him in this desire, become equal with Him, and merge with Him. This way you reach out to Him and this is the real meaning of any Mitzva.

In our world, observing Mitzvot is necessary only to fulfill the act and place Kabbalah studies above it.

CORRECT THE AIM

Q: You often use the term, "aim." Which should I prefer when the aim contradicts the **Mitzva**?

A: A Mitzva is a correction of man's inner intentions, which makes the phrasing of the question incorrect. We need not correct anything but the aim, meaning our intent to delight ourselves alone, the aim for ourselves.

Man's nature is not to take anybody else into consideration, and to work only for himself. That is man's essence. Our only duty is to alter that nature, and that is the only thing that we can call "correction."

There can be no contradiction between a *Mitzva* and an aim. The *Mitzva* is a gradual process of correction of the aim, from "for me," to "for the Creator." Man must correct that aim at all cost. The mechanical acts that a person performs in this world, which are called *Mitzvot*, are not spiritual *Mitzvot*, but customs whose actual spiritual meaning is unintelligible to us.

EVERYONE MUST PASS CORRECTION

Q: I understand that one Kabbalist can do the work of seven billion people. But I don't understand why everyone (including women, children, old and young, retarded, etc.) must feel the pull toward the Creator and go through the 125 degrees to accomplish the final correction.

A: The structure of the collective soul ~ the First Man ~ consists of parts that are called *Galgalta* and *Eynaim* (*GE*), and parts called *Awzen, Hotem, Peh* (*AHP*). *GE* are the vessels that a Kabbalist works with in our world. They are vessels sufficient for the unconscious preparation of everyone in the world to have a point in the heart. But after that, everyone must travel alone. By "everyone," I mean every individual soul.

There are partial and incomplete life cycles, and there are those who walk in pairs with other cycles and thus correct one another, such as a retarded child and its agonizing mother. We cannot see the goal and the common correction of souls that are linked like that because they are very complicated and involve many cycles.

We are not supposed to occupy ourselves with these matters, as they only divert us from the main issue: if we are given a place, a life and an understanding of the goal, we must act!

When you attain the goal, you will understand everything, whereas now it will only confuse you, causing you to possibly miss your chance in this life.

Thus, our desires to understand what is happening do not match our level. They are sent to us from Above so that we will fight them, not follow them.

ONE HUNDRED AND TWENTY FIVE DEGREES

Q: To what extent can you separate between each of the 125 degrees? Let's take, a Kabbalist who has reached the spiritual world and is in, for example, *Bina* of the world of *Assiya*. Is the Kabbalist aware of exactly where he is?

A: Since even the smallest part of reality is comprised of all the other parts, it is thus made of ten *Sefirot*. Therefore, in the very first attainment, there is already awareness of all existence, since the whole existence is no more than ten *Sefirot*, only 613 times higher, clearer and more detailed.

In other words, after reaching the first degree, one can already sense all the parts of reality, but in a way that's appropriate to the first degree.

The three degrees of the soul's development - conception, infancy and adulthood~ exist in each of the 613 degrees. Of course, unless one has gone through all three states in the lower degree, one cannot attain them. But after the cycle of conception, infancy and adulthood, a person can already understand all the situations, even to the end of correction.

However, the end of correction itself is unattainable because it has no parallel in lower degrees. The end of correction is the last degree. It is called "the coming of the Messiah," which comes after the Light that corrects the evil forces, the shells.

THE WAY TO CHANGE

Q: Can I change myself without studying Kabbalah?

A: No. Changing means attaining the attributes of the Upper Light. That is why only through the Upper Light, which shines from Above, can the correction be performed. This is why it is the only way to change yourself.

ONLY THE SCREEN CAN CORRECT US

Q: Why do you say it is impossible to improve one's character? I think one can improve one's character with the help of psychology, but it is a waste of time. If there is something negative in a person, it must be the best thing for their correction.

A: It is correct that nothing we receive at birth can be corrected. The Creator initially designed it in a rigid, unchanging form. Hence the name. *Domem*, deriving from the word, *Dmama* (stillness).

The only thing that does change is the intention behind a spiritual desire, namely, our attitude toward the Creator. Only the intention "for His sake," born in us as a result of our efforts, is new. The rest cannot be changed.

It is only revealed in us according to the need and ability to create a new intention, "for the sake of the Creator." That is how we study it – there is the vessel, the Light, and the screen that is created by us.

THE CAUSE OF FASTING IS MISINTERPRETATION OF KABBALAH

Q: Rav, Kabbalah does not deal with physically observing Mitzvot. But if I want to change, push myself forward, and rise spiritually can I use the system of fasting for that purpose, such as 5 days of fasting, then a break and so on continuously? Or is it of no use at all? Naturally, in addition to the fasting, there would be Kabbalah studies, listening to lessons, etc...

A: Fasting will never help you improve yourself or become spiritual. It will only make you think of your "spirituality," nurture your vanity, and make you demand a reward from the Creator ...

I suggest you have a big snack and move forward! Eat right, keep fit and study Kabbalah.

OUR BEHAVIOR AND THE SPIRITUAL WORLDS

Q: In your articles and books you repeatedly stress that our behavior in this world is in no way connected with the spiritual worlds. Therefore, one may conclude that man can pass the barrier between our world and the spiritual world, and still behave immorally in this world (commit serious crimes, treat people badly, and so on). Is this true?

A: Since all the corrections must be carried out within, achieving the goal of creation means correcting the desire. No external actions can be defined as such. Only changing the desire itself from "for one's own sake" to "for the Creator's sake" is regarded as a correction.

Only by inner efforts can people bring about such changes in themselves and attract the surrounding Light. When their properties are thus changed, it will lead them to the Creator. Any outside pressure is only superficial.

We see how external restrictions fail to make us better (correction facilities, jails, etc.). They only conceal the vice and make us unable to quickly correct it.

Hence, unlike all other educational systems, Kabbalah calls upon man "to study with the proper intention in a group, with genuine books under a Kabbalist's guidance, attract the powerful Higher Light, and achieve the goal in this very lifetime."

The Light itself changes us; there is no other force capable of correctly doing it. Thus, Kabbalah is the only means of correction. When the time comes, all immoral traits will be mended, but for the time being they are needed exactly as they are. The evil was made by the Creator and one should not destroy it, but rather turn it into good.

Q: Can it be said that the changes in character are actually an expression of what was already in them? Though these previously hidden traits seem new, was their "changed character" actually sitting inside and only now surfaced?

A: We are surprised when normally reserved Englishmen or Germans suddenly turn into barbaric murderers. Here are some insights on this:

There is a story about a man who tried to convince a Kabbalist that man's nature could be changed. He said that even cats can be made well mannered and invited the Kabbalist to see this for himself. The guest came and, upon his host's invitation, the doors opened and cats dressed as waiters began to bring in the dishes. Everyone cried out in amazement, but while no one noticed, the Kabbalist took a mouse out of his pocket and set it free. When the cats saw a mouse on the floor, they abandoned everything and rushed after it.

We are caged within our nature, and correction is possible only if we receive the power to change from the outside. Any inner power is a part of our nature; hence it doesn't correct us, but only puts on an external disguise.

GOOD DEEDS COME ONLY FROM ABOVE

Q: What does doing good deeds in our inner work mean?

A: Good deeds are everything that leads towards the purpose of Creation and towards uniting with the Creator by matching our properties with His. Every act of correcting our souls and assisting other souls as parts of the collective soul is called a "good deed" because each one reveals that "Thou art good, and doest good."

Q: How can you aspire to do good deeds when you know in advance that it's impossible?

A: Try it and see. How else can you expect to know who you are?

The Light comes as a result of our efforts, and only if we aim for the good can we learn how bad we really are. So if we believe we are good, and testify to it, we reveal precisely what phase of spiritual development we have reached.

The most important thing to remember is to read as much as possible; this way you'll feel your true nature much faster.

SENSING THE GOOD

Q: How do I avoid pain?

A: The Creator leads the world and is in constant control of it. There is nothing in the universe but the Creator. Creation is beneath Him and the Creator is the sole ruler. There is no other force but Him.

We fully grasp this when we become Kabbalists, but only our readiness and how much we can adapt our mental attributes to the Creator's Light will determine whether or not we receive what the Creator wants to give us.

The less we can adapt to the Light, the more we suffer. The aim of the Creator is always for the best, but our own senses turn good into anguish when our attributes do not match those of the Light.

It all depends on our own attributes. If they match what we receive from the Creator, we feel the true intention of the Creator. The wisdom of Kabbalah reveals how we can alter ourselves until we reach a perfect match with the Creator, ultimately feeling only the good and the eternal.

Kabbalah teaches how to receive correctly from the Creator, and feel what's coming to us from Him.

CHANGE: A REINCARNATION

Q: Why is it that, when you are in a certain situation, you cannot even imagine the possibility of a different situation?

A: Every situation is considered a life cycle. If the situations are extreme, they are called a "catapult," meaning the running around of the soul from one end to the other after the body dies. The sensations of the self and the people around one in every situation are called a "world." Thus, each time one enters a new state, that person is actually in a new world.

The ego, whose root is in *Malchut de Ein Sof* (*Malchut* of the infinite), does not change. What changes is the screen over the ego. This changes the extent of its connection with the upper nine *Sefirot*, the attributes of the Creator. That way, when *Malchut* feels that the nine *Sefirot* are outside it, it feels itself in a completely separate world. If it weren't for those nine *Sefirot*, *Malchut* would only feel the pleasure or the lack of it in itself.

But when it bonds with the attributes of the Creator, it feels Him in them. That feeling can be either conscious (when a person is in the spiritual world), or unconscious (if one feels only this world). It can be felt inwardly (in the senses) or outwardly (concealed), and we call it "the world," or "my world."

Thus, you can see how miniature changes in your natural attributes, in your smallest particles, generate a completely different picture in you. That picture is so different, it makes it hard to say that we are dealing with the same person. And indeed, these are two different people. Their insides are different, but their outside - the physical body - remains the same. That is why it is said that at any given moment, meaning after every change, we are different, reborn.

CONTRADICTORY OPINIONS

Q: Why is it that I always doubt ideas that I myself presented a minute ago?

A: The truth is that everything changes within you all the time. The contradictions in you astonish you, and indeed it is astonishing to see how such many contradictory views can exist at the same time in one person, especially when changing from one minute to the next.

This, in fact, is how you are taught that everything is given to you from Above, that everything stems from the Creator, where all the contradictions merge into a single perfection.

And it is thanks to that merging, and your closeness with the Creator, that you'll be able to attain the contradictions within you.

ESTIMATION AND SELF-SCRUTINY

Q: How can I get used to analyzing after each act? If I fail to analyze it, does it mean that the act was superfluous?

A: Only reading Kabbalah over many months can bring you to feel and appreciate what goes on inside you, assess your thoughts and examine your actions from the point of view of the Kabbalah. Then the scrutiny will begin, meaning the ability to criticize yourself from the perspective of the truth.

Before one attains this ability, a person is like any other beast, because there's nothing within but one's animate nature. Only when the seed of the future sublime soul appears can a person appreciate self correctly. Only then does one stop being a beast and become a man, for "man" is that part of God within us.

A NEW BRAIN

Q: Since I've begun reading Kabbalah books, I feel as though my brain has been reprogrammed. It seems that all my moral values have been turned upside-down. I think more and more about simple questions whose answers I thought I already knew. Can you explain what is happening to me?

A: What you are experiencing is the beginning of an understanding of new values, a new appreciation of the world around you, a new and more mature approach to life. These changes take quite long time to happen, because it is impossible to make such drastic alterations instantaneously, and to bring a person from this world to the next. This is because the human brain, the nervous system and the physiological systems, the links and the relationships with the outer world, all lay heavily on us and present a counter-weight.

But you have already begun the changes in the soul, so keep asking your questions. That way you should begin to feel the first results of the study on your inner world.

DURING THE ASCENT

Q: When I feel myself in ascent, when I feel a purpose in the spiritual work, do I have to remind myself that the revelation of the Creator is only in my corporeal vessels, and start looking for deficiencies in that state in order to avoid falling?

A: An ascent is meant to be a springboard to rise even higher, not to descend. Read a lot and as regularly as possible to find in the texts what you could not see before. Do not, under any condition, enjoy the feeling of the ascent itself. Instead, control yourself, and along with the feeling of the ascent remember the very cause of the ascent and the contact with the source of that state.

The whole difference between the first and last conditions of creation is in man's sensation of the Creator. It is like the example of the host and the guest: the guest takes what's been prepared for him, but he doesn't feel who gave it to him. Only the feeling of the giver differentiates the two situations.

That is why we must try not to get disconnected from thoughts about the Creator when we meet with obstructions. The disturbances that He sends us are all in order to strengthen our relationship with Him.

The minute you forget about the Creator and focus only on the sensation of pleasure at your situation, you will begin to decline because the pleasure will be for yourself and not for the advancement.

It is not self-affliction, but rather a learning process meant to link the cause and consequence together. You can learn the rest from the article, "There is None Else Beside Him."

NEW DESIRE, NEW CORRECTION

Q: The spiritual world is a world of altruistic desires. Our world (this world) is a world of egoistic desires. One who puts a screen over the desires of this world and acquires altruistic desires of the world of *Assiya* will never be able to want the sensations of "for oneself." If that is the case, how can we ever climb to higher worlds?

A: Everyone has private desires that were given to them from Above in order to feel them in this world. These desires can be measured for quality and quantity. When we can restrict them (avoid using our desires only for ourselves), that is when we cross the barrier, the gateway between this world and the spiritual world.

The ascent to the higher degrees comes after we acquire a screen ~ after the correction of the intent to receive for ourselves, over the new and greater desires to enjoy. Afterwards, these desires are used as much as possible, as long as the intent is to give to the Creator, to enjoy for Him. By doing so, we bring Him as great a pleasure as He brings us.

You're right. If one has nothing to correct, one cannot rise. If one altered the aim on the new desires from "for me" to "for the Creator," only then can one ascend.

The ascent is the receiving of a new egoistic desire and its correction. It is the alteration of the intent from "for me (shells)" to "for the Creator (holiness)." The measure of the ascent corresponds to the intensity of the corrected desire.

Once a person has been given a desire with the intent "for himself" and has corrected it to an aim "for the Creator," that person rises to a higher spiritual degree. The old desire, however, is replaced with an even greater new desire with the intent for himself, and again the intent must be corrected. That is how we progress.

THE RIGHT AIM

Q: How do I create the right intent within me?

A: In order to feel the Creator, we must build within us the intent to receive pleasure in order to benefit Him. For this purpose, we must read the right texts. There is only one force that can free us and bring us out of our nature and place in us the right aim – the reforming Light of the Kabbalah.

There are special books that were written especially for that purpose, and only there is the Light strong enough to reform. These are the writings of Rav Yehuda Ashlag, Rav Baruch Ashlag, the writings of the Ari and the Zohar (written by Rabbi Shimon Bar-Yochai).

ADAPTING, PREFERRING, BUT NOT WAIVING

Q: Can you say that relinquishing the pleasures of this world shows that one has a desire to live in the spiritual world, or is that not enough?

A: The Upper World, meaning man's sensation of the Creator, is a better state than the state of this world, so we must aspire to it as something perfect and not out of fear of punishment.

In this world, too, before we attain the Upper World as something sublime, we indulge ourselves with pleasures. In fact, this is necessary in order to spiritually develop and build the right kind of connection with the Creator. A person who nullifies the desire for pleasure cannot continue to develop.

For this reason, it makes no sense to reject this world. We must simply learn how to accept this world in order to enjoy it in a complete and eternal manner. Here is where we can utilize the wisdom of the Kabbalah, and for that purpose it is good to do the following:

1. Feel the Upper World, meaning the Creator.
2. Be convinced that the Upper World is far better than our own.
3. Understand the method of adaptation to that state.
4. Realize that situation and be perfect and eternal in every way.

THE NEED FOR CONTACT

Q: You always recommend reading. What can I do if it's impossible to read at some point in the day, yet at that time I feel a need to bond with the Creator?

A: At all times and under any circumstances you can find the Creator within you, calling you to bond with Him. The problem is that the connection keeps cutting off. The Creator wants to deepen the connection, so the minute a person gets in any kind of contact with Him, He immediately erects obstacles along that person's way. This is done so that a person will sustain the contact despite those obstacles, and thus strengthen the bond.

It's true that man cannot always sustain contact, but he'll gradually succeed.

BEFORE THE REVELATION

Q: What can be done when I still don't have a permanent contact with the Creator? Can you feel the Creator before there is a screen?

A: It is impossible to anticipate the next step. On the contrary, creation is purposely made in such a way that we cannot foresee the next step, otherwise we'd be like a thief who runs before the crowd yelling, "Catch the thief, catch the thief!"

You needn't be sorry for the things that are still not corrected in you, things that prevent you from moving forward to bonding with the Creator. In fact, it is precisely that regret that pushes you to continue working on your nature and wish to be redeemed from it, from the intent "for yourself." That separation between your heart and your mind, between the desire to enjoy and the intent "for yourself" will indeed happen.

It is written (Psalms 126, 1): "When the Lord brought back those that returned to Zion, we were like unto them that dream." This is a transition stage similar to when a child is born; it comes over us from

Above without our being aware of it. But past the barrier the work is entirely different.

Only intensive reading of genuine Kabbalistic texts hastens the way. I recommend that you read the Introduction to The Study of the Ten Sefirot (Breaking the Iron Wall, item 155).

ATTEMPTS TO FEEL THE SPIRITUAL

Q: I'm trying to feel the restriction, the screen and the corrected desire. Is it possible to implement them in my everyday life?

A: Anything you think you can implement, implement. Otherwise, look around you. It does not matter that later you will realize that what you see is not exactly accurate.

Use incorrect analogies; it doesn't matter. In our world, everything is allowed because this world is here to teach, and the mistakes we make in it are not considered mistakes. Rav Baruch Ashlag always used to compare it to how in the past, when paper was expensive, a child would be given a piece of slate to write on so as not to waste precious paper.

At any given moment, we are faced with a different picture of the world. Each new degree is a negation of the previous. Therefore, take your sins and your mistakes in the right proportion ~ you should correct them, because without doing so you cannot rise to the Creator. When you use your desires with the right intent, you will rise up to the most perfect and eternal state.

CONFIDENCE AND FAITH

Q: Fear of disappointment stops us from being happy in the present. Does it also hold back my progress?

A: For Kabbalists, attack is an ongoing operation. The fear is not the fear itself, but a fear that results from the lack of ability to feel the purpose.

Feeling the purpose is called "faith," and it is faith that gives you the confidence to tackle pain. The disciple becomes a creature clinging to the purpose of life only to the extent that he or she can glorify the greatness of the purpose of creation. Therefore, if we work on glorifying the goal, nothing seems scary.

In addition, what is important about the goal is its connection with the Creator. After all, the Creator Himself is the goal! If you constantly strive to reach the goal, send for thoughts about Him within you, link anything that happens to you with Him, and then you can really do anything. You will acquire confidence, and the fear will leave.

There cannot be disappointments if the perfect and eternal leads you to Him. So all you need to do is to demand to feel Him!

THE AWAKENING OF FEELINGS

Q: Ever since I was a kid, I believed my feelings weren't real. They awaken in me a sensation of boredom and a desire to escape them. I want to feel something real!

A: This is a correct perception of the world we feel. The world is not felt for what it is, but more like a dream, as King David wrote, "When the Lord brought back those that returned to Zion, we were like unto them that dream," (Psalms 126, 1).

When the Creator returns us to Him, we feel that until that time, we were dreaming.

UNNECESSARY FEARS

Q: Is there something I should not touch while I am working on myself?

A: I don't understand the fears and worries of those who think that during the study of the Kabbalah we can "touch" something dangerous, something beyond our understanding, or even fall to dangerous places.

These fears are unfounded, and only a complete revelation of the universe can change our inner world. It forces us to change because we can no longer lie to ourselves, and a deliberate concealment on our part creates inner compromise, which stops the whole process of change and spiritual development.

When I first started to study with my teacher, Rav Baruch Ashlag, I was amazed at how deeply a person should dig. Bring everything to the Light, be afraid of nothing (although it can be very unpleasant!), and then ask the Creator to allow you to see even deeper.

THE RIGHTEOUS AND THE SINNER - CONSTANT STRUGGLE

Q: When the righteous "look" at the sinner, the sinner disappears briefly, then returns to "pay a visit" more wickedly! And as soon as the righteous close their eyes, the victorious sinner is back. How can I keep my righteous vision ever vigilant?

A: This is the constant inner work of the righteous and the sinner in us. But it is said that there is no need to try to destroy our sinner. Instead, we should turn that person into a righteous person. Then, the work will start to be creative. The work itself continues beyond the barrier and until the end of correction.

HOW DO I AVOID FALLING?

Q: It is probably impossible to avoid falling altogether. But can we predict the falls before they come? After all, one never falls immediately. If that is true, perhaps it's possible to try not to fall, or at least make it easier. Can the attempt to avoid falling today help me in my future situations?

A: There is no remedy against descents, and there cannot be one. That is because a descent is a fall into new desires of self-reception. Once corrected, they bring you up to the next degree. Each "next degree" is different from its former degree, in that you receive stronger desires. As a result, the power of correction "to please the Creator" is more intense.

They say that "holiness increases and never decreases," but prior to correction, each new desire with the intent "for my own pleasure" seems like a descent to us, or a fall. However, That specific addition, once corrected, will seem to us to be the cause of the ascent.

The new desire is received when we fall into the stock of desires for pleasure, which is in us by the nature of our creation. Only then do we slowly begin to live with it and correct it, hence the falls. In fact, this is how we receive the substance for correction.

It is, however, possible to avoid a fall in many cases, meaning to receive the new, uncorrected desires without a spiritual decline and loss of contact with the Creator. This requires a different method: you consciously control the situation, choosing to face by yourself a stronger desire for pleasure, thereby strengthening your contact with the Creator.

The method is to search within for the deficiencies in your intents while still in the ascent, thus avoiding the need to wait for the Creator to "drop" them on you.

There is a story told by Rav Baruch Ashlag about an old man walking along, bent downward as though searching for something, knowing that there are still many desires for self-indulgence that he has yet to encounter in order to correct them and thus rise.

We define our own situations, according to our own feelings. Therefore, we can and should aspire to exit a situation that we define as a "fall." We are where our thoughts are.

But other than that, a fall is any thought that is not of the Creator, but of other things. It doesn't have to be a bad feeling, or one of depression; it can actually come while you are in a good mood, desiring to enjoy life, but without a connection to the Creator and the purpose of creation.

Therefore, the beginning of the fall can occur when we feel at the top of the world. Suddenly, in that blissful situation, we disconnect from the thought of the Creator and simply enjoy our good fortune.

At that very moment, even unconsciously and uncontrollably, the fall begins, even as we are still enjoying life. Suddenly, we realize that the fall has taken place, and that we are already down.

So let us learn from this old man, who, while still on the ascent, is already looking for ways to improve his situation. He begins to criticize his thoughts and his connection with the Creator, specifically when he is filled with the Light of Wisdom. Because he so badly wants to find his deficiencies (in his intent "for the Creator"), he doesn't fall because he turns all thoughts that are not of the Creator, if they ever come, into a correction, which then leads to a further ascent.

SPIRITUAL ASCENTS AND DESCENTS

Q: What does it mean to say that a descent brings another descent, and in between we will not feel any ascent take place?

A: When a person regards every situation as a descent, meaning when one is dissatisfied with everything, it is an excellent situation. If that person were satisfied with the present situation, progress would stop. Clearly, it would be best if one didn't stop at all until the end of correction!

But if it is one long descent is it felt as several descents, with no ascents between them? It must be that the ascent is felt as several separated ascents because it relates to several areas: aims, the form of the pleasure, the feeling of disappointment in former goals, and the giving of new meanings to old values.

Generally speaking, all these are excellent situations. It is through them that the desires are created, and the vessels in which to perceive the Creator. After all, there is nothing more opposite to man than the Creator. Therefore, ultimately, the Creator is sensed only in the opposite sensations to those sensations that we feel toward ourselves.

AN ABRUPT CHAIN REACTION

Q: Please explain the meaning of "One sin leads to another."

A: "One sin leads to another" means that one violation leads to another. Man receives pleasure from theft, stealing someone else's Higher Light for himself. Damaged vessels start demanding more, consequently, "he who receives 100 wishes for 200, he who receives 200 wishes for 400."

When we fall to a lower level, it generates overall weakness and leads to further falling. The new and lower surroundings tempt us with new sins (receiving for ourselves) distancing us from the Higher Light and obstructing the Light's influence on the vessel.

ADAPTING TO SPIRITUAL DOWNFALLS

Q: When downfalls come, I start cursing the entire world and lose the desire to live. Afterwards, while reading your articles, I feel ashamed. But the downfalls return, and they are very deep, and there is no way to get used to the fact that it's only a game sent from Above, just an exercise. Any advice?

A: Practice and experience will turn feelings into wisdom and you will begin to evaluate the states you are in not just from your feelings, but also mentally, measuring, changing and comparing them, and seeing the connections.

Everything comes with time. How much time it will take to balance between the feelings and the brain, to long for the Creator not just emotionally but also mentally, depends on the efforts you apply.

STICKING WITH THE ASCENT

Q: During a spiritual ascent, when you're supposed to think about a lower situation, does that mean that you have to artificially descend to that situation?

A: Only the evil force pushes us to suffer and "eat our own flesh." Never, under any circumstances, should you look for lower situations because "one is where one's thoughts are." The lower the situation one is tied to, the more distant one is from the Creator.

Q: Is it true that when in low situations, it is good to remind myself of good situations?

A: No. It's not good to remind yourself how good you felt during the ascent, because you've already fallen from that. If you now rise up again by remembering that ascent, it is not a correction or a new distinction. Quality-wise, your current degree will be no better than your former one.

Therefore, it is best to search for new reasons to rise, make new assessments about the greatness of the Creator, the purpose of creation, and the nothingness of your own situation, etc.

SPEED AS FREQUENCY OF CORRECTIONS

Q: In Kabbalah, there is a notion of "speed of passing states." Could you please explain what "speed" is in the spiritual sense? And how can we feel that it depends on us?

A: In the spiritual realm (of sensations), advancement is defined as "the changing of feelings," determined by changing the attitude toward the Creator. The subtle nuances of these relations, "I vs. the Creator" form in us the sensation of spiritual motion. All the other changes are either not spiritual or preparatory.

In other words, movement is a changing of intentions from "for me" to "for the Creator." The frequency of such changes determines the speed of the movement in the spiritual realm.

DISCOVERING THE LIGHT WITHIN THE DARKNESS

Q: I've realized how selfish I am to people around me. It is terrible! I dream about changing. Is this the right request; is that the prayer

that He awaits from me? After all, I want to correct my relationship with people, not with Him.

A: You describe your situation correctly and analyze it well. You're right. Now you are being shown that one of your attributes is bad, but you are not yet shown how it feels compared to the qualities of the Creator.

The Creator is still hidden from you, and you still don't feel Him. But it is through that comparison, through the gradual discovery of your negative attributes, that you'll begin to feel the Creator as something opposite to your own nature on the one hand, and as something near, soft and kind to you, on the other.

Then you'll understand the principle of "as far as light excelleth darkness" (Ecclesiastes 2, 13). We are all vessels, and therefore can only understand the Light as something opposite to us, or else we would feel it as pleasure and not as another attribute.

HE AND I

Q: How can I go through all these difficult times?

A: If I feel something negative about myself, at first I am infuriated. I want to scream, to be free from the distress. Then I calm down and try to understand that the Creator sent this sensation to me for a reason. If I prepare myself ahead of time to realize that everything that happens to me comes from the Creator, that He is the One who sends me the problem, along with the sensation that it comes from Him, that situation is called "concealment of the face."

And we awaken, because we are now faced with a problem. It is not only a blow, but a special message from Above. Here begins our spiritual work. We, who cannot see that there is a message from the Creator that comes along with the blow, are more like animals.

If we understand that the Creator is the Source of this blow in order to wake us up, we begin to relate to things from the perspective of "the point in the heart."

We must always try to remember that there are only two realities in the world: "Him" and "me." Even after you have accepted that everything that happened to you came deliberately from the Creator, there is still a great deal of spiritual work to be done.

The first thing to remember is that you must never simply settle for the understanding that the Creator sent you this message, and then calm down, and continue as though nothing happened. By doing so, you are seemingly erasing that message, and are waiving a chance for advancement that was given to you by the Creator.

FROM DESPAIR TO BLISS

Q: I feel bad for not having a true desire, one that doesn't let me sleep. Can we genuinely say at some point that we have done everything we possibly could to attain our goal? How can we reach it?

A: It is as Baal HaSulam writes: "There is no happier moment in one's life than when one finds oneself completely desperate of one's own strength. Meaning, that he has already toiled and done everything he could possibly think of and found no cure. For then one is worthy of a genuine prayer for the Lord's help, because one knows for certain that one's own efforts will be of no avail. But as long as one still feels that something might still be done, one might still be able to do, one's prayer is not complete."

Therefore, it is necessary to quickly make the full amount of effort, in quality and quantity, in order to attain complete awareness of the necessity of God's help. But other than that, it is always vital to work on the need to attain the purpose; otherwise all that you will harvest is despair.

Here is a winning recipe: Read, translate and help spread the Kabbalah (the most helpful of all), pray and ask of the Creator, as much as possible, and what the mind will not do, time will.

CHANGING SITUATIONS

Q: How do situations change? For example, when we feel powerless and realize that this is our true state and there is nothing we can do about it at the moment, how do we exit to another situation? Or should we accumulate a certain number of such situations until the Creator Himself delivers us, because we are passive and cannot demand strongly?

A: Our changes and ups and downs do not depend directly on the amount or quality of our labor, the power of our study, or the work of our group. We can never see that the increase in changing situations depends on our labor because we cannot see the difference between our current and future situations.

Sometimes, although we put in a great deal of effort, we suddenly feel the next situation as harder and harsher, or we suddenly experience rapid progress, while we have done almost nothing!

Only in the future, when we have passed these situations, will we understand their causes and effects. Therefore, we must go on regardless of the immediate results, because the explanation will be given only at the end, when its necessity will also be understood. However, we are built to always want rewards for our actions, the response that we think we should get. Over time, we gradually gain patience and experience, even when we do not get an immediate answer to every question. One simply toils on.

ON WHOM DO WE DEPEND?

Q: After having read the Rambam, whom do I ultimately depend on, myself or the Creator?

A: Everything is in the hands of man, and everything is in the hands of the Creator ("all is foreseen and permission is granted"). This is exactly what The Rambam dealt with. One should say before the act that everything depends on him: "If I am not for me, who is for me?"

But faced with the outcome, one should say that it is the Creator's will and the Creator's doing, since "there is none else beside Him." We are always within the boundaries of time and cannot perceive how it is possible to be outside them. Therefore we cannot imagine how everything can depend on us, and at the same time depend on Him.

WHERE'S THE "I"?

Q: It is said that in the beginning of every act I should say: "If I'm not for me, who is for me?" and at the end I should say: "There is none else beside Him." How do I relate to emotions during the act, and where am I in my decisions?

A: Exactly because we still lack the sensation of the sameness between our "self" and the Creator, we should artificially awaken a situation where we are, so to speak, completely cleaved to the Creator, as though there is no difference between us and the Creator.

Then there cannot be the question, "Who is the performer, me or the Creator?" By awakening the state of adhesion and with our power of will and yearning for the Creator, we will begin to, over time, actually feel that state.

But that does not conclude our work. Progress is possible only through contradictions. Therefore, during the act and before it, we should ignore the existence of the Creator and force ourselves to act, not in false pretense, but as though the Creator is really gone.

These exercises are necessary because suddenly, in that phase, we begin to "believe in the Creator," "to be righteous," although we cannot actually feel the Creator.

Q: Why does man prefer to believe, rather than to act directly and realistically?

A: It is because the evil forces, the shells (our corrupted desires) that are not cleaved to the Creator intentionally stop us from acting. This makes it possible for us to try to correct these thoughts and desires.

You might say that all these obstacles originate in the Creator: in the beginning, He sends us thoughts that He exists. It is His obstacles that prevent us from acting. At the end, He sends us thoughts that He does not exist, and those, too, are obstacles that we must overcome.

All these obstacles regarding the presence or absence of the Creator exist solely to give us a chance to make an effort. That effort corrects our thoughts and our intentions.

Ultimately, man sticks with the thoughts of the Creator. He does not follow the thoughts of the Creator, but rather cleaves to them, meaning that man's thoughts and the Creator's become identical.

Baal HaSulam once wrote about it in a letter:

"I have already said on behalf of the Baal Shem Tov, that before a Mitzva is performed one mustn't think of private providence, but on the contrary, one should say," If I'm not for me, then who is for me?"

But when the act is done, he must believe that it is not by the might of my hand that I deed that Mitzva, but only through the grace of God, who planned it for me in advance, and I was compelled to obey.

So it is with matters of this world, because spirituality and worldliness are alike. Therefore, before a man goes out to the market to earn his daily bread, he should remove his thoughts from Providence and say: "If I'm not for me, who is for me?" and do everything other people do in order to make their daily living.

But at night, when he comes home with his pay in his hand, God forbid that he should think that because of his ingenuity he made that profit. Even if he had been lying in the basement the entire day, he would still have made that same amount, because that is what the Creator had in mind for him and that is the way it must be.

And although these ideas seem to contradict one another and are unacceptable, still man must believe them, because that is what the Lord had stated about him.

And that is the secret of the unification of *Havayah Elokim*. *Havayah* is private Providence, where God is everything and needs not the help of dwellers of clay houses. "*Elokim*," in Hebrew numerology equals "nature," where man behaves according to the nature that He had imprinted in the corporeal heaven and earth.

When man keeps their laws as all other animals, but along with that believes in *Havayah*, that is in Private Providence. By that he is found to be uniting the two in one, and thus brings great contentment to his Maker and illumination in all the worlds."

Now we can understand the three aspects: *Mitzva*, sin and choice. The *Mitzva* is the place of holiness, the sin ~ the place of the evil side, and the choice, which is neither *Mitzva* nor sin is what holiness and the evil side fight over.

When man makes choices that do not fall into holiness, he makes that whole place fall in the hands of the evil side. And when he gets stronger and performs unifications with holiness, he makes the area of the choice a holy place again.

I have interpreted the words of our sages ~ "the healer has been given permission to heal" ~ according to that, meaning even though the healing is undoubtedly in the hands of the Lord and no human counsel shall move Him from his place, still the holy Torah tells us that He "shall cause him to be thoroughly healed (Exodus 21, 19)", meaning to tell you that it is a choice, the place of battle between holiness and sin.

So we find that we are obliged to take over that choice and turn it over to holiness. And how is it taken over? When we go to see a doctor, and the doctor gives us a remedy that has been tested a thousand times, and when the medicine works and we are cured, we must still believe that without that doctor the Lord would still heal us, because the length of our lives has been predetermined, and instead of praising the human doctor, we should praise and thank the Lord. By doing that we take over the choice under the authority of holiness.

Other matters of choice fall into that category, too, which is how the boundaries of holiness are expanded, until we suddenly see our full stature and we are all in the holy palace.

I have explained that matter to you several times before, because that issue is an obstacle to many people who have no clear concept of private Providence. They want to trust instead of work, and furthermore, they want to eradicate the questions from their faith and receive signs and omens above nature, and for that they are heavily punished.

That is because since the sin of the first man, the Lord has presented a correction for that sin by uniting *Havayah* and *Elokim*, as I have explained. That is the meaning of the words: "In the sweat of thy face shalt thou eat bread (Genesis 3, 19)."

It is natural that what one attains with great efforts, one finds hard to say that it is a gift from the Creator. Thus, there is room for one to make an effort to completely believe in Private Providence, and decide that even without these efforts, one would still achieve all that. By that that sin is sweetened."

ME OR THE CREATOR?

Q: How do you reconcile the contradiction between "everything depends on me" and "everything is predetermined by the Creator"?

A: All these "exercises" of how and what to think before an act and after, are needed for the preliminary feeling of the Creator, in order to get a grip on His Presence. Because we cannot yet feel the union of our self with the Creator, we should force ourselves into that feeling, and only then will we be able to feel the unity with the Creator.

Before and during any act, we should completely overlook the Presence of the Creator, and pretend He is nowhere near us. What stops us from acting that way rationally? Why do we suddenly begin to believe that the Creator will help and try to be righteous?

The answer is that the evil forces, the shells, (our corrupted desires) did not unite with the Creator and deliberately prevent us to do so. This enables us to make an effort and correct these thoughts and desires.

Of course you might say that all these disruptions come from the Creator. He first sends us thoughts that He exists, which is in fact an obstacle, and finally He sends thoughts that He does not exist, which is in fact another obstacle. All these obstacles are there to urge us to try to correct our thoughts, because ultimately, our thoughts and the Creator's unite.

Not only do we follow the thought of the Creator, but we unite with it, meaning our thoughts and the Creator's don't take the form of cause and effect, but are simply the same.

REWARD AND PUNISHMENT

Q: If the Creator exists, He must be looking over everyone with eternal love. Why, then, are there so many who are punished?

A: Your question only indicates the place you're in, because we can only draw conclusions from our own degree of development. If we rise spiritually, everything will change for us: our conclusions, our opinions and even the way we see the world. We will see the world as something good, perfect.

However, in your current situation, you can only see a fraction of reality, where it is very hard for you to justify and understand the Creator. I know that from my own experience.

Let's wait until the Creator is revealed to you, and then you will be able to justify Him. He who justifies the Creator is called "righteous." One must become a complete righteous to discover the Creator and His actions and know everything about Him, in order to justify Him.

For that, we must be identical to the Creator because we can only know if we become like Him, out of equivalence of form. I suggest you read Baal HaSulam's Introduction to The Study of the Ten Sefirot.

CORRECTING THE SENSES

Q: Is there a Kabbalistic technique of behavior through which we can "soften" or limit the reception of evil?

A: Everything comes from the Creator. In principle, only one thing comes out of the Creator: simple Light, total goodness. In our corrupted senses we feel it according to our equivalence with it, ranging from the total opposite, to what it really is.

We perceive the difference between us and the Light as pain. That pain can be unconscious, as when a person doesn't know why the world is in such pain, or it can be conscious. This occurs when we begin to feel the Creator and feel that the Creator is not a source of pain, but rather a source of pleasure, and the reason for the pain is the difference between our qualities and those of the Creator.

The way to delivery is quite simple ~ study only the writings of Rashbi (Rabbi Shimon Bar-Yochai), the Ari and Rav Ashlag. Our pain will gradually fade and instead of asking, "Why don't I have...," we will begin to ask "Why don't I have love for Him?"

Afterwards, we will feel the "pains of love" ~ the desire to cling to the loved one. In the meantime, these are just words (and pretty worldly ones, too), but only when we have attained these situations can we understand their spiritual meaning. Sometimes even ordinary people feel they are experiencing these situations and begin to write about them.

In any case, I urge that you read a lot, without specific order. Read everything that we have published, and as a result, you will go through a variety of situations that will teach you how to live.

Your connection to a leader, a rav, a Kabbalist, is a must. Otherwise, in a moment of weakness, you might get distracted. You'll return to Kabbalah, obviously, but it can take a very long time, perhaps several lifetimes.

CONSCIOUS WORTHLESSNESS

Q: I try to do things that the Creator needs, but then I begin to feel self-loathing and disgust. Everything I ask seems false, but still I go on as though something is pushing me from behind. Is there another alternative for me?

A: There is only one choice: to go on reading Kabbalah books and listening to our music. Also, exercise for an hour or so, as much as you can, with the aim that it will help you come out of your situation.

What the mind cannot do, time will. These situations are experienced by anyone on the path, and there will be many more such reactions. It is called "the recognition of evil," the recognition of the worthlessness of our nature.

Afterwards, embarrassment will be replaced with genuine shame, which we mentioned as the reason for the first restriction. Generally, I can advise you to put your thoughts on paper; this – accelerates these situations, speeds your awareness, and therefore changes them. In short, – it will help you pick up the pace.

OVERCOMING INDIFFERENCE

Q: What should I do when I suddenly begin to treat circumstances that come to me from Above with indifference: I just don't feel anything, not the pain, and not the pleasure that I would normally feel. What is that situation? Should something be done about it, or will it go away by itself?

A: All the feelings are given to you from Above. And they are necessary. You will see that for yourself, if not now, then later on. During such times, the most important thing is to look at yourself from the side and see how there is nothing you can do with yourself.

For that purpose you can get all sorts of situations from Above... you'll see that without reward, without pleasure or a goal, you cannot even lift a finger. Your mood, your goals and your view on life can be changed instantly from Above. You must examine these situations.

Kabbalah is the study of the nature of creation, a study you perform on yourself, your flesh, your pain and your joys and aspirations—from the finest to the most gross.

It is not easy going through stages of indifference, but in order to accelerate them, the best way is to be in a group of people who are like you, who study Kabbalah as you do. Do something with them, anything at all, for example, give classes in Kabbalah or help with circulation. Any physical act that is aimed at the purpose helps a great deal in overcoming a state of indifference. Our job is to pick up our pace.

STATES OF INDIFFERENCE

Q: Why is it that instead of enthusiasm, I suddenly feel complete indifference?

A: Any person who begins to be aware of the purpose of creation, the attainment of Him and the means to do it, is in fact being given an invitation from Above to study the wisdom of Kabbalah. The rest is up to you.

Whatever you feel (and it doesn't matter what it is, because you'll experience many different feelings, ranging from complete indifference to anxiousness) is given to you so that you can advance. Therefore, the only answer is to go on studying diligently, regardless of your changing moods and desires.

INNER STRUGGLE

Q: Why is there a difference between the understanding of the mind and the feeling of the heart? Why is it that after a person has already followed his heart, because he couldn't go any other way, he finds that his mind was right? Why this struggle in me and how do I cope with it?

A: What happens within you are inner examinations of yourself and the beginning of the study of your self. It is quite possible that you have performed this analysis of yourself earlier, before you began to study Kabbalah. Psychologists deal with this, as well.

The difference is that psychological analysis is not done under the influence of Kabbalistic texts, but by studying ourselves within the framework of this world, in the degree of the human mind.

When one studies Kabbalah, one's entire analysis is a consequence of the effect of the surrounding Light on one's soul. Therefore, you will eventually relate your feelings to the contact with the Creator. Read more, especially parts of the material that you like. It is also good to read Psalms. Search for a discussion of similar situations in the articles.

You'll see that you're going through what they went through. You're progressing toward the goal, although the road seems confusing, tiring, tedious and empty. Nonetheless, it still leads you toward the goal, toward eternity and perfection.

TRUE AND BITTER, OR FALSE AND SWEET?

Q: When I read Inner Reflection, I wanted to enjoy myself, but instead I began to feel desperation and a guilty conscience. Why?

A: The heart can either feel pleasure or pain. The brain analyzes true or false, and you are the one who must choose which is more important: the truth (however bitter), or falsehood and sweetness. That choice is in everything you do, and it is a factor in the process of your correction, your inner change.

THOU SHALT NOT KILL

Q: What is the most effective way to stop enjoying for myself and start enjoying for the Creator, without killing my desires?

A: One cannot change one's desires, as they are given from Above. He cannot even change His aim directly. It is said that "the Light reforms." So the results only gradually become apparent through efforts in the study, and through the attempts to be connected with the rav.

You will acquire the sensation of the Upper World, the Creator, and make your progress by yourself, through the desire to receive strength from Above.

"RESTRICTION" -- THE GATEWAY TO SPIRITUALITY

Q: Provided I strictly follow the condition of the first restriction, how many years will it take me to at least get a feel of the Upper World?

A: The minute you can perform the first restriction of the desires you are given and not use anything for yourself, but for the Creator, you will feel the Creator and the Upper World, according to the strength of the restriction you performed and the number of desires that were corrected on that restriction.

If you can later on turn your previous corporeal aim from reception for yourself to spiritual aims of reception for the Creator, you will perform spiritual acts with those desires. You will take control, instead of being guided by the Creator.

THE TIME OF PREPARATION

Q: It is promised that within one life cycle, a person can go through all the stages, beginning with the first desire for spirituality and ending in the completion of correction. In case the cycle is not completed, wouldn't it better to just "kill the time"? After all, this life was given for the sole purpose of correction!

A: In his Introduction to The Study of the Ten Sefirot, Baal Ha-Sulam says that within three to five years a person can reach the Upper World and begin to climb the ladder. But that is only ideally. In real life it takes twice or even three times as long to succeed.

What I am saying now refers to souls of the 1990's, but things should take less time in the 21st century because the souls that descend today are a lot closer to spirituality to begin with.

"MY SONS DEFEATED ME"

Q: Why is the last phase of the four phases of development characterized as an argument with the Creator?

A: The maturity of the soul and one's desire are determined by one's desire to rise above one's current level. The still level is characterized by a lack of independence, the vegetative is more independent, the animate, more independent than the vegetative, and man is the last of these phases. Man actually consists of these four phases.

On the still level, man does not change and remains in the state he was born at. On the last level–the "man" in man–he wants to leave his receiving nature and fight the Creator, who has given him that nature. The Creator created the receiving nature, and man forces Him to change it.

BLAMING THE CREATOR

Q: How is it possible to avoid disappointments along the spiritual journey? After all, it is more convenient for us to think that the Creator deprived us by not giving us a desire to come near Him, so we justify ourselves and blame the Creator. But if we understand that, can we correct these processes inside us?

A: There is nothing in us that should not be there. We remain precisely as we were created, but if we try to correct ourselves, we correct the way in which we use our attributes, those we were born with. All we change is the intent, from doing "for us," to doing "for Him."

So you needn't complain about your preliminary qualities, and if you were put here, you might as well look around you and start doing something about it.

Q: How is it possible to avoid the letdowns during the spiritual journey?

A: The letdowns are unavoidable. They are actually positive, because they are a sign of your dissatisfaction with your desire for pleasure. They are signs that you're going in the right direction. A person who works for self is full of energy because that person believes that this way promises eternal bliss.

Q: But it is easier for us to feel that the Creator deprived us.

A: The question is, how do we react once we feel the dissatisfaction with our condition: do we blame the Creator for not pampering us, or do we ask for help against our own nature?!

Q: ...and then we justify ourselves and blame the Creator.

A: Reverse the order. Blame ourselves and justify the Creator. There is an inner contradiction when we blame the Creator for not letting us draw near. Nearing the Creator means that we are in a state where we want nothing for ourselves, but take everything that comes to us as the best possible thing, because we believe that everything extends from the Creator.

So what request is there to talk about?

Q: It is easy to blame the Creator for not giving us a desire and a way to approach Him.

A: If we continue to say that the Creator doesn't "let us approach Him," then that is exactly the situation where we have something to ask. We must ask that the Creator render more qualities of love for our fellow creatures, so that we will be completely satisfied with how the Creator leads the world, and instead of cursing Him, we will bless the Creator.

We can certainly do that.

Being in the left line is necessary to reveal new attributes of self-reception. After that, we correct them, become filled with Light and knowledge, and thus rise above our former state. It happens all the time.

We can only accelerate the speed of the ongoing process and cut down on our lingering at each phase. It all depends on our adaptation to a certain situation.

Whining and blaming the Creator is easy because it relieves us of acting or making an effort. But what the mind does not do, time will. Everything passes, and we will gradually get used to these changes and begin, to a certain extent, to control them. In any given situation, we should act as it says: "Whatsoever thy hand attaineth to do by thy strength, that do" (Ecclesiastes 9, 10).

Even if you don't know how to do it, it doesn't matter. Just do it. Even the most misunderstood, mistaken act speeds up the pace and brings you closer to the next degree, which is always closer to correction than before.

BREAKING THE SCREEN

Q: It is said that the higher the *Sefira,* the greater its desires and screen were before the breaking, and the lower its sparks fell at the loss of the screen. Why?

A: A higher *Sefira* means a greater desire and thus a stronger screen to match it. Of course, if the screen is lost, a greater desire remains bare. What's left is a greater desire for the self than in the lower *Sefira,* whose screen and desire are smaller.

Hence the rule: he who is spiritually greater has greater desire. And if he falls, his fall is deeper, and he becomes worse. It is the same way in this world, but in the spiritual world the distances (differences in attributes) between ascent and descent are enormous.

If you really put your mind to it, you can go through all the passages and advance without paying attention to your moods and your inner mental state.

WHAT IS SPIRITUAL FAITH?

Q: Faith should replace all the senses, as though the entire reality were laid before one's eyes, despite the absence of the sensation of the Creator and His guidance. Is this not blind faith?

A: You mustn't believe blindly in the Creator, since faith is acquired only through the screen, which is the sensation of the Creator. There is faith that is the Light of *Bina*, Light of mercy, and there is whole faith, which is called the Light of Mercy with the illumination of *Hochma*. The latter is the one we want to attain.

Then the vessel/soul–man–is in its perfect state at the end of correction, after it has returned to its root, the Creator.

INCREASING THE IMPORTANCE

Q: How can you intensify the importance of the purpose of life and the greatness of the giver?

A: Baal HaSulam answers it this way: by studying, in a group, and under the guidance of a kabbalist rav.

The studies must be made up solely of texts that were written for the exclusive purpose of bringing one to the Creator from the very first word.

Why do you need a group? All the souls are, in fact, one soul, divided into many parts by our physical sensations. Spirituality "pours," so to speak, from soul to soul, and if there is a strong bond between the members of the group, their body does not pose an obstacle on their path toward the Creator.

On the contrary, it is through overcoming the disturbances of the body to the contact between souls, that the feeling of spirituality intensifies to the extent of being able to sense the Creator.

The rav must be a Kabbalist, a disciple of a renowned Kabbalist from whom he had received the exact method of the study, studied it himself and completed at least some of the way.

FAITH ABOVE REASON

Q: What is this method called "faith above reason?"

A: There are three paths one can take: above reason, within reason and below reason. Reason is the self of man, his concepts, his mentality, and his education.

Below reason - is action without self-criticism or examination. It is a state where reason is not taken into account; fanaticism, faith at all cost, is accepted without examination. The more capable a person is of disconnecting the mind and going by faith alone, the closer the faith is to being "below reason."

This expresses itself in fanaticism and training that people follow blindly, beyond question and doubt. This method is used to teach certain habits that people keep for life. Therefore, the more a person is prone to "faith below reason," the more stupid such people become, to the point where they begin to believe in miracles and similar phenomena.

Within reason - means that a person examines and accepts only that which is suitable for one's conception of reality. It is an inner faith, a state where a person relies on reason, senses and everything available from the inner nature.

Above reason - means that a person examines data, sees that it opposes one's perception of reality, but accepts it anyway, even if it is against one's better judgment and understanding. Why? Because this reason stems from the Upper One, Whom one trusts more than self.

All our modes of operation are narrowed down to "faith above reason." The higher the degree, the more one gives. We cannot understand it; we cannot see how we can attain such a high degree, put in the effort, and find the energy to nourish that toil.

However, it is possible with "faith above reason," despite the desires and the understandings of the body, because the desires of the body belong to the current degree, whereas we wish to climb to a higher one. Therefore, we are given more and more knowledge in the form of disturbances, and the more we relate to them with "faith above reason," the wiser we become.

In fact, we rely on that reason for our progress, using it to rise "above" it. That knowledge remains within us as a basis we trample on. Thus, we grow wiser and wiser from one degree to the next. You will gradually understand this through your own experience.

If Kabbalists simply tried to erase those disturbances as ordinary people do, they would remain in "faith below reason." But they examine them, face conflicts and work against them, which is why they gain knowledge against the faith, and build the faith over the contradictions, over the desires of the body. That is why they can understand things that are beyond our conception.

In other words, the spiritual world opens before them, because they acquire the screen with "faith above reason."

"FAITH ABOVE REASON" IN THE CONTEXT OF GROUP WORK

Q: How does "faith above reason" work in the context of the group?

A: We must always keep the Creator in the background of the image of the world as we see it. We must always try to think of the Creator in our subconscious. Then our thoughts will be in the right direction: because we are with friends, who are also in a state of searching for the same goal.

That is why everything I get from someone in my group today is probably a disturbance that I must confront with faith above reason, and accept what he tells me, justify him. By justifying him, I rise to a higher spiritual degree.

To go with "faith above reason" means that I accept and agree with my heart and soul with everything that happens to me. When one of my friends criticizes me, I should accept everything that comes from it as good and true with "faith above reason," because I cannot see the actual truth with my egoistic vessels.

When we manage to move a few steps forward when doing these seemingly simple exercises, meaning when we try to receive everything that comes to us as the desire of the Creator, we begin to feel how the Creator relates to us.

That is still not a revelation, but it is the beginning of our spiritual contact with the Creator. That is how we begin to connect with the Creator.

We understand that the Creator is now hidden, and sends His messages through the people around us. Thus, we begin to feel the involvement of the Creator in everything that happens in our lives.

This is a genuine feeling, and this contact becomes permanent, and the key factor in our lives. This is the way to the entrance to the spiritual world, the strengthening of the contact with the Creator and the rise to a higher degree.

A COMMON GOAL

Q: Why do we need to agree with our friends?

A: When we see that our friends are right, we don't have to justify them. We simply have to accept their thoughts and agree with them. Thus, we acquire new knowledge. This is also the case when love makes us agreeable with another. In both cases, we do not go through any process of correction.

If it is not an external reason (a boss at work, pain, loss, love etc.) that makes us agree with another, but because we must work together for the same goal in order to attain it, we will make a thousand tests for the sake of unification to discover which of us is right.

But after that, regardless of the consequence, we will agree with our friends. That decision is called "faith above reason," because we accept it against our better judgment.

Why would we do this? Because the goal necessitates it. The facts support our opinion, and we accept our friend's opinion against our common sense and because of our common goal.

ATTAINING A HIGHER SPIRITUAL DEGREE

Q: How can I attain a higher spiritual degree?

A: How do we rise from degree X, to degree X+1? In our world, a person can only raise one's physical body. In the spiritual world, a person raises one's spiritual body and one's aims. For that, we must be able to alter our aims to fit the new spiritual degree.

But if all of our feelings change, how will we be able to change ourselves? The way to do it is through "faith above reason."

We behave against every value, understanding and attribute that we have in an X spiritual degree, and blindly accept all the attributes of the X+1 as true, although they completely contradict our nature and seem completely unreal and unnatural in our current condition.

The abilities of a higher degree allow us to give more, and to become even more detached from our own needs. At the moment, we may be incapable of it; it seems unnatural. We think that only a madman could do this.

However, we must accept them with faith above reason, and adopt them as our own. If we succeed, the Creator will raise us to the next spiritual degree, closer to Him, and we thus become an embryo in the next degree.

Like an embryo in its mother's womb, we agree to unite with the Creator with our eyes shut. There are no other means to come to a higher degree.

Now we can understand why it is impossible to do this without help from Above. We must aim at "faith above reason" instead of trying to understand with reason and logic, even if it were possible.

Within a group are always opportunities to accept a friend's opinion. The group should become a place where one becomes mentally ready to advance with "faith above reason." We must constantly practice on one another in order to understand what "faith above reason" really means: to accept the opinion of another, even if we completely disagree with it.

When I examine my own friend's attitude toward me, I always start the analysis with my intellectual ability and my desire for pleasure. I cannot ignore the situation, I cannot forgive, but I must come to a point where, although I completely disagree with him, I accept his idea because I want to reach the goal with him.

I must not compromise. We have to fully acknowledge the evil. If I don't understand the origin of my knowledge, how can I ever rise? And over what?

If I don't understand the opinion of my friend, how will I accept it? I have to analyze everything and accept his idea, although I vehemently object to it, although it pains me, and makes me suffer and hate.

It is true that my friend is just as much of an egoist as I am, perhaps even a bigger egoist, but that should not matter. We must focus on practicing, on trying to accept our friend's ideas over our own.

We thus have an opportunity to do something with "faith above reason." However, after we decide to accept a friend's reason, we agree with them heart and soul. It is new knowledge, in a higher spiritual degree, which now becomes our own.

Rav Baruch Ashlag writes in his essays about how the group works. He says that when a group of Kabbalists is founded, they get a chance to practice the relationships within them, hold grudges, and finally rise above them, because it is the only way by which they can rise to a higher spiritual degree.

THE BOUNDARIES OF LOVE

Q: Loving is dangerous. The minute someone realizes you're willing to do anything for them, they take advantage of it. Isn't there something like that in the relationship between the Creator and us?

A: Love can only exist where there are no boundaries! But if it is un-bounded, it awakens disrespect and perhaps even hatred in the loved one. We find examples of that in the way children treat parents who are totally devoted to them. Therefore, in order to reach absolute and lasting love, the Creator created a system of inter-relations between Him and us.

At first, both He and His Love are concealed. This is done to pre-vent a situation where, after realizing how much love is available to us from the Creator, we begin to hate Him.

Therefore, we must first come to a state where we want to give ev-erything to the Creator, and only then will we be able to sense correctly, without harming ourselves, the love of the Creator. We will then be able to receive from the Creator and express our eternal love to Him.

This is an eternal and unchangeable state. For that reason, the first commandment in the Torah is to fear God, and the second is to love Him. The Zohar says that the fear does not relate to a fear of losing the love, because the fear of losing is selfish. The fear is a spiritual attainment of the question, "Have I done everything I possibly could for the Creator?" It is much like a mother treats her child, except in this case, our attitude toward the Creator becomes the same as His attitude toward us.

You must understand that to perform an act of kindness means first and foremost to exit the boundaries of the desire to be kind only to yourself, and to be able to perform acts of kindness, regardless of how you feel. In this situation, any desire to give yourself pleasure, whatever form it takes, will not destabilize your desire to continue doing good.

Thus, it all depends on *who* does the good act and not *for whom* it is done. The question is, what are one's intentions when one performs an act of kindness? Does one mean to benefit the person for whom one is doing the act, or does one mean to be rewarded for it?

If there is a link between an act of grace and a reward, the grace is not a grace, but another way to receive pleasure through a third party. That is what we call, in our world, "love." But true spiritual love can only be attained after the first restriction, meaning the restriction of your own desires to receive for yourself.

That is the correction of our desires through the screen, because only if that correction takes place is the link between the desire (the act of the receiver) and the pleasure (the response of the giver) broken. That correction can only be attained through the wisdom of the Kabbalah.

WHAT IS THE BARRIER

Q: It feels so good when you can love, and so bad when you can't. Does the pain of not being able to love go away when I cross the barrier or only at the end of correction?

A: The pain stems from your natural desire to enjoy yourself in this world, and it will be gone even before you cross the barrier. The barrier is the relinquishing of the thought, "for me alone." In fact, it is the relinquishing of every single thing in this world. The abandoning of the thought, "for me alone," already relates to spiritual desires and pleasures.

AGONY IN THE SPIRITUAL WORLD

Q: In our world, man suffers the agony of this world, and in the spiritual world, the spiritual agony, which is much harsher than the pains of our world. How can one agree to replace lesser pains for greater pains?

A: Spiritual pains are pains of love, pains that are linked with the question, "What more can I do for my love?" They are called "sweet pains." These pains never diminish; they exist so you can feel the pleasure of giving, the adhesion with the Creator.

NO LOVE WITHOUT FAITH

Q: This is how I understand what's written in The Book of Zohar: a true love is faith in the true Creator. Faith in the true Creator is the true attainment of the Creator. The true attainment is a true understanding. The true understanding is when a person sees, or distinguishes, or learns – and at the same time, if his attainment is correct-that what he attains is love for the Creator and faith in Him, since without faith there can be no love.

A: You're right. There's nothing I can add!

The method of attainment of the Higher World is natural, since we discover it by ourselves, in ourselves and do not receive it from Above as a book. Upon discovering it in ourselves, we describe it and use it to shorten the way.

We can go the same way without the books, but it would take much longer. There are people in our time who have suffered a lot and, as a result, suddenly began to understand and feel the spiritual. There are also people who, like you, have a premonition of it.

But it's not a genuine, definite attainment that enables you to govern yourself and your surroundings. In order to understand faster and better, we need books to guide and teach us. In the end, there is nothing more natural for one's soul than revealing the Creator, since the soul is a part of Him.

FEELING THE CREATOR

Q: What is our work?

A: When I enjoy myself, pleasure fills me entirely and I become a slave to it. I can no longer control myself or my actions. In such a situation, my attributes are not complete, because I am willing to do anything for pleasure.

If I feel unhappy about the world around me, I must see that it is the Creator Who is giving me this sensation, so that I can make up for my dissatisfaction with my egoistic desires in my spiritual aspiration for the Creator.

Instead, I have to relate to the current problem as though it is not a problem, but rather the best possible situation for me at this moment. I must take it as a given situation and agree with it.

When that happens, my dissatisfaction is replaced with faith that everything is sent by the Creator and that it is all for the best. When that happens with a member of the group who has offended you, look at things through his eyes, put his thought and desire into yourself, agree with him, because you want to be like him and like the Creator.

It doesn't matter who it is or what spiritual degree he has reached, if you want to be free of your egoistic desires and feel the desires of the Creator, then you already want to free yourself from your egoistic vessels and feel the Creator.

THE REASON FOR THE REVELATION

Q: Rav Ashlag speaks in his articles about the importance of the feeling of the greatness of the Creator. We have a natural inclination to want to serve a greater person than ourselves, so it is obvious that the body will surrender to that demand. But greatness is where there is kindness, whereas the kindness of the Creator is concealed from us. Let us assume that the Creator is almighty and guides everything. But if the world is full of pain, how can we see His greatness? The king is great because of his graceful acts toward his subjects, not because he is in power. How then can we see the greatness of the Creator?

A: You're right when you say that if the Creator would reveal Himself to us, we would surrender, as it happens in our world. The only difference is in our goal. The Creator will not be revealed for any other purpose but the correction of the world. We want the Creator to reveal Himself because we want to be certain of His existence, but that should only be for correction.

If one asks the Creator to disclose Himself for the purpose of correction, the Creator will appear before him as a performer of kindness. In response, one immediately will feel an unbounded love for Him.

CHAPTER 5.
THE DESIRE FOR PLEASURE:
DISCOVERY AND CORRECTION

UNLIMITED DESIRE

Q: Why do we need the principle, "to be filled for the Creator?"

A: This principle allows our desires to stay alert and not wither. After a meal, we are normally satiated and our desire disappears. Just imagine what it would be like if we could have a great meal, and only increase our appetite. The more we eat the more our will to receive increases.

That is why we need the principle, "not for myself, but for the Creator." Only in that situation does our vessel become unlimited, and during the spiritual progress we experience feelings that are indescribable to ordinary senses. Because the pleasure we have in this world is, as Kabbalists describe, a minute Light, a spark that comes down to this world; it is not even a dim Light, not to mention an infinite one.

The desire for advancement does not go away with the evolution of spirituality. On the contrary, your desires keep growing and so do your abilities. That is why you begin to receive satisfaction, meaning the Light, in an increasing degree.

PLEASURE - LIFE OR DEATH

Q: You write: "Although it seems contradictory, the Light of life, the very source of our pleasure, can also bring death. The reason is that a pleasure that is 'for me' is felt only in part of the vessel, thus generating the opposite result – death. When the pleasure is 'for the Creator,' it is felt in the entire vessel." My question is: how can a feeling that is felt only in part of the vessel bring death? Why can pleasure "for me" enter only a part of the vessel?

A: After the first restriction, the Light cannot enter the desire – the vessel - because the screen stands in the way. If the screen can withstand the desire to enjoy in the vessel, in other words, if it can build the intent "for the Creator," then according to the measure of that intent, which constitutes the strength of the screen, the Light enters the vessel. This is the only possible way to fill up the vessel ~ the soul.

The purpose of creation is to fill up the vessel with Light through the screen. If the Light encounters a vessel that does not have a screen, it returns to its origin (because of the first restriction). When the Light touches a vessel that does not have a screen, that vessel immediately begins to want the Light for itself, regardless of the source. Then it is called a "shell," "impurity," and "death."

SOURCE OF DESIRES

Q: Please tell me about material and spiritual desires. Does the environment determine all our desires? And what if there is no environment? Is it death?

A: Everything is determined by our inner *Reshimot* (spiritual recollections) or by the environment (education, advertising, friends, etc.). See the four factors of man's development and freedom in Baal HaSulam's, The Freedom.

Q: And what about the basic desires of humanity? Is this the only thing we have?

A: Each of us obediently plays a tiny role in this grandiose mechanical show, feeling "what passes on us" and finally becoming prepared to sense the end result.

Q: How did great Kabbalists sustain and develop their desire for the spiritual while being alienated from humanity? Or was it their way of distancing themselves from the desires obstructing the road to the goal (money, respect, power, etc.)? What was happening to the spiritual desires at the time of such estrangement?

A: The great Kabbalists felt humanity as no one else did, absorbing its suffering and aspirations, and were closer to it than anyone.

Q: How can one grow desires within? From inside? Is it possible?

A: This can be achieved only by studying and contributing efforts towards anything relating to Kabbalah and by being constantly connected to it.

Q: What is the reason for the lack of desires? I am referring not to the feeling of an empty vessel; instead, it is a feeling that there isn't one.

A: If you are struggling with this and do not succeed, then you have to go through this feeling and it will pass. Bow your head, but don't consent to it, just go on as if you do have desires.

THE AWARD IN PEACE AND PERFECTION

Q: Why is the reward in peace and perfection?

A: It is said that peace and tranquility is the ultimate state. Why? Because the work for the sake of giving is regarded as a reward. If giving is desired, then the award is there.

Take sexual intercourse or eating as the crudest examples. These processes require a great deal of effort. But since nature thought of an immediate reward, life and procreation became possible. We do not think of the effort, since the reward, the pleasure itself is so great.

Or take a mother who enjoys feeding her child. Even if she is a queen, she will not turn down the pleasure of the act. She doesn't feel it as an effort. And if a person changes vessels from being aimed at reception to being aimed at bestowal, one naturally feels pleasure from giving, and experiences peace and tranquility from such an act.

SOURCE OF SPIRITUAL DESIRE

Q: When I began studying only a year ago, I seemed to be very close to the spiritual. I could almost feel it. But now I have a question: where does my desire arise for something I can't feel, know or see? Why do I want it? After all, everyone around me says it doesn't exist...

A: The point in your heart is leading you and it will not let you stop. There are more and more people these days who feel these desires. What should you aspire for? You should return to your root in your emotions, to the place from which this point in the heart came to *Adam*, the collective soul. You should want to return to the state of unity with the Creator.

DESIRES AFTER THE END OF CORRECTION

Q: Suppose a Kabbalist has completed his personal correction. He then continues to climb from one level to the next. But in order to rise spiritually he will probably need to fall. So what desires does such a Kabbalist go down to?

What kinds of desires exist after the end of correction?

A: In the Introduction to the Study of the Ten Sefirot, Baal Ha-Sulam describes all the levels that we must go through in our spiritual development. When we complete the correction of our personal vessel, meaning our soul, we continue to correct our connections with other souls in the collective soul of *Adam*.

Then, as they also complete their corrections, the souls rise to the level of the end of correction and even higher, to levels that have never been described, because they are called "the secrets of the Torah." It is impossible to study these, or to disclose them to others.

Material and Spiritual Pleasures

Q: I teach Kabbalah in a small group I organized by myself. My students, beginners in Kabbalah, asked me about the difference between physical and spiritual pleasures. Please help me formulate a clear answer, since I myself feel a bit confused.

A: Spiritual pleasure is:

• Endless, since it created the vessel and, therefore, can fill it completely.

• Eternal, because it is perceived in the intention "for the sake of the Creator," which is never lessened upon filling with pleasure, and hence is everlasting.

• Not concealed from the vessel behind all the worlds (the Hebrew word *Olam* derives from the word *Haalama*, concealment); hence it is not weakened to the level of Minute Light. The tiniest spiritual pleasure is billions of times greater than any physical one, meaning one that is received for oneself.

The result of receiving the Divine Pleasure consists not just of the pleasure itself, but of a feeling of unity with the Creator, sensing Him, which is an additional pleasure.

The result of feeling the Creator is grasping Him, becoming all knowing, encompassing the entire universe, which is an additional pleasure.

CIRCULATION OF KABBALAH
AND THE DEVELOPMENT OF THE SOUL

Q: I would very much like you to clarify the meaning of "Kabbalah circulation."

A: Man acquires any science about himself and his world by researching himself and his surroundings.

Anything he can't understand, but wishes to, he compensates for with fantasy, based on analogy, speculation, and rational continuation of whatever is already known. But however hard one tries, it is impossible to speculate and imagine that part of the universe that one never felt within. Analogy will not help either, since one's senses never experienced anything similar.

Kabbalah creates, or more accurately develops, a new sense. And only in the process of its development does a person begin to feel "that" world. Only then is it clear that no fantasy could possibly help one imagine it.

One cannot convey one's feelings to others who do not have this sense. To those who do have it, one can pass it along only to the extent that this sense has been developed in them.

Hence, on the one hand, Kabbalah is a science because we develop a sense of the surrounding space, and research it using a strictly scientific method. On the other hand, Kabbalah differs from all other natural methods, as it is impossible to research that world without first acquiring the special sense for it. Only to the extent that one feels that world, does one begin to feel and perceive everything differently.

One who doesn't feel it is unable to imagine it. The meaning and the goal of "circulating Kabbalah" is to cause man to feel the need to develop his soul.

"Circulating Kabbalah" gives us a method for such development and teaches us how to use the newfound sense. That is why Kabbalah is a special science and not a religion.

THE EVIL FORCE - THE FORCE OF THE CREATOR

Q: I was surprised to read in the *Haggada* (tales for Passover night) that Pharaoh made Israel come nearer to the Creator. How is a negative force capable of working for the Creator and against itself?

A: Pharaoh *is* the force of the Creator. It is a good force that takes a negative appearance in us, as it says: "Two angels lead one to the goal - the 'good' and the 'bad'."

The whole experience of progress in Kabbalah pertains to the acquisition of new forces of bestowal. If man had only good inclinations, he would never be able to advance. For that reason Pharaoh, the evil force and man's evil inclination, which allows man to take from it greater desires for pleasure, correct them and rise even higher.

Therefore, it is important to relate to Pharaoh as the Force of the Creator that was given to us for our assistance. Pharaoh promotes us by awakening in our egos a desire to advance and develop materially. From awakening that desire, we begin to understand that material progress doesn't give us anything, and that true development is spiritual.

When, under the influence of Pharaoh, we begin to develop spiritually, we search in the spiritual world for a vessel to be filled with the desire for pleasure. Thus, our own egoism, Pharaoh, is the motivating force behind everything. This is because it is impossible to receive the Upper Light in our will to receive; it is impossible to sense the Creator, the infinite pleasure.

Instead, we can only enjoy the (very small) pleasures of our world that, once gone, leave us feeling emptier and even more dissatisfied than before.

Pharaoh must motivate us to spirituality, so that afterwards, when we receive the spiritual delight, he will take it for himself. In our world, Pharaoh motivates us to receive pleasure using our regular desire to please ourselves.

In the *Haggada* of Passover, he is called the "old Pharaoh." Then it is said that a new king rose in Egypt, and this is the Pharaoh who takes us to spirituality, and then takes receives it himself.

In fact, contrary to the pleasures of this world, one can receive spiritual pleasures only in a vessel called "faith above reason," meaning with the intent to enjoy in order to please the Creator. Pharaoh pushes man to receive spiritual pleasures for himself. But man cannot receive such pleasures directly, so Pharaoh takes man toward spirituality, study and labor.

When one finally receives the Upper Feeling, Pharaoh comes and takes man's attainments through the alien thoughts that are sent him.

Q: How does it happen?

A: After the attainment, there suddenly appears a thought to use what one has attained for oneself, such as to enjoy the status of a "sage," or a Kabbalist, draw people near or drive them away, gain respect, influence, etc. By so doing, Pharaoh takes for himself all the spirituality that one has worked so hard to attain, through the vessel of faith above reason, and into his own private vessel of joy.

What benefit does this offer us, then? *It is through Pharaoh that the Creator motivates man to new efforts.* But once man has attained a new spiritual sensation, he loses it again because Pharaoh puts in him yet another new desire for self, instead of the desire to bestow. In this way, man will enjoy the spiritual pleasures he has acquired.

Q: Why does Pharaoh succeed?

A: The will to receive that the Creator created is entirely in the hands of Pharaoh, who can always raise new desires to receive, greater than the small desires to bestow he had acquired in the previous degree.

This way, Pharaoh gives man an additional will to receive that is greater than the will he has corrected thus far. Pharaoh plants in man, through his desires, the desire for pleasure of the next degree in order for him to correct that, as well. That way, he enables man to continue with the process of correction.

All that man can see is how his work is wasted. Furthermore, man feels that each time he acquires a greater attainment, he falls from it and plunges deeper still in his own selfish desires, where he discovers an even greater desire for pleasure than before.

This process repeats itself time and again, and each time Pharaoh brings man to such desperation that he cries for the Creator to save him from the hands of Pharaoh. At this point, Pharaoh's work is done, and he appears before man as an angel, an emissary of the Creator.

SHORTENED EXILE

Q: Baal HaSulam **writes about a premature spiritual birth. How does this happen and can it be prevented?**

A: The exile in Egypt was supposed to last 400 years, to match the four degrees of the development of each desire. Instead, it lasted only

210 years. As a result, Israel had to experience three more exiles: Persia and Media, Babylon and the current and last exile.

An early exit from exile, from pregnancy, is called "abortion." But this also happens in the collective development of the souls, through their evolution from Above downward, meaning even before they are born as creations. That is why we don't ascribe it to the creation, but to the development of the creation within the Creator. This occurs before the creation has developed enough for an independent existence outside the Creator.

In other words, as creations, we do not feel ourselves equal, independent or free to choose our actions. We begin our existence as creations after the breaking of the "First Man," and only through the process of the evolution from down upward.

We have to go through the degrees of our development according to the evolution of the soul. We must do it as it evolved from up downward, except that the return is in the opposite direction: from down upward – meaning toward the Creator.

WAS THE EXIT FROM EGYPT PREMATURE?

Q: The books of Kabbalah maintain that the exit from Egypt was made prematurely, and that there are farfetched historical consequences to it. Did the premature liberation prevent a possibility to attain spiritual attributes in due time. If so, is it like a child who was supposed to be born, where preparations were made for labor, but then everything was ruined because the child was born prematurely and died at birth?

A: Theoretically, that situation exists during the creation of the worlds from up downward. Baal HaSulam describes it as a "dead infant" because the liberation (the process of birth) happened not in due time, but prematurely.

This means that, one is not quite ready to assume the spiritual attributes of giving and bestowal. Although given forces of bestowal from

Above, the "infant" was still not in a state to accept them. The "dead infant" could not acquire spiritual attributes, although everything was ready for him. That is why there had to be three more exiles. But when the souls rise, there is only evolution toward a greater correction, from below upward, to the degree of the Creator.

EGOISM AS A SPIRITUAL DESIRE

Q: Why are Jews such egotistical people?

A: Jews, Israel in the spiritual sense, are those who aspire for the Creator. Naturally, they need a special desire for that. The desire for spirituality is the greatest of the desires in this world. Therefore, the smallest spiritual pleasure is greater than all the pleasures of this world. Hence, in order to want spirituality, you must be the greatest egoist.

Q: I face an inner contradiction. On the one hand, spirituality is about loving your fellow man, altruism and bestowal. On the other hand, in order to develop in spirituality, we must acquire greater desires to please ourselves than the ones we have right now.

A: Our reality in this world is that the desire for pleasure is limited to minute pleasures, whereas the sensation of the Creator, which is the spiritual world, is about immense pleasures. Therefore, people who aspire to spirituality must possess immense desires.

But these desires must be identical to the pleasures that stem from the Creator, meaning that we will not want to please ourselves, but to render pleasure. The wants of man and those of the Creator must be identical.

If we want to give as much as the Creator, to that extent we can sense the Creator and enjoy Him. Man's soul is made of small desires to give, called "Israel," and great desires to receive, called "Nations of the World."

In the first stage, *Katnut* (infancy), man discovers within only the small desires to give. He corrects and fills them. Then, in the stage of *Gadlut* (adulthood), the greater desires to receive join in.

In our world, this process happens on a worldwide scale: Israel, meaning the Jews, must first reach spirituality, and all other nations must follow. But in this pyramid, too, are exceptions.

There are also incarnations, association and dissociation of souls. Therefore, it would be unwise to draw general conclusions from the above. (I recommend reading the Introduction to The Book of Zohar in that context, from item 66 on).

DESIRE FOR PLEASURE - WITH A SCREEN

Q: Can you say that man is farthest from the Creator because his will to receive is greater than that of a stone, a tree, or a cat?

A: By nature, the greater the desire for pleasure, the farther man is from the Creator. The smaller the desire, the nearer man is to the Creator. But if a person corrects himself, he begins with the absolute nullification of his desire to enjoy and uses it only in accordance with the measure of the screen, which he acquired.

Therefore, in a corrected state, the greater the will to enjoy, the more a person can resemble the Creator; and the smaller the will to receive that is used (with a screen), the farther one is from the Creator. During the study of Kabbalah, when the will to receive grows, the measure of the screen grows with it, which is the aim to please the Creator, rather than yourself.

Thus, a great man, a Kabbalist, has a great desire to enjoy, but a corrected one.

PAST PAINS

Q: Why do we get pleasure when reflecting upon past pains? In fact, they even seem to bring us more pleasure than the pleasures of the past, especially when shared with someone.

A: Because the events of the past have been corrected (mitigated), we feel sweetness in those old pains. It is a bit like our path: it isn't sweet, because we want and suffer. But when we attain our goals, we take pleasure in the love for the Creator and our encounters with Him in past pains and disappointments.

It is like a person in love who yearns to meet his loved one and finally does. The intensity of the pleasure is a measure of the intensity of the yearning, the ability to aim the yearning at the desired object, and its duration.

In general, if one shares one's feelings with another person, the two create a common vessel, a larger vessel for sensations. There is an additional feeling in that vessel: that of the other person. That is why it is more pleasant to share an experience than to experience something alone.

FROM MATERIAL PLEASURE TO THE SPIRITUAL

Q: I feel that there are a great many pleasures and that people around me are having fun. Are these pleasures considered small or great, compared to the spiritual pleasures you speak of?

A: Man is born to our world with very small desires that gradually grow: soon there is a desire for a family, power, respect, and knowledge. Yet, these are only experiences of this world. The desires demand of the brain their necessary amount of development. In other words, the mind evolves to the degree that is necessary to satisfy one's desires.

But if we should desire spirituality, if we suddenly feel that we want something not available in this world, then we begin to search for it.

We are directed to Kabbalah from Above. (Quite often we are directed elsewhere, toward other "spiritual techniques" which means that we must go through still other phases of development. It might take several more lifetimes before we arrive at Kabbalah).

Finally, when we begin to study Kabbalah, our every desire begins to grow within us. We become more egoistic, and therefore smarter. Greater worldly desires are born, especially sexual ones.

As the sages of the Talmud say: "After the ruin of the Temple, the taste of intercourse was left for the workers of the Lord alone." This means that the true taste of sexual pleasures remains only among those who grow spiritually.

To a person who is not proficient in the structure of the worlds and who does not know the Upper Guidance, it sounds like the complete opposite, but to disciples of Kabbalah it is clear that in our world, the pleasures and desires are tiny. In fact, the higher we rise toward the Creator, the greater our desires and pleasures become.

YEARNING

Q: If a person badly wants love from the Creator, is that an egoistic desire?

A: Of course it is, but what's wrong with that? Look at yourself reasonably, appreciate yourself according to the degree you're actually in, don't demand too much of yourself and don't take on yourself impractical tasks, or those that are beyond your ability. If you can't perform them, it's a sign you still don't know their true meaning.

In the first period of the development of the soul, below the barrier, man gets to know his egoistic attributes. He realizes that he is distanced from the Creator and develops a desire to be with Him, for his own pleasure, as it says: "...for I am love-sick" (Song of Songs 2, 5).

If that degree is completed, it leads to a passage through the barrier to the spiritual world. The passage through the barrier is the response to the immense egoistical desire to enjoy the Creator that evolved in man.

THE BIRTH OF A WILL

Q: You said on one occasion: "The spiritual ascent is a long and rough road. You need to be born anew at every single degree, until you resemble the Creator in your every trait."

As I understand it, to be born is to feel a new attribute of the Creator. If the soul feels a new attribute and situation, does the old one still count?

A: Every new degree is born on the basis of the past. You might say that on the basis of negating a past situation, the need for a new situation is born, because the old one has exhausted itself.

There is a passage from the *Keter* (will to bestow) of the lower *Partzuf* to the *Malchut* (will to receive) of the upper *Partzuf*. That passage means birth: the appearance of a new attribute of reception that has now been acquired again. Thus, the birth we speak of is a birth of a new desire.

The life expectancy of that desire is the time it takes to correct it. Immediately after that, a new (higher) situation (desire) is born.

A COMPLETE WILL

Q: Once I tried to picture a situation where I lost everything: my job, my home, my health, etc. but I took it as something good, as something necessary for progress and suddenly felt a great relief. Can such self-persuasion help, and should it be done consciously on a regular basis? Is it, from the perspective of the Kabbalah, the right thing to do? After all, the will to improve one's health is an egoistic desire.

A: Many people have these feelings and thoughts. But to those who seek a way to the Creator, such feelings are intentionally given in larger amounts to make them feel that they need the Creator and want His Revelation. This is true even if this evolution comes as a result of an escape to save one's own skin, such as escaping a threat to one's life, financial bankruptcy, public disgrace, etc.

The Creator initially uses the ordinary means that He created for man in order to bring him closer. The purpose of everything we have is to bring us closer to the Creator. Redemption depends solely on our beginning to feel the Creator, and the expectation that the Creator will be revealed before us. But man's will does not tend to accept the termination of its being "the owner," nor the necessity to give up control over man.

This condition was also made by the Creator so that man would hate his receiving nature. Why? Because it contradicts the giving nature of the Creator so much, that man would want to eradicate it.

It is only because of man's recognition that everything opposite the Creator is negative that we finally surrender and plead before the Creator. The Creator did this initially so that our desire for Him would be complete.

CHANGING THE INTENT

Q: You write about the deletion of surplus desires, but on the other hand, you say that there are no surplus desires, that no desire should be eradicated, but that man's egoistic nature should be mended to match that of the Creator (altruistic).

A: The term "deletion" refers to the change of the intent from *Lo Lishma* (not for Her name) to *Lishma* (for Her name). Through the change of the intent, the will to receive acquires a completely different outer shape. If, for example, a person wants to kill, that desire could be used positively, such as by working in a slaughterhouse.

Q: I can't ascribe spiritual intents to several of my aspirations. Is it right to delete a corporeal desire that cannot be joined with a spiritual intent, the aim "for the Creator?"

A: You should never dig into your uncorrected desires. "One is where one's thoughts are." Think of the Creator, of His Thought, and His Greatness. Only the surrounding Light, which comes through your study, can change you; you cannot do so by yourself. Therefore, don't even try; it is not the right approach.

Unfortunately, not all people know about Kabbalah and therefore think that bad thoughts and desires can be deleted. Kabbalah teaches that only prayer to the Creator and the response from Him will give you the strength to rid yourself of all the deficits.

CHANGING THE CORPOREAL DESIRE

Q: I find it hard to see myself, after so many years, changing my corporeal nature to a spiritual one. How does it happen?

A: Man begins his journey toward the Creator out of personal interest – in a state called, "*Lo Lishma*." Then, through the effect of the Upper Light, he suddenly acquires a new intent: "for the Creator" (also called, "*Lishma*"). The change in man's intent is not possible any other way but through the effect of the Light. The effect of the Light can be awakened only through a systematic effort in the study of the Kabbalah in a group.

Ultimately, man indeed receives a possibility to fill himself up without limitation with the pleasure he yearns for, but he doesn't have the ability to receive it, due to the limitation of his own nature. Only when he exits his self does he acquire the ability of infinitely receiving. Therefore, the wisdom of Kabbalah is a science that teaches how to receive from the Creator.

The change in the attributes complies with the principle, "You have labored and found, believe."

I made efforts and found means, I made efforts in the group, connecting with it truly with an aim for myself, but ultimately the Light came and corrected me. I regard it as finding, because I couldn't have exited my nature previously, while I was still captivated by it.

CROSSING THE RED SEA

Q: It is very hard to apply the first restriction over all my desires, so I wanted to ask if it is possible to work with each desire separately, one by one, without restricting all of them at once?

A: We are all born with a certain quota of corporeal desires: desires to enjoy for ourselves. These desires can be satisfied with a greater amount of corporeal pleasure or with a lesser amount, by limiting the desire. But all that has nothing to do with the type of will to receive that is necessary for entering spirituality.

When we enter spirituality, our will to receive grows in quality; we want to take pleasure in the Creator and not in pleasures of this world, which are mere costumes over the pleasure that comes from the Creator.

In each spiritual degree, we are given a greater portion of will to enjoy, which we must overcome. Each additional desire should be used in our search for a connection with the Creator. As we are gradually granted new, greater desires, we should first gather our strength in order to refrain from using those desires for ourselves. That is called "making the first restriction" on the given desire. Thus, we acquire a screen and can already use that will for the Creator and not for ourselves.

From this we learn that in each degree, we should gather strength to perform the first restriction over the desire of that degree by ourselves.

Only once, when man first exits the sensation of this world and enters the Upper World, does he receive a screen over his corporeal will to enjoy. In other words, the first time we cross the barrier between the physical and the spiritual world, we acquire the intent not to use the corporeal desires for ourselves. It is a special moment, called "the crossing of the Red Sea," that comes after the exodus from Egypt, meaning after one has been freed from one's nature.

Through that passage, man crosses over to the spiritual realm, where he senses the Creator. The sensing of the Creator is the attaining of the Upper World.

CHARACTER, ATTRIBUTES AND HABITS

Q: Is it risky to allow yourself to be moved by a film or a book that does not contain even a shred of spirituality, and use them for relaxation? And what about my less positive habits? How will I deal with those?

A: There is nothing you can do with yourself. Your reactions and what you are today will also remain later. You will begin to change inwardly as you delve deeper into Kabbalah, but your character will remain the same.

The Book of Zohar says that your character has nothing to do with your natural desire to enjoy. Your character is expressed as your responses to stimuli. Once you change your goal, you will perceive a different reality. So step out of it and begin relating to things differently.

Today, you can only say to yourself that everything comes from the Creator. Later, you will sense it very clearly. Then you will not have to say anything to yourself, your new attributes will determine that.

You must think only of rising to the degree of the Creator. If you think about your own negative characteristics, by doing so, you are accusing the Creator, because the thoughts of an uncorrected person are also uncorrected, since "one is where one's thoughts are."

Therefore, it is best not to think of yourself, but of the Creator. This way you are already in Him.

ENVY AND LUST

Q: What do I do with my jealousy, with my lust? Does the Kabbalah correct such attributes and the relationships between people?

A: During the study of Kabbalah, you are gradually influenced by the surrounding Light that changes you. It first happens in small portions, and later on it becomes a perpetual process. Over time you might appear to be more egotistical, because you react differently to external stimulus, relationships and pain, and people tend to interpret it as carelessness toward them. In fact, you have simply begun to understand the meaning of what is going on. You do not cry anymore like others do, and you do not panic. On the contrary, you want to give everyone more and more, but you do it in a special way, through the correction of the universe through yourself.

This love for mankind, the greatest there is, can seem like pure egotism. Even though you relate to people around you like a loving father who will not give his child a knife to play with, others will not understand you. In general, Kabbalah can be understood only by personal experience. Unfortunately only people with spiritual attainment can enjoy this type of experience.

LYING TO THE RECEIVING NATURE

Q: What do I do if my will to receive doesn't let me do what I intend to do? Can you lie to it, or use some trick?

A: If you're trying to make your will to receive (your nature of enjoyment, satisfaction, simply living) accept your position, it means that you have come up with some "bait" through which you promise it pleasure. This will allow you to do as you intended.

It's as though it is happening not within one person but between two people who lie to one another, just as the Torah and other holy books seem to speak of many people, when in fact they refer to various attributes of the same person and the connections between them. .

The questions that are resolved there are very similar to yours: what to do, can man lie to his own nature, and, in general, which is the best way? Therefore it is recommended to read a lot. Remember, "Whatsoever thy hand attaineth to do by thy strength, that do" (Ecclesiastes 9, 10).

Man must try everything even before the receiving nature discovers that it takes no pleasure in it, and only then will it agree to ask things of the Creator...

Q: Does it matter what makes you stop being an egoist?

A: At first, the aim is for me, *Lo Lishma*. Man confuses working for the Creator with working for himself. But it is precisely that situation, which allows him to make an effort. As a result of the effort comes the Light that corrects from Above, and man begins to understand what it means to be "outside myself, to work 'not for me', but 'for the Creator'."

222

Those questions should be asked, but the answers are feelings that go along with the corrected vessels. *The question is a vessel; the answer is a Light.* In the meantime, the answers are only good for calming yourself down and encouraging you to make an effort.

In general, man grows like a baby, which unconsciously imitates adults. Actors learn the same way. In fact, any study is based on repetition; you learn that which you still don't know, the degree you have not yet reached. That process is called, from *Lo Lishma* to *Lishma*; from "for me" to "for the Creator" - from the sensation of this world to the sensation of the spiritual world.

THE "GOOD WILL" AND THE "EVIL WILL"

Q: How can you tell what causes each ascent, and does it have any meaning in the spiritual work?

A: Two angels take one by the hand to the purpose of creation: on the right-hand side - the "good will," the desire of the Creator to bestow; on the left-hand side - the "evil will," one's own will to receive. They both come from the Creator, Who is the source of everything, but the difference is in the way His bestowal descends upon us: either directly and openly, or indirectly and secretly.

Is the reason that important? Can one always understand it? Perhaps it is better to consider that from this minute on we will "charge ahead" and not be so absorbed in the past, in search of the reasons for the current situation. Such a search indicates that we live at the expense of our past attainments, in debt, and afraid of the task we have been assigned to do, afraid to stay alone with ourselves.

DISCOVERING THE REAL ME

Q: Can other people see that I've become more egoistic, even though the changes are within me?

A: Everyone is born perfect, meaning we all initially have everything we need for correction and development. We are like a seed of wheat, containing all the information that is destined to develop. All that is left is to nourish the seed so that it reaches its potential.

That principle also drives man's character, his worldly traits, and his spiritual traits. Man's soul first appears as a tiny spot, a "point in the heart." After the study of the Kabbalah, it swells to the proportions that have been set for it in advance, and becomes a whole *Partzuf*.

All the evil that is now apparent in man was there before, only concealed, because he didn't have the necessary readiness, the strength and the need for correction. Because of that, the evil begins to show during the study of the Kabbalah.

Within everyone around us is also that evil, but we are so blind to it that not only can we not feel it, but some of us even regard ourselves as righteous. When the time of correction comes, we will all discover our true natures, and only through our corrections will it be possible to attain the Creator.

When we discover our evil traits, we get irritable and dissatisfied because we don't want to feel that way about ourselves. But other people don't understand what is going on with us, and will never link it with the revelation of evil because they have never experienced that process themselves.

HIDDEN FROM OTHERS

Q: Everything that was in me before is now coming out in the open. Do others see this as well?

A: What lies hidden inside us, in the point in the heart, at the seed of the soul, is our uncorrected nature. It first appears in small portions and then gradually reveals itself to the senses to a greater extent. But we must correct our traits bit by bit. Therefore, those of us who study more diligently discover our nature more quickly and in greater portions. We recognize our nature as bad, and we are repelled by its presence.

Kabbalah is an applied, experimental science. Everything we now know about the spiritual world and the Creator we learned from Kabbalists, people who enter the spiritual world by self-correction, and feel it within themselves the way we feel our world. They tell us of their discoveries in their books, where we can read about the spiritual world.

Kabbalah, as we've said above, is an applied science. If we do not learn from our own experiences and do not work on correcting ourselves, we cannot understand what we read in books. Thus, because they speak of things that have no expression in this world, we will know nothing about Kabbalah.

For this reason, Kabbalah is called "The Wisdom of the Hidden" because we cannot see the hidden, only the revealed. Being scientists of Kabbalah does not mean reading many books, but rather attaining the upper degrees of revelation. The extent of the revelation of the Upper One reflects the degree of the Kabbalist.

Although the will to receive becomes revealed further and further until it reaches its true limitless measure, it is invisible to others. It is impossible to see various kinds of pressures in behavior, impatience toward empty, meaningless things, the rejection of ordinary pleasures, which appear childish, etc.

These changes are mainly displayed outwardly in one's impatience, as Kabbalah does not tolerate empty philosophizing or discussions about theoretical and intangible concepts.

EGOISM IN SOCIETY

Q: When we begin to study Kabbalah and advance toward spirituality, we discover within us hidden egotistical traits that hadn't been apparent before. Will those traits affect ours whole behavior, increasing our selfishness towards others?

If that is true, how can groups of people that advance together exist? How can people maintain relationships if they become so "evil" during the study?

A: You are right. When a disciple advances, the will to take for oneself grows, otherwise how can there be any advancement? Each degree exposes another layer of uncorrected desires with the intent "for myself" and one rises by correcting the intent from "for me" to "for the Creator." The newly corrected desires consist of the new degree to which the person has now risen.

But then, Kabbalists would always feel themselves "bad" compared to the people around them. And that would have been true, if that were an addition of desires to take pleasure in material things. Indeed, one discovers such desires, too, but they are neither the most important nor the biggest of man's problems; they are not the ones he should wrestle with.

If you want to eat, drink or sleep more, don't worry about it; it is a temporary phenomenon during a spiritual descent, when there are no other pleasures.

The situation is that man is given more egoistic desires to enjoy the spiritual world, and we should wrestle with what rebels against the Creator, or as Pharaoh said, "Who is the Lord, that I should obey His voice" (Exodus 5, 2).

The most important thing is to confront thoughts against faith and doubts about Providence or the uniqueness of the Creator.

It is true that the physical desires grow as well, but that is done on purpose, in order to divert us from the correct battle against that which really distances us from the Creator.

The most important thing is not to change the object against which we are fighting. We must fight not the desires of this world, the desires of the animate nature, but rather the disturbances that keep us away from the Creator.

A shell is an impure thought, an impure aim against the Creator. It exists only in the spiritual world, along with—and against–purity (sanctity), not against physical temptations. Therefore, in a study group, although the egoism increases, it is expressed in personal interferences in the aim toward the Creator, not as ambitions to become a leader, for example. It is simply that, out of the awakening yearning for the Creator, each person wants to contribute more to the group.

Rav Yehuda Ashlag writes that the group must form the basis for the future society. Today such societies can be established on a small scale and the Creator rewards such a society with great help and personal care.

"ONE IS WHERE ONE'S THOUGHTS ARE."

Q: I read in an article written by Rav Baruch Ashlag that the only way to escape situations of spiritual decline and unawareness is to examine the current situation while still in a state of ascent, and understand that nothing is lower or more distanced from the Creator than one's existence as a beast. In this state, we lack the ability to evaluate our situation under the dictatorship of worldly desires. What does it mean to inquire, to purposely decline to a lower degree?

A: One must never search for lower situations because "one is where one's thoughts are." The lower we decline, the more distanced we become from the Creator. Always try to feel the contact with the Creator and leave the rest to Him.

If, for the purpose of progress, we should be dropped low, then the Creator will create that situation, but man himself, wherever he is, should want only to remain close to Him.

Only the Other Side pushes man to agonize and torture himself from within. The reply to it should be prompt: always try to be happy, to reach adhesion, high spirits and enthusiasm in the search.

The thoughts and conditions that affect man, whether positively or negatively, are brought to him from Above. They are spiritual forces, which we call "angels." With regard to spirituality, our bodies are considered dead.

Much like a vehicle, the body can only respond to spiritual forces. The angels can point the body (one's desire to receive) in the "wrong" direction, away from the aim toward the Creator; they break our contact with the Creator by afflicting the body with dead-end thoughts, lack of purpose, emptiness or fatigue.

The holy Zohar writes that the angels that control us do not have souls and can be fooled. It is our goal and our responsibility to maintain contact with the Creator despite the disturbances; therefore, the angels that bring us "bad" thoughts can be fooled. Since the body understands only mechanical movements, start dancing, even by yourself (as Rav Baruch Ashlag used to do with tears in his eyes). You will see how easily the body comes out of its negative state.

SELF AWARENESS

Q: When I face a certain situation, my self wants to react. If I think that my response is not real, can I change my response?

A: Beyond all the calculations, now and in any situation, you will ultimately act the way you will because you are who you are~and you cannot act any other way. Only in the next degree of development will you understand why you acted the way you did.

Therefore, in these situations I simply advise plenty of reading of the recommended texts to direct you, consciously or unconsciously, to understand what is going on. Generally speaking, people don't think about such questions as: "What is actually leading me?" They're only bothered with "How do I get what I want?" On the other hand, you are already at the beginning of a process of understanding and self-recognition.

SPIRITUAL DIAGNOSIS

Q: You once wrote that man couldn't assess his own mental state. You said that to diagnose it correctly, he should exit his current situation, change it and only then be able to see what kind of mood he was in.

I think there are two problems here: The first is that in his new situation, he will have to go back to the past, meaning he cannot live in the present. The second is that if he cannot evaluate his situation, he is in fact captivated in that situation, a slave to his own state.

A: It is obvious that man cannot objectively diagnose the current spiritual state he is in, because he always diagnoses it out from whatever desire currently affects him. So how does one evaluate one's mental state?

We cannot evaluate our own situations correctly, but at the same time we cannot believe other people because they, too, are controlled by their desires.

Q: Practically speaking, man should see what he must do at any given moment. But sometimes he doesn't know how to react to what happens to him. Should he remain passive and wait for a situation to go away, or should he try to react, to mend at all costs?

A: Only the Creator knows and only He can give the answer. We must turn to Him with this request and demand an answer. In Kabbalah it is called going "above reason," meaning above our knowledge and understanding.

Every step we make, if it is genuine, should make us rise to the next degree. But the thoughts and desires in the next degree are not just opposite to the ones in the current degree; they are completely different!

Q: But still, how do you attain the next spiritual state?

A: This is what happens during the search for an answer from the Creator: there is a certain act in the spiritual world, whereby the lower part of the Upper *Partzuf* (spiritual entity) descends to the upper part of the lower *Partzuf*. The Higher *Partzuf* is called "Creator," and the lower *Partzuf* is called "Creature," man's current degree.

In other words, man should try to feel with all his might that part of the Upper *Partzuf*, which is in him, and hold on to it. He should ignore all other thoughts, or go against his thoughts and desires and accept those of the Upper One. Then, the Superior Degree raises man to its level.

From that, we learn that our entire inner content, our thoughts and desires are given to us in order for us to rise upward through them.

ASPIRING TO THE TRUTH

Q: Sometimes it happens that a certain situation makes me so angry that for days I am infuriated. I try to analyze the situation, seemingly objectively, and understand that it is my primitive egoism speaking and not the inspiration for the truth, for spirituality.

How can I learn to interpret those feelings? After all, in order for me to turn to the Creator and ask for His help in correction, I need to see that my egoism is completely at fault.

A: When we read the books of Kabbalah, we accumulate its wisdom only in theory. We believe that this way we accumulate knowledge and experience. After all, that is what usually happens in our lives when it comes to learning anything–there is the study; there are exercises, experiments and training.

However, none of these things exist in spirituality. If a person does not physically and emotionally experience a situation, no knowledge, preparation or exercise will help.

Even people who do not study Kabbalah and have never even heard about the purpose of creation, advance toward that purpose during their lives. But they advance slowly, over millennia, unaware of the process. During the study of Kabbalah, everything we feel as something from above is perceived in our senses, just as we feel the corporeal things.

The Upper Senses take the form of regular, corporeal sensations; sensed not only in the soul, but also in the entire body. So when examined from the outside, we might appear to be in a good or bad mood, nervous or calm.

If, before the Kabbalah, you could share your thoughts and feelings with others, today you must not speak of your internal situations with anyone, because they all stem from your personal spiritual journey. You can ask your rav about them, in special situations, when a certain state might cause problems, such as wanting to leave Kabbalah, break away from the group, or leave your spouse, etc.

Any situation that is sent to you lasts just long enough for you to recognize it as such. That length of time is not for you to decide. It passes and is replaced by another necessary situation, which is sent to you from Above. Even as I answer, everything is already changing within you...

The power, the rhythm, the speed of your motion toward spirituality depends on you, but you cannot measure it. I remember that I once told my rav, "I'm making such great efforts and nothing changes!"

At that time, I did not understand his answer–that within us are many quick changes, which for ordinary people who do not study Kabbalah would takes years, perhaps hundreds of years of ordinary life, to occur. So have a little patience and try to have more fun.

A SIDE VIEW

Q: What do I do if my ego does not allow me to do things for the Creator? I terribly regret it, but there is nothing I can do about it. Does this mean that as far as internal work is concerned, all that remains for me to do is to watch it from the side?

A: Over the course of our spiritual development, the Creator shows us our essence, our nature, and the difference and distance between the Creator and us. As we advance, we feel our inferiority with growing intensity.

We see our traits as negative and relate to them differently than other people relate to their traits (if they ever do). We examine ourselves and compare ourselves to the Creator. The Upper Light already reaches us, but not - as yet - very strongly, not openly. It appears just enough to make us feel the difference between the Light and ourselves.

Read more of the material that you feel close to and it will help you through this time. You will still encounter various situations in the future, and for this reason our sages have said, "Much knowledge increases pain."

VICTORY OVER THE EGOISM

Q: Through a continuous spiritual quest, I have comprised a new theory about Kabbalah. It is The Theory of Shapes. It has an immense spiritual impact; it is full of mystery and secrets and with it one can triumph over one's egoism.

A: Man cannot defeat his egoism or his desire to enjoy for himself, because that desire is imprinted in him. The aim "for himself" permeates his every cell, starting from the still part of man, through the vegetative, animate and even the speaking, which is the intelligent part of man, the soul (or desire). Man simply cannot correct the intent from "for me" to "for the Creator" by himself.

Only when we understand our inability to correct our aim by ourselves and badly want to correct ourselves can we begin to ask the Creator for that miracle. When He sees that our only desire is to rid ourselves of the intent "for myself," He reveals Himself to us.

When we see the eternal power of the supreme and almighty Creator, we become permeated with the desire and the strength to change our intent from "for me" to "for the Creator."

This operation is called "The Light in it (the Kabbalah) Reforms." The Light is the Force of correction, which comes down to man from the Creator. The desire to correct your own nature, to know yourself and understand your "I," can only be satisfied through Kabbalah.

With any other way, you will indeed try to change something within you, but it will not be the true desire to change your nature of self-indulgence, although you might think that that is exactly what you are seeking to change.

There is no other theory and no other practical method! But if you want to explain your theory to me, I am willing to read it and together we will interpret it. If one has put a lot of effort into ridding self of one's nature, the theory, even if incorrect, is worthy of attention. Perhaps I can still show you the right way.

REWARD AND PUNISHMENT

Q: I have several questions: Is man neither rewarded nor punished for his actions in this world, since he has no free choice over his actions? Aren't the Creator's decisions and actions in the spiritual world influenced by man's desires? Are our desires the only ones that influence our world? Are man's desires his essence?

A: The essence of man is his will.

1. Man's desires do not influence the Creator.

2. Only the Creator decides what to do with man.

a) Man is neither rewarded nor punished for his actions in our world, because he is not free to do or not to do them.

b) Everything that happens in our world happens according to the Will of the Creator.

At first, man must act as if the Creator does not exist, and everything depends on him alone, meaning that he alone determines the outcome of things and not the Creator. But when the act is done and the result has been determined, he must then attribute everything to the Creator, as "There is none else beside Him."

INFLUENCING THE CREATOR

Q: Do our decisions affect the Creator?

A: No.

Q: Does only the Creator decide what we must do?

A: Yes. Ordinary people do not influence the Creator, because they have no means to do so. They have no screen. But he who becomes a "man" in the Kabbalistic sense of the word ~ a person with a screen-can influence the Creator and the entire creation. He becomes the leader of creation in place of the Creator; an equal partner to the Creator.

As long as you have not become a "man"- a person with a spiritual degree- and are still captivated by your corporeal nature, you are incapable of making any decisions because all you can see is this world.

What do you see before you that would enable you to decide what to do? In this world, you are given the illusion of freedom, and are taught to behave like a blind kitten. When that truth is revealed to you, you'll see how wrong you were.

The Creator is almighty precisely because He gives man everything: freedom of choice and the strength to act, understanding and attainment of the laws of reality. Upon choosing spirituality, man wishes to cleave to the Creator. This desire stands far above his self-benefit; it pertains to the attribute of being "for the Creator."

In other words, man sees the Creator as the ultimate good and wishes to serve Him.

FREEDOM OF CHOICE

Q: Where and how is the freedom of choice expressed? During one's life, when exactly does one choose, and what should one choose?

A: The choices that we have in the course of our lives are narrowed down to the discovery of the causes that compel us to study Kabbalah. Besides the study of the Kabbalah, all other occupations that we pursue are considered animate because they are transitory and expire when the physical body does. As human beings, we have freedom of choice only in our decision to study Kabbalah. There are three reasons that compel us to study Kabbalah:

1. Reward and punishment in this world;

2. Reward and punishment in the next world;

3. For the Creator ~ when we are driven by the desire to resemble the Creator in His ability to give (to attain the attribute of bestowal). For that purpose, we study Kabbalah as a means to attain the altruistic goal: the will and the desire to bestow upon the Creator.

Because of the above, spirituality is higher than us; it is above the boundaries of time and space. We cannot convince our bodies to give to the Creator because our bodies immediately retaliate with the question, "What will I get out of it?" By their very nature, they cannot understand any better.

Thus, we have no choice but to ask the Creator to give us the desire and the will to bestow; to act and to think regardless of considerations of self-gratification. If we focus all our thoughts and desires on attaining that trait, the Creator will replace our corporeal nature with a spiritual one.

Then, in contrast to when we could not understand the possibility of working for others, now we cannot understand *not* working for the Creator.

THE LAWS OF NATURE

Q: What has the correction of the 613 desires to do with the unchanging laws of nature?

A: Everything that appears to be happening around us is but a reaction of our senses to the Upper Light of the Creator, or better put, to His Attributes. We cannot feel our surroundings in and of themselves, only our reactions to things outside of us. That external "something," the Light, or the Creator, does not change. We ourselves change constantly, and so do our responses to the Outer Light. This makes us think that something is happening all around us.

In fact, we change only in order to satisfy our sensation of deficit. Yet, when we attain the Attributes of the Creator, they no longer form a hindrance on our way to the Light; instead, we become like the Creator—unchanging and at complete rest.

Of course, the physical and spiritual laws of nature do not change; they only develop and add to the collective, simple law, which is the Attribute of the Creator: benevolence. All other laws express physical, spiritual, biological and chemical aspirations that accompany the substance and the desire that yearns for self-gratification.

These laws, which do not change until the end of correction, will then be felt as something completely different, each by our own stature, just as today we interpret situations differently from one another.

PREPARING FOR A BRIGHTER TOMORROW

Q: **What if a person is jealous of someone else because they are regarded as being at a higher spiritual level?**

A: There is a good reason for the verse, "When writers vie, wisdom mounts."

Jealousy is one of the most important means of spiritual development. Baal HaSulam speaks of it in a preface to the book *Panim Meirot u Masbirot*. It is most important to use it correctly, meaning not to desire that others have nothing, but to desire that you will have what others have.

The pleasure is in the self-recognition, in the attainment of the entire universe within you. Even today, the things you discover about your external surroundings are perceived in your current vessels. However, you are, as yet, incapable of feeling the full power and magnitude of our world, and still cannot discover the huge world that is concealed from us: the feelings, the communication between people on a spiritual level, the laws of nature, and the collective force, which we call "Creator."

If we could feel these things, it would mean that we are at the state of the end of correction (*Gmar Tikun*). That would mean that we are all prepared spiritually, have corrected our aims for the current situation, and are now ready and willing to discover and comprehend the Light of the Creator. The end of correction means that each and every person has corrected his tools, his sensations; that each has a screen, and that now each person is ready to start living.

As we understand it, this means the end of correction, because there is nothing more to aspire to or to live for. Can we refer to our present situation as life? No. This isn't life in the true sense of the word. It is only a process of correction, a preparation for the work ahead. The wisdom of Kabbalah unveils true life before our very eyes.

THE BEST SITUATION

Q: **How does** Baal HaSulam **relate to human life?**

A: There are prisoners who have food and water and are content with life. They need nothing more. They don't even want to leave their prison. But then there are others who are free to walk the earth, yet feel as though they live their whole lives in prison. They would give anything to break free.

The difference between these two approaches to life results from variations in our spiritual development, the development of our souls.

Baal HaSulam writes that there are people who think only of themselves, or the well- being of their families, or even that of their city or town. Others think of the wellbeing of the whole nation, and yet others of the whole world.

Yet, how can one picture that the whole world is imprisoned while being free to do whatever one wishes, without feeling that in fact, there is no freedom of choice, that one is limited in every way, as is the entire world?

As a student of Kabbalah, my primary goal is to perceive that I am imprisoned, that the cage limits my freedom, and that I should do anything to get out of that cage. I begin by seeing that outside the cage there is another life, fuller and more beautiful than I could ever imagine. I realize that without that beauty, my world until that moment has been dreadful in its emptiness. The soul cannot evolve in such a world.

If you try to see yourself living outside of that cage, try to feel the spiritual freedom; it will be easier for you to understand the means of getting out of your current situation.

The wisdom of Kabbalah is not opium for the masses, because opium means deception. Why was the use of drugs prohibited all over the world? Because drugs create an illusion of freedom, with severe consequences. Man feels that he is in a completely different situation; he purposely misleads his own senses. Kabbalah accomplishes exactly the opposite. The first phase in the study is the opening of the eyes, making one see the world for what it really is.

In fact, man is always in the best possible situation, yet he feels the complete opposite, because he can only understand his own reactions, his own corporeal attributes, which are self-centered and limited in scope and abilities. These are attributes that have not been corrected through Kabbalah. The system taught by the wisdom of Kabbalah is a process of gradual spiritual evolution, the discovery of the Creator through the screen.

CHAPTER 6.
SOUL, BODY AND REINCARNATION

HOLOGRAM · THERE'S A LIKENESS

Q: I'd like to hear your commentary on the following ideas. It's written: "A soul is a part of the Creator. It's just that the Creator is whole and a soul is a part. Like a stone separated from a mountain, where a mountain is whole and a stone is a part..." Following this comparison, I just wonder if an analogy with a hologram could make a relation between the Creator and a soul easier.

Hologram is a photographic image of a 3D object, which not only registers the intensity of a radiating wave in a certain point, but also its phase. An interesting feature of a hologram is that it not only registers a 3D image on a 2D material, but if you split it into many pieces, even the tiniest piece will contain the *entire* image with all its characteristics (though diminished respectively).

If this analogy is correct, could it be useful in enabling technically minded people to understand?

A: "A soul is a part of the Creator. It's just that the Creator is whole and a soul is a part. Like a stone separated from a rock, where a rock is whole and a stone is a part..."

This means that a desire splits the entire Light into parts, since it consists of parts. It is like children making "sand cookies" with their tiny molds. The "sand" in our example is the Light; the "molds" are egotistical desires, which by their egoism split the Light into fractions inside the "molds."

A hologram may sometimes serve as a good example to stress that each randomly taken part of the spiritual realm consists of all the parts, only in miniature proportions according to the part's level. Your analogy is a good one!

THE SOUL AND THE PHYSICAL BODY

Q: Where inside the body is the soul?

A: It is impossible to describe what the soul is and where it is in the body just by observing it with our minds. That is because within us there is now only the "animate soul," the force that sustains us. There is not an organ in our body that is capable of feeling the soul.

Q: The philosopher Deckard argued that the soul is where the "third eye" is, whereas Yogananda maintained that it is in the brain.

A: You are trying to convince me that the soul is somehow connected with the body and that it is, for example, where the third eye is. Perhaps you agree with Yogananda that the soul is in the brain, and thus you ascribe the brain activity to the soul because you, as yet, do not understand what a soul is. The soul is a desire in which the Creator is felt, a desire that enjoys with the intent "for the Creator."

Q: Will it be possible in the future to dismantle body parts and rebuild the body from spare parts? Does that mean that it will be possible to build a biological robot that will attain the spiritual world and a soul?

A: You can replace everything in the physical body, but that has no influence whatsoever on spirituality. Spirituality means unity with the Creator. It is not in our flesh and blood bodies. In the armies of the past, it was common to believe that if a warrior killed his greatest enemy and ate his liver, he would acquire his courage and strength.

Q: This might sound absurd, but I read that in the East, when a holy man is about to die, his disciple asks permission to eat a part of the teacher's body after his death. Is there a spiritual meaning to that?

A: You have already answered your own question, because from your words it is understood that the beliefs of the East maintain that the spirit is in the substance. That comes from a complete unawareness of the actual root of the spiritual forces.

Humanity is now awakening to all kinds of clairvoyants, eastern shamanic theories, and charlatans. This is happening so we can experience them and realize how false they are, thus bringing humanity as a whole to Kabbalah.

THE ANIMATE SOUL

Q: Science has already succeeded in cloning the biological body, but what about the soul?

A: The soul has no connection with our corporeal body. Our physical body can exist as a biological, "animate" body, with an enlivening force called the "animate soul." But that has nothing to do with the Upper Soul.

We do not ask ourselves why there are cows, chickens, or cats, and what kind of soul dwells in them. Yet they too have souls, but their souls are simply the animate force that sustains them, the same force that sustains our own bodies.

Therefore, the body can be cloned and there is no problem with that. In the future, all organs, and eventually the whole body, will be cloned. But the soul does not depend on the body because man receives a soul according to well-defined spiritual laws, on which physical and biological sciences have no bearing.

There are many people in our world whose Upper Soul does not exist at all. That soul is called the "point in the heart." There are people who have it, and there are those who still don't. By the way, we cannot know who has it and who does not.

OUR BODY AND KABBALAH

Q: What is the meaning of the assertion that there is nothing in common between Kabbalah and our bodies in this world?

A: Indeed, they have nothing in common. The human body is like the body of any other animal, whereas the soul is the desire to be filled with the Creator, meaning to delight "for Him."

The desire replaces its intent from enjoying "for itself" to enjoying "for the Creator." It changes from being a receiver to being a giver, although the act of receiving pleasure remains the same. In that case, the desires of the Creator and the creature are alike –both are giving.

Thus, by the fact that the soul is filled with the Creator, meaning it receives for Him, the soul is called "a part of God above." Only that desire can be filled with Light, meaning the sensation of the Creator.

The Creator created only one thing: a desire to enjoy. That desire is divided in several parts:

1. Desires of the world of *Ein Sof* (infinite world) - the greatest desires.
2. Desires of the world of *Adam Kadmon*.
3. Desires of the world of *Atzilut*.
4. Desires of the world of *Beria*.
5. Desires of the world of *Yetzira*.
6. Desires of the world of *Assiya*.
7. Desires of "this world" - the smallest of all desires, which operate with the intent "for myself."

Our substance is a small desire for pleasure. The soul evolves in us gradually. We develop our lowest desires through desires for food, sex and family. Then come the desires for wealth, respect, control and power; then for knowledge. If we have developed these desires over thousands of lives in our world, we get from Above a desire for spirituality.

To the extent that we develop that will correctly, we receive from Above an admission into the Upper Spiritual World and acquire new desires to act "for the Creator." By realizing these desires, we receive the Light–the sensation of the Creator.

DRESSING THE DIVINE SOUL

Q: What happens to the animate part of the soul after our death?

A: In "The Preface to the Wisdom of Kabbalah" Baal HaSulam writes that all that exists, except for the Creator, is the desire to receive pleasure; and all distinctions between the created beings are determined by the degree of this desire. The Creator fixes it in each being, and since there are four levels to the desire, there are also four groups of beings: still, vegetative, animate and speaking (man).

Only stage four has an independent desire. The rest are auxiliary, "mechanical" ones. Hence in all the worlds, including ours, there are still, vegetative, animate and speaking. Only man has free will, and is therefore obligated to correct himself with the help of the screen, and change his intentions from "for oneself" to "for the Creator." If desired, man corrects the preceding stages three, two and one, meaning the animate, vegetative and still.

Man has within an animate stage and a man stage, in which the man stage is his soul, developing from "the point in his heart" to its full size at the end of correction. Man's biological body and his animate soul are similar to those of animals and have the same fate: according to the degree of cooperation with the Divine Soul, the animate soul rises to correction, and, as we learn, they dress one another, merging into one.

ALL ABOUT THE SOUL

Q: **Where is the soul and what processes occur in it between each descent to this world?**

A: Kabbalah, being the revelation of the Creator to the creatures in this world, does not deal with these questions. It describes only what we must experience in this earthly life. We learn by ourselves what happens outside our lives by studying Kabbalah. But there is nothing about it in the books, since we must know what we need for correction, not to satisfy our curiosity. Study and you will see.

Q: **Are the questions about changing the soul and receiving a soul relevant only after crossing the barrier?**

A: The changing of the soul happens inside the soul; changing the states is called "soul incarnation." Roughly speaking, the vessel itself stays unchanged (although not entirely accurate, it is easier to explain it this way).

Q: How does the soul separate itself from the body?

A: Nothing is separated, because a soul is never connected to a body. In man's feelings, it is perceived as moving from one level to another. This feeling is called "a separation from (some part of) an egoistic desire," or "the death" of a body.

Q: How does the soul transfer into the collective soul of *Adam*?

A: The soul never actually left the collective soul; it simply stopped feeling it, since it corrupted its spiritual feelings by acquiring an egotistical desire. But in the process of desiring correction, the soul corrects its feeling and becomes able to feel its true state in the collective soul.

Retrieving this feeling is called "the ascent up the steps of the spiritual ladder" from our world into the world of *Atzilut*.

Q: How is the individual soul separated from the collective soul?

A: As the soul acquires additional uncorrected egotistical desires, it loses its feeling of the spiritual world, interpreted by the soul as a separation from the collective soul. As a result, the soul starts to feel a more crude desire in itself, called a "body." This is felt by the soul as birth in the biological body.

Q: How does the soul get into a body?

A: If you mean the biological body, then the soul has nothing to do with it. But if by a body you mean desire, then if the desire is egoistic, it is called "a body of this world," and if the desire is altruistic, it is called "a spiritual body." All these questions are explained in The Introduction to the Book of Zohar.

Q: How can a collective soul be "*Adam*" if it was "broken?" A broken jug leaks... It is impossible to retain anything in broken pieces...

A: Nothing disappears: all the states are saved and have equal rights to exist. Hence there's a state called "*Adam*" before the splitting. After the splitting, fractions of *Adam*, which are separated souls, descend into our world, and ascent to their root, the "primary *Adam*."

Q: Does one have a soul prior to crossing the barrier, or just a fraction of a soul?

A: Before crossing the barrier, man has only a point of longing for the Creator (the point in the heart), among all other longings (heart) for the pleasures of this world, which are felt through our five senses. Upon crossing the barrier, the point starts to grow, ascending 125 steps of the spiritual ladder of the five worlds. As it reaches its root, it finds its original place, except now it is 620 bigger than before.

Q: Can knowledge directly received from the Creator be argued?

A: If it is indeed received as a result of Divine Revelation, it is true for the person concerned and can't be argued. But this is subject to change during one's spiritual ascent. Nothing is absolute!

A RENEWED SOUL

Q: Is the soul fixed in the body, or does it change?

A: Let me simplify the explanation by saying that the soul is fixed and never changes, because otherwise one cannot even begin to understand what happens with the soul and compare its varying situations.

There is another basic question that comes up: if the soul does change, that would imply that one soul works, while another is rewarded. It is very hard for beginners to accept that, because they think it is unjust. But generally speaking, souls do change all the time. Each moment there is a new soul.

A soul is something indefinable; it is the corrected desire that constantly changes and unites with other parts of itself, other parts of souls. In the end, after having been corrected, all the souls will unite and be filled with the Creator.

Therefore, the differences between souls exist only in the sensations of uncorrected souls, meaning only during the process of their correction and only when they sense, through their natural attributes, where there is a demand "for me," and perform the calculation, "Who does the work and who receives the pay?"

DRESSING IN THE BODY

Q: I have read many explanations about body and soul. Does the Kabbalah recognize the process of a dressing of a soul in the body, and if so, how does it explain it?

A: "A soul dressed in a body" means that a person suddenly feels drawn to something exalted. That attraction is misinterpreted. One senses some surrounding Light, which indicates that the person is inside something very big, and is rather lost in it.

Everyone feels this preliminary sensation, but after a person experiences that sensation several times, it diminishes because one learns correctly, studies the Kabbalah correctly and begins to create within vessels that will help one feel spiritual sensations.

A person thus stops being like an embryo in the womb (a state that exists in a beginner) and becomes more and more mature. Emotions are then redefined and analyzed, and thus one grows farther away from that preliminary situation.

Instead of wanting to be "enveloped" in something higher like an embryo, one should aspire to attain the Upper One himself, to consciously be in Him and try to move forward independently. That can be possible only if the person begins to acquire a spiritual vessel for progress called the "screen." That is exactly what Kabbalah teaches.

Q: At what point does the soul dress in man?

A: The soul is not dressed in man from the beginning. In the final stages of one's incarnations, there evolves a desire for greater and greater pleasures: fame, fortune, and knowledge. Then there begins to evolve a desire for an Upper Force, for the Creator, for something outside the individual.

Then, all worldly satisfactions begin to pale. This is already a phenomenon that characterizes the surfacing of the soul. At that stage, the search begins for the source from which one can satisfy oneself, which can only be found in Kabbalah.

When does this happen to us? That depends on our maturity. It is not a question of age, but of the number of incarnations we have gone through and the root our soul comes from.

We are all individual parts of one collective soul called "*Adam*." The soul dresses in the body. Everyone has a unique, special soul. That is, it may take one person fifteen life cycles to attain spiritual sensations, while another would need only five. One may need to experience horrendous torments, while another will have it very easy. It all depends on the purpose of the soul and its initial state.

When the desire for the Upper Force appears, one should do one's utmost in order to satisfy it and develop it correctly; otherwise it might be taken away, perhaps for several lifetimes.

Q: Are you actually saying that there are people without souls in this world?

A: There is a force that revives every biological body, called "the animate soul." But when Kabbalists say "soul," they refer to a vessel, a screen that enables contact with the Upper Force, the Creator. When a desire for contact with the Upper Force first appears in man, it is called "the impregnation of a soul." If man does not have the desire for the Upper Spiritual Force, it means that that person does not have an upper soul.

It has nothing to do with one's physical attributes, only with one's inner readiness to bond with the Upper One.

Q: So are there people without a soul?

A: In each of us there is a "fetus" of a soul, but the question is whether it has come to a situation that necessitates its growth. If the fetus has not yet come to that state, a person will not feel any desire for spirituality, for the Creator. But if the fetus has come to that state, a person feels a need to know the purpose of his life. Without the answer to that question he simply cannot go on living.

From this point forward, the advancement depends on man alone. Some people develop their souls, meaning attain the sensation of the Upper World, within a few lifetimes, and others must incarnate hundreds of times. It depends on the society that a person chooses for himself to develop in.

THE WORLD OF THE KABBALIST

Q: While dressed in the physical body, does the soul exist only in our world?

A: That is not necessarily the case. Take, for example, the physical body of a Kabbalist. In his emotions (his soul) he might be in the world of *Atzilut*, but his physical body remains in our world, with all its maladies, desires, habits and characteristics.

HOW MANY SOULS DOES A KABBALIST HAVE?

Q: Baal HaSulam (Rav Yehuda Ashlag) wrote that he would not have been able to attain his degree if the Creator had not placed the soul of Rabbi Shimon Bar Yochai in him. Before that he had his own soul, and after that, the soul of Rabbi Shimon entered him. Did it unite with his original soul, or did he have two souls in one body?

A: The body is born, lives and dies in this world. There is a force that sustains it, with its unique attributes, character and skills. Together, these qualities form a being in our world that is no different from a beast. Animals live amongst themselves, separated from one another, but not as much as people, because they are not as well developed. The level of development is determined by the amount of the variations in that creation.

For example: stones of the same kind are no different from one another. Among plants of the same kind there are minor differences. One can already recognize unique characteristics in animals, and these are apparent in man in every aspect. But all of this can be attributed to the same sustaining force~the animate soul.

Everything that happens to man in his past, present and future belongs to this world. There are people who can predict the future, see the past, sense diseases and so on, but all that relates only to our world, to the animate soul.

Spirituality is above the body, above the desire to take pleasure in material things. It is therefore not connected with the body. A "body," in Kabbalah, means "desire." If a person has acquired a screen, he feels the dressing of the Spiritual Light within.

The sensation of the Light, the Creator, within such a desire is called a "soul." The Light changes according to the screen, and any change in the screen is called a "reincarnation of the soul."

A person in our world has only the animate reviving force, as do all other animals. If a person gets a desire to take pleasure in the Creator, a desire for the Upper One, a screen may be obtained by studying Kabbalah (there is no other way), and one will then receive a spiritual soul in addition to the animate soul. The animate soul does not change, but the spiritual soul changes all the time. A Kabbalist has two souls: the animate, and the spiritual.

Naturally, a Kabbalist is born with the animate soul and only later attains the higher, spiritual soul. It is said that everyone must come to the degree of Moses, meaning they must attain a soul such as that of Moses. Everyone must come to complete adhesion with the Creator and unite with the spiritual root that is in *Partzuf Adam ha Rishon* (the First Man), which contains all the souls within it.

THE ROLE OF MAN AND THE ROLE OF THE SOUL

Q: Are we born with a predetermined task that we live with and that we willingly (or unwillingly) perform, or, as the Ari explains, can we attain a soul by labor, effort and prayer?

A: It is not up to us to decide what soul we will be born with, what attributes we will have, and with what task or role we will come into this world. From childhood, we begin to unconsciously advance towards our task, through our environment and the circumstances we are given.

If the task deals with connection with the Creator, then at some point if we have matured through past lives, we will begin to search for something higher than our own world. That is how all Kabbalists started and that is how you will start.

What will happen next? That depends on the effort you'll make. Ultimately you will attain the degree of Moses, who received the Torah on Mt. Sinai, but when that time comes, in this life or in ten or a hundred lives from now, depends on the quantity and, even more so, on the quality of your efforts.

THE GENDER OF THE SOUL

Q: Does the soul have a gender, like the body?

A: The soul does have a specific gender: male or female. That attribute extends from the root of creation, from the very beginning. *Zeir Anpin* (male) and *Malchut* (female) of the world of *Atzilut* are the prototypes of the genders in our world, and there are no greater opposites than these.

Throughout the system of creation, built from up downward, there is a division, a separation into a feminine part and masculine part. The lower the degree of creation, the coarser and simpler it becomes, and the more overlap there is between the masculine and feminine parts.

For example, in plants there is almost no division by sex. But the more the creatures develop, meaning the higher up they are on the ladder of evolution, the more distinct they become.

In the spiritual world, this oppositeness is very obvious. One does not cancel the other, but complements it. Without the feminine part, the system of creation is inconceivable. The masculine part depends on the feminine part and waits for it.

Q: Are the souls of men different from those of women?

A: Yes, it is true that men and women have different kinds of souls. But the souls of men are neither better nor worse than those of women. They are simply different kinds of souls, and hence their corrections are different.

Q: What is the difference between feminine and masculine souls?

A: Regardless of the physical body in our world, masculine and feminine souls are two types of parts of souls that comprise the spiritual *Partzuf*, also called the "right" and the "left" of the *Partzuf*. A Kabbalist who climbs the spiritual ladder alternates between the masculine part of the vessel and the feminine part. Consequently, at one time the Kabbalist has a masculine soul and at another time, a feminine soul.

An example of that is the soul of the First Man. It broke into 600,000 parts and then into a great many more. However, the content of the original *Partzuf* is retained in every one of them, turning each part to a minute *Partzuf* of its own. All the attributes and the forces of the entire creation that were concentrated in the first spiritual *Partzuf* now exist in every little spark of it.

Those sparks are called "souls" of people. Each has its own origin in the First Man and each comes from a different *Sefira* or a sub *Sefira* within the ten *Sefirot* of the First Man. Those souls divide by masculine and feminine souls, and clothe the appropriate corporeal body accordingly.

We are born with only a certain task. Our corporeal-animate characteristics do not change, whereas our inner-spiritual attributes change according to our correction. Thus, a woman may experience masculine spiritual situations, but on the outside, her body, which is the dressing, the clothing of this world, will remain a woman.

In the spiritual world, however, the soul experiences corrections both in its feminine part and in its masculine part. In our world, the body is fixed and retains its gender – male or female.

SOULS OF LEADERS OF THE WORLD

Q: Do evil leaders and dictators in our world have no spiritual souls, since they were destined to punish mankind?

A: All souls are a part of the soul of the First Man. The soul is a part of the Creator from Above because it is filled with the Light of the Creator, depending on the extent of its correction.

We cannot see what actually happens to the souls, and certainly not to the souls dressed in bodies of leaders of this world. All of these people, good or bad, are simply robots in the hands of the Creator to serve His purpose in this world.

It is said about them that their hearts' destiny is fully in the hands of the Creator ("The hearts of ministers and kings are in the hands of God"). Therefore, everything that happens should be ascribed solely to the Creator.

Q: What connections have they with the "forces of darkness," of impurity?

A: The systems of holiness and impurity exist only to serve the purpose of creation. You can only speak of systems of holiness and impurity in relation to those who are progressing in Kabbalah. Otherwise, one might think that, besides the Creator, there is another authority. Those two systems exist only to sustain one program – the design of creation.

SOULS OF JEWS AND INCLINATION TO KABBALAH

Q: Kabbalah belongs to all souls, yet Kabbalah is attributed specifically to Jews. Why?

A: Every Hebrew (*Ivri*, from the Hebrew word, *Ever* (passage), meaning one who wants to cross the barrier between our world and the spiritual world), or Jew (*Yehudi*, from the word *Yechudi* - meaning one who wants to unite with the Creator), or Israeli (Israel, from the Hebrew words *Yashar-El* -meaning "straight to God," meaning he who wants to go directly to the Creator), takes two lines from Above, and bit by bit builds a middle third line.

The *left line* consists of one's uncorrected attributes; the *right line* consists of the attributes of the Creator that one by one are shown to us from Above. The *middle line* is the result of the correction of the left line using the right line.

The result of one's work, one's spiritual ego, is the Hebrew, the Jew and the Israeli, in everyone now on this earth. As a result of the law of Root and Branch, there is a great inclination to correction among people who are called Hebrews, Jews and Israelis. But it is only an inclination.

Those Jews (of this world) who do not implement this inclination are considered to have a greater will to receive for themselves than do non-Jews. Therefore, we can only speak of inclinations, not about a person having two souls. The revelation within us must come with great effort.

Other nations also have a growing number of people with an inclination for spirituality. This is because we are approaching the end of the correction of the world, which will occur when Jews, meaning those who are called Jews in this world, will fully correct their nature. Then, all other nations of the world will follow them and correct the left line through the attributes of the Creator, as the prophets have proclaimed.

THE POINT IN THE HEART

Q: Are the soul and the point in the heart different names for the same essence?

A: A desire that is created by the Creator to enjoy Him (the Light) is called a "soul." That desire remains in perfect form and complete adhesion with the Creator as it was initially created. In order for the soul to attain that situation in its own right, and to equalize with the Creator independently, thus becoming like Him, the Creator separates it from Himself by rendering it with opposite attributes to Him.

Ultimately, the soul stops feeling the Creator, the eternity and perfection, and clothes a corporeal body with a will to enjoy for its own pleasure. Through this will, the soul feels what we call "Our World." In order to feel its true, original, and complete state again, the soul must develop within it similar attributes to those of the Creator, as though giving birth to them, creating them.

In its original and complete state, the soul consists of the same volume as the Light that descends from the Creator and is filled by it. The more detached the soul grows from the Creator, the smaller its desire becomes. At the farthest distance from the Creator, there remains only a point (in size and power) and we can feel only our own will to delight our animate bodies. That point, however, which is in each and every one of us, can start "talking!"

The original soul is divided into 600,000 parts. Each of them evolves gradually from a point to a vast spiritual vessel (620 times greater), over the course of 6,000 consecutive corrections, called "years" or "degrees."

When it first appears, the soul is felt as a point in the heart, at the center of all desires, in man's ego. The soul exists within everyone in this world. But what soul? At what level? That is something we must all discover.

Q: Why are there so many bodies in the world, but only 600,000 souls?

A: Most people in our world don't have a spiritual soul, only an animate soul, like any other animal, which is enough to sustain them. But in them, there is also an embryo of the future spiritual soul, called the "point in the heart." The heart is the desire to take pleasure in everything around us.

Throughout history, and through their many lifetimes, humans develop desires for physical pleasures, and then for wealth, power, control, and knowledge. Following those desires for worldly pleasures, generally called the "heart," is the desire for spirituality.

The desire for spirituality seems to appear within the animate desires, hence the name, "point in the heart." Of course, those desires have nothing to do with the heart in our body. If we planted a new heart in someone, it would not change a single characteristic in that person‒ even if we implanted a new brain. The spiritual sphere has nothing to do with our biological body.

But the point in the heart is not the soul (yet). It is more like a human drop of semen, from which the embryo develops and the child is born. The point in our heart is like a drop of desire, a yearning for supreme attainment, for the Creator. If a person begins to develop it, it grows like the semen that has evolved into a fetus. When it becomes independent, it is called a "soul."

Q: What does it mean to receive a soul?

A: The soul is born out of spiritual semen, which is developed by the Light that descends on a person when studying Kabbalah. The point in the heart then begins to inflate and expand under the influence of that Light, and finally evolves into ten complete *Sefirot*; a complete structure called *Partzuf*, or a *Guf* (body) of a soul. The Upper Light is drawn into those ten *Sefirot*. This is how a person begins to feel the spiritual world, the Upper One, the Creator.

600,000 SOULS

Q: You said in your lectures that only 600,000 souls descend to this world. How is it possible to explain that the number of the physical bodies in this world is much greater and reaches some seven billion? How do 600,000 souls divide among all the people on earth?

A: There is only one soul in the world, called "*Adam ha Rishon.*" The soul of the *Adam ha Rishon* consists of 600,000 separate parts. Each part is a separate soul that is corrected when it joins with other parts, other souls. In order to join with other souls, the aim "for myself" must be canceled, because a spiritual bond and full unification is the exact same thing.

By revoking this aim and joining with other parts, with other souls, each part, each soul acquires attributes from the primary soul— that of *Adam ha Rishon.* A soul bonds with the Creator to the extent that it can bond with other souls. That fills the soul of *Adam ha Rishon*, because the attributes of the Creator and the corrected attributes of the soul equalize.

600,000 is a symbolic number. At the first breaking, the soul of the creature, called *Adam*, broke into 600,000 parts. Then, over many generations, it continued to break into the following smaller parts:

- Cain and Abel
- The tower of Babylon
- The rest of the generations

In addition, the souls constantly go from one body to the next, divide and unite, because they are in fact one soul divided only by our individual feelings. The will to enjoy for itself only is imprinted in them. You might say that there is only one soul, which is filled with Light, but because of our imperfection, we feel ourselves as separate parts of it.

At the end of correction, all the souls that feel separated will unite with one desire and one thought, one delight and one Creator.

THE SOUL CALLED "ADAM"

Q: How is it possible that in our world there are 600,000 souls, yet at the same time we learn that there is nothing but the creature and the Creator?

A: The soul is the desire to delight in the Creator. In other words, it is the Light that comes from Him. A desire to receive is called a vessel. The purpose of the Creator is to satisfy that desire for pleasure with Himself, provided the soul itself wants it. When that happens, it will feel pleasure. The Creator solved that problem by distancing the soul from Him. When the soul moves away from the Creator, it begins to want to draw near Him of its own accord. That gradually creates in it the desire for Him.

The created soul is called "Adam." It is, in fact, the one and only creation. *There is nothing in the universe apart from the Creator and Adam, who is the creature.* Adam was divided into 600,000 parts that were dressed in people in this world.

In the beginning of the spiritual path in this world, there is a change in a person's desires: the desire to delight in pleasures of this world turns into a desire to delight in the Creator. It is the greatest egoistic desire of all.

Once beyond the barrier and inside the spiritual world, each part goes through a correction of the aim from "for me" to "for the Creator." The extent of the correction is the extent of the fulfillment with the Light of the Creator until the soul is finally completely full. That sensation cannot be described in words; it is a sensation of eternity, wholeness, equivalence of form with the Creator. It is the purpose of creation.

CHRONOLOGY AND KABBALAH

Q: When, according to the conventional calendar, did **Adam's** fall occur? Is it worthwhile trying to reconcile the contradiction between the archaeologists' beliefs and the Creator's Words? Or is there no contradiction at all?

A: According to the Hebrew calendar, the count of descending broken parts of the vessel (soul, *Adam*) into our world, and their incarnations, began in year 0-0-00. Before that, no descending of souls occurred, since the vessel was not broken. I am describing this in the words of this world, but you won't be able to comprehend it unless you grasp it by yourself.

Archaeology points at the bodies that existed before the year 0-0-00, but there was no descending of the broken parts of *Adam* into those physical bodies. Baal HaSulam, in his article, "The Solution," which describes the solution to the society of the future, writes that the Earth was formed from gases. These condensed through millions of years until they produced a hard substance.

Then life appeared on it: vegetative, animate, and human. Only afterwards did the soul, or, rather, the broken parts of the soul, *Adam*, start to descend into man. *Adam* consists of the upper part, called "Israel," and the lower part, called "Nations of the World."

These parts are also gradually revealed in each of us, first in the people of Israel, the descendants of Abraham, and then in the nations of the world. Our task is to correct these parts in us and combine them into one construction.

THE CHRONOLOGY OF THE SOULS

Q: To which part of *Adam ha Rishon* can we attribute the souls that descended before Abraham, GE or AHP?

A: Before Abraham, there were souls in which the combination of GE and AHP did not require correction, meaning they had very thin *Aviut* (coarseness, or the will to receive). Such souls descend into our world even today; they suffer in this world, and prepare themselves for the awakening of the point in the heart.

Abraham the Patriarch was the first to feel this point and begin to work on his correction. Consequently, Abraham was called the first *Ivri*, from the Hebrew word Ever (to go over), meaning he who wants to cross the barrier between our world and the spiritual one.

In addition to the soul of *Adam*, our bodies are kept alive by an animate soul precisely like that of any other animal. However, this soul is unchanging and need not be corrected.

THE CORRECTION OF THE SOUL OF THE FIRST MAN

Q: The collective soul~the First Man~is a complete, rigid and uniform framework. Still, the souls that comprise it are adaptable, connected and mixed with each other. How can you explain this?

A: The framework is indeed rigid, but the ties within are flexible, because the whole universe and the soul of the First Man (*Adam ha Rishon*) are built from the name of the Creator *Y-H-V-H* (*Yod, Hey, Vav, Hey*).

1. The tip of the letter *Yod* - *Keter*.
2. The letter *Yod* itself - *Hochma*.
3. The letter *Hey* - *Bina*.
4. The letter *Vav* - *Zeir Anpin*.
5. The letter *Hey* - *Malchut*.

The First Man is a spiritual *Partzuf* that broke in 600,000 parts. When its screen broke, the aim "for the Creator," which linked all the parts (desires) together under one goal, was gone. Without the screen, the parts want to receive for themselves instead of giving together to the Creator and thus moving upwards. Now they do not have the understanding, the desire or the will for it. The mutual desire is indeed gone, but the framework is not.

What was extinguished was the screen that ties everything into one action, like a group that works together and is then dismantled.

Q: Why do the parts of the First Man correct themselves separately instead of as one soul?

A: It is only possible to overcome one egoistic desire (*Reshimo*, or imprint) at a time, and not an inclusive desire of all the *Reshimot* together. What matters is that the breaking was done deliberately, so that the creature, the soul, would break to pieces. In this way, the soul will begin to feel those situations that cannot be felt otherwise, when they are not mixed with the attributes of the Creator.

Our work begins from the lowest point in the universe, at the end of the evolution of creation, upwards. Anything that happened before us serves as preparation for us. The breaking of the First Man into parts is necessary for the attainment of the soul. The correction of the breaking is necessary for the birth of the vessel and its fulfillment with Light.

Q: Which parts are corrected first, and which come later?

A: The souls are divided in two: a part that can bestow, called "Israel," and a part that receives for itself, called "Nations of the World." But since they must be created first, their uncorrected nature shows in their full and actual power. That is why Israel appears to be worse than the Nations, although when the nature of the nations is revealed for the purpose of correction, it will be apparent just how much worse it is than Israel's.

Everything that happens in the world relates to the correction of the souls and their parts. This constitutes the entire reality. We cannot accurately assess what is happening with each and every one of us because all souls are linked together.

THE SINGULARITY OF THE SOUL

Q: How does the fact that each soul is unique and receives the Light according to its own characteristics, agree with what you write. You say that Kabbalists feel all the worlds equally?

A: We all have the same five sensory organs. Because of that, our ability to feel and our understanding of the outside world are identical. What we feel through our five senses is essentially our desire to enjoy.

That desire is found not within any specific sense of the five, but consists of five desires for pleasures:

1. Animate pleasures from sex, family and food.
2. Pleasure from wealth and social status.
3. Pleasure from power (control) and fame.
4. Pleasure from knowledge.
5. Pleasure from the Creator.

Those five desires exist in all of us in different combinations and they combine to create a collective desire for pleasure in man. According to the proportion of desires within our collective desire, each of us experiences different feelings. This is where the uniqueness of people comes from.

The entire universe is comprised of ten *Sefirot*, each comprised of ten inner *Sefirot*, and so on, indefinitely. For that reason, each particle in the universe that we take will always be comprised of ten parts, or *Sefirot*. But the proportions between the parts are always unique to that component.

THE MULTITUDE OF *PARTZUFIM* AND BODIES

Q: After the breaking of the First Man (the collective soul), 600,000 parts were created. Why, then, are we so different if each of us forms a similar part of something uniform and whole?

A: The vessel, or body of the First Man, is comprised of ten *Sefirot*. The whole body of the First Man is, or dresses on, the thirty *Sefirot* of the worlds of BYA (*Beria, Yetzira, Assiya*): its head (*Rosh*) in *Beria*, its throat (*Garon*) in the six upper *Sefirot* of *Yetzira*, its body starts from the *Chazeh* (chest) of *Yetzira*, down to the *Chazeh* of *Assiya*, and its legs (*Raglaim*) start from the *Chazeh* through the end of *Assiya*.

The characteristics of the *Sefirot* are different from one another and are linked with one another only by the intent "for the Creator." If the intent breaks or vanishes, then the link between the parts of the body is gone and each characteristic finds itself on its own.

What ties all the parts of the body, or desires, together is that we are all comprised of the same desires, but each of a different kind, character and shade. The fundamental attributes of the creatures are the same, but the first nine *Sefirot*, from *Keter* through *Yesod*, mix with the tenth *Sefira*, with the *Malchut* of each of them, in man's ego, in different combinations in each of us. They mix by well-defined signs and groups. In this way, they cause the creation of races, nations etc.

THE DEVELOPMENT OF THE SOUL

Q: How can I know which degree my soul is in, in the course of my spiritual development?

A: If you work on yourself, you will gradually begin to sense your spiritual situation. Later, you will begin to feel where you are, at what spiritual level your soul is located, and your spiritual state. This is possible because you are building your situation and determining your moves and the degree of your spiritual progress.

In order to perform the next step, you must know exactly what is happening right now, or you cannot progress in the spiritual world without doing yourself possible harm.

CHOOSING THE WAY

Q: Are there any TRUE ways, besides Kabbalah? If so, then what are they and how many? I guess I've been hopping from one thing to another for too long. I am trying to find something to stick with, but until now, all my efforts have failed.

A: Only you can understand yourself and choose your way and your purpose in life. Everyone does this independently, choosing in accordance with how developed one's soul is at the time of making a choice.

When I asked my teacher if being with him was the right place for me, he told me to test myself. He never coaxed me, as is done in all religious streams, never pulled me to him, since that could only do me harm. So you should work it out yourself. I can only wish you to do it actively, constantly comparing and verifying all possible ways of development with the feelings in your heart.

Above all, do not lie to yourself. Consult your heart and do what it tells you – that will be the right choice. Go this way until you change, develop, and grow out of your uncertainty. It is a permanent process till the very end of correction. Good luck to you!

WHAT LIMITS A SOUL

Q: **First, a man is limited by his nature, egoism. In the spiritual world, man is limited by the root of his soul, *Malchut de Atzilut*. Or does this root not limit the possibilities of a soul?**

A: Acquiring the screen enables us to free ourselves from the slavery of egoism and understand that the intention "for myself" is foreign, artificially created in us from above with the purpose of letting us rid ourselves of it and discover how free, eternal and perfect it feels to be in the intention "for the Creator".

WHERE DO WE COME FROM AND WHERE ARE WE GOING?

Q: **What happened with the First Man later on? Did he live for 930 years and then die? If this is what will happen to us, then why hurry? We will always have time to disappear...**

A: We do not disappear and we are not going anywhere. Everything is here, in this place, but in different dimensions, and therefore unfelt. There is no such thing as being born from nothing. In the beginning, the Creator created the worlds. Only after was man created. Everything was preordained that man would sin and lose his spiritual degree, falling to the level of our world.

All our souls are parts of one collective soul named *Adam*. Each of us must correct our part of *Adam*. We must correct it alone, of our own choice, on a route that is called "the path of Torah." Otherwise, we will be forced to mend ourselves on a "path of torment."

No one will be allowed to merely exist because the goal is clear, even though the road may take longer or shorter, and be more or less pleasant. By our terms, the goal can be expressed in centuries of torment and slaughter, instead of pleasure. It is worthwhile to hurry up and attain the sensation of the right path. That path is the best for both you and the Creator. It is the way of justice, which brings with it pleasure and completeness.

NEW SOULS

Q: Are we new souls?

A: Baal HaSulam writes in the article, "The Freedom," that each generation consists of the souls of the previous generation, but in new bodies. This is how mankind evolves. Souls accumulate experience from generation to generation, so that everything we study as scientific discoveries in this generation, and all experience and knowledge that is acquired is imprinted in the next generation as an obvious, indubitable fact. That is why children are smarter than their parents.

Indeed, there is reincarnation, but certainly not for bodies. The souls are what return, but only in the human body. The process of reincarnation can be understood only by attaining the Upper World, by studying Kabbalah. In the Upper World, souls without bodies are tied to the Kabbalists, who are not burdened by the body and can exist in our world and in the spiritual world simultaneously. Therefore, the laws and actual attainments of reincarnation are only open to Kabbalists.

LIFE CYCLES

Q: How many lives does a person have to live?

A: It depends on the individual. You can calculate the number of lives needed for man if he advances against himself, by the force that necessitates him to advance. But one cannot foresee how many lifetimes will be spared when the hastening of the way is one's own choice, one's freedom.

Our souls continue to return and clothe new bodies until that moment when we are able to control ourselves completely.

In the Kabbalah, there is a field called "incarnation of souls." It deals with the incarnations of each individual soul: how many cycles it has to go through before it reaches its peak, and when it is in full control of itself and fully participates in the creation of the world. But let us assume that your soul needs seventeen more cycles to attain its completion. In reality, you can go through them within one lifetime; it all depends on the pace of your advancement.

One cannot say how many cycles each soul will have. It is our own choice. Therefore, each one of us can, in this lifetime, experience several additional cycles and cut the road of correction much shorter, and experience a level of existence completely different from that of today, where we will not feel the transition between life and death.

Q: When does the soul dress in a physical body - is it at birth, or at another time?

A: The dressing of the soul in our biological body does not relate to the physical age of the body. When a person begins to feel a desire for the Upper World (by desire, I mean a genuine yearning for the Upper World), it means that a soul has clothed him.

REINCARNATION

Q: Is reincarnation the appearance of a new soul, which brings about the birth of a new person?

A: We do not count people like we count cattle heads; not by physical heads, but by spiritual heads, meaning by their desires and their aims. If those desires and aims have transformed in quality, we have a new person before us!

Q: But I've read in several other places in your books that reincarnation means there are many appearances of the souls in bodies in our corporeal world, and that this occurs until they reach their individual end of correction.

A: It is true when you speak about the unification of the soul and the body, at which time the body is like a cover, a shirt for the soul.

Q: In your book, you write: "Just as we must seemingly serve our egoistic desires (our inner "Nations of the World"), so we serve all the nations of the world in the physical world. Our spiritual state is what determines our situation in this world." Is that really so?

A: To the extent that we serve our inner desires in order to enjoy them, instead of serving the Creator, we are not serving ourselves, but the nations of the world. They are the ones that enjoy the fruits of our work, not us. Therefore, we have to know that we are the only ones who can change our fate, and only through the spiritual world, through inner change and self-correction.

Rav Yehuda Ashlag writes about it in his "Introduction to The Book of Zohar" (item 66 through the end).

PREVIOUS LIVES

Q: Is the experience from past lives kept somewhere when we die?

A: In the article, "The Freedom," it is said that what one has acquired in this life becomes a characteristic in the next. But the information can also be transferred in an opposite form from the one it took in the previous life, because matter itself rots and vanishes between the two life cycles.

Q: If a person did not attain anything in past lives, where is the root of that person's soul?

A: Any moment in one's life, even if the person simply exists, is already a correction. That is because we are under the authority of nature and suffer from it, even if unconsciously, and so does the entire creation: the still, vegetative, animate and man. It is said in the Talmud that if a person wants to take a coin of a certain value out of his pocket, but instead finds a coin of a different value, it is already a pain for him, because he feels that his desire was not satisfied. Thus, the amount of pain is precisely determined, regardless of our feelings.

But we have the ability to choose, and to make our own efforts to accelerate the correction. When that happens, we will begin to feel our pain consciously and discover its root cause, and can then conclude that it is advisable to change our intentions in order to get rid of the pain.

Because of that, as we draw nearer to the purpose of creation, we change every minute of our lives. For that reason, each life cycle always seems different. Besides, there is the need for constant renewal of the links between the souls. Otherwise, the connections would not be fixed and there would not be the correction of the collective soul, which is the unification of all the souls.

RIPE SOULS

Q: I told my relatives about Kabbalah, but they wouldn't listen. How do I open their hearts?

A: There are two types of people, meaning souls:

1. Those who are in their preliminary stage and still do not feel the need for spiritual elevation. They are called "Still" - inanimate - in the spiritual sense of the word, because they do not correct themselves, they do not move toward spirituality, like the still in our world. In fact, this term accurately describes the souls of all the people in the world, except for a few hundred Kabbalists and their disciples.

2. Those people (or souls) that have received a desire for spirituality from above, because it is their turn to start approaching the Creator. They find Kabbalah, begin to study and correct their attributes. In their new attributes, the corrected ones, they receive the sensation of the Cre-

ator the spiritual world. The question, "What is the meaning of my life?" is what motivates them. It is because of that question that they grow spiritually. They attain the Upper Worlds (in ascending order) - *Assiya* - *Yetzira* - *Beria* - *Atzilut* according to their efforts.

One who attains the degree of the world of *Atzilut* is called a "Man," and before one attains the degree of Man, one's spiritual development is respectively: *Assiya* - still; *Yetzira* - vegetative; *Beria* - animate.

I suggest that you do not try to persuade anyone, and in general refrain from speaking to people who oppose or do not wish to hear, as you will not convince them. A person should come to Kabbalah when ready. You can offer others a book, but nothing more. If they react, then the seed (the point in the heart) already exists in their soul. If no response is returned, then perhaps in a few life cycles the person will want what we want today.

ONE'S SOUL SHALL TEACH ONE

Q: Is it true that there are souls that are connected to the "wisdom of the hidden" and souls that are connected to the "revealed wisdom?" Does each soul have its own spiritual root, by which it can fulfill itself?

A: You are quoting from the words of Rabbi Shimon Bar-Yochai, who speaks of a corrected aim of man's desires, "for the Creator," meaning those who are already in the process of climbing the ladder from our world to the infinite. To such people there are two types of soul: one that is named "The Revealed Torah," which stems from the term, *Ohr Pashut* (lit. Simple Light), and the "Wisdom of the Hidden," which is revealed on certain conditions.

There is indeed a meaning to the words of Rashbi (Rabbi Shimon Bar-Yochai) that relates to our world as well: one who is drawn to the revealed Torah should study only that, and one who takes after Kabbalah can study Kabbalah. I always stress the words of our sages: "One's soul shall teach one," which means that the soul shows us where to find the origin of fulfillment.

Kabbalists think that people should develop freely. Freedom in the Torah means a simple observance of the commandments and laws, as long as one is not ready for something else. But if one has a desire to reach for the Creator, a desire for spirituality, that individual should be provided with all the conditions for spiritual growth, and should not be stopped or scared off.

Kabbalah states that a person must freely choose that part of the Torah~ revealed or secret~according to the ripeness of his soul. There was a great rav by the name of Noam Elimelech who said: "Kabbalah alone kept me in Judaism." That is because his soul has reached beyond the phase of the revealed Torah, and if he had not received that fulfillment he could not have truly existed.

One should find oneself. That is the only thing that Kabbalists encourage, whereas those who follow ideas and beliefs blindly, purposely forbid it.

BIRTH AND CORRECTION

Q: Man is born in our world through the joining of a physical body with its spirit, which may already be at a certain level in the spiritual worlds, meaning, by definition, it can already have a screen. Why, then, is there a need to start from the beginning in the physical world?

A: Every birth in our world signifies a correction of the corporeal level of desires. Even if a person studied Kabbalah in the past and reached a certain level, but not a final one, that person must be born as a baby, suffer, learn, and arrive at Kabbalah from the beginning. But the student will very quickly return to the level of the previous life and continue from there. There is never a repetition, only new corrections and additions to the previous life.

A PHYSICAL BODY AND A SPIRITUAL BODY

Q: What is the connection between our body and the spiritual bodies?

A: Anything that happens to the physical bodies in our world corresponds with what happens to the spiritual bodies in the spiritual world, or in spiritual desires. Outside the corporeal world there are only desires called forces, bodies, souls, *Partzufim*, etc.

A spiritual body is a desire with an aim "for the Creator." It thus turns out that to the ordinary person in our world with a corporeal body, there is no spiritual body. But a spiritual body, that intent, can be acquired through the wisdom of Kabbalah, which teaches how to acquire a screen, the aim "for the Creator."

A spiritual body evolves gradually, according to the correction, in the following steps:

- Conception - when a person is willing to nullify the self completely before the Creator, be dependent on Him and totally accept His Rule;
- Delivery - the ability to perform the actions alone, instead of through the Creator;
- Infancy – the period when a person gradually begins to perform certain actions, while the rest are still left for the Upper *Partzuf* - the Creator;
- Adulthood - a state of complete equivalence of form with the Creator in the current degree.

SOUL, MIND AND CHARACTER

Q: What happens to a soul that is dressed in a smart person and how is it affected by such a mind and character?

A: The body and the evolution of intelligence in no way affect the soul and its development, meaning the correction and fulfillment with the Light of the Creator. The fact that the soul and the body are "linked" in one person does not mean that the body influences the soul, because the soul is a desire to give (bestow), something which does not exist in the body's nature. In principle, the soul must change in a person, it must be corrected. This is why it is sent to the lowest level of creation - this world.

The body gives the soul something "extra" that allows it to exist until a person is able to identify with the soul rather than with one's corporeal body: the mind and character. Every habit and characteristic that has to do with this world and exists in all people requires no correction.

A person should not suffer because of one's characteristics and should not change them in any way, but instead should make contact with the Creator, which is our goal. Character has no bearing on that.

I advise everyone to research the Creator, study His deeds, His powers and the spiritual laws, instead of delving within self. "One is where one's thoughts are." Therefore, one who is adhesive with the Supreme is *in* the Supreme, and one who lowers self to lower attributes and suffers from them, "eateth his own flesh."

Salvation and correction come from Above. A person must only extend upon self the influence of the Upper Light, and that Light will correct everything that needs to be fixed.

The character does not change. Man's characteristics remain the same, because the will to receive exists in us. The will to receive takes a different form in each of us, in character, in perception of life and in desires. The form of the will does not change, only the aim and the use of it, from receiving "for myself" to an aim "for the Creator."

The conception and the birth of man and everything he does in this world arouse no response in the spiritual worlds. They have no effect whatsoever on the soul, because everything in our corporeal world is born and reveals itself before us by evolution from the movement of Upper Forces from up downward, as described: "There is not a grass below that does not have an angel above, that strikes it and says to it: Grow".

Only our desires to draw near the Creator have any effect on Above. A desire to draw near the Creator is a desire to equalize with Him in His desire to bring us pleasure. These desires are called "raising MAN." If we want to do everything for the Creator, as He wants to do for us, if we ask of Him to give us a chance to do it, than that prayer is felt in Him and He responds to it.

CHANGING THE SHIRT

Q: Is there a physical death in Kabbalah?

A: There is no death. Just imagine that you begin to feel another life besides this one, a life in which you also participate. Previously, the additional life was hidden from you. Now, suddenly you begin to feel that you are living in another place, a different relationship. The latter becomes so important to you, so vivid and clear and strong, that eventually, this life loses its meaning and is pushed aside.

When a person crosses the barrier to the spiritual world, it becomes the center of one's life. The person begins to reevaluate his or her life, and begins to relate to it on a completely different level. Situations such as physical life and death become akin to the changing of a shirt. That is how my teacher (Rav Baruch Ashlag) always described it.

Q: Is there anything after death?

A: You must be asking what happens after death to a person who is not a Kabbalist, because if he were a Kabbalist, meaning of some spiritual degree, then while in this life he would know how to maintain contact with all levels of creation.

What degree does a person who never studied Kabbalah feel when passing away? One feels the lowest degree, much like people who experience clinical death feel. It is a tiny sensation of freedom from the corporeal body; nothing more. Kabbalists feel that freedom a billion times more vividly than ordinary people feel it after death, even while still alive!

SLEEP AND DREAMS

Q: Is the passage to the spiritual worlds done during sleep and dreaming?

A: The wisdom of Kabbalah deals with the study of the laws of the universe, the structure of the soul and the management of the worlds. Your questions about dreams relate to the physical animate state of man. There is no connection between dreams and spiritual forces. Dreams indicate what happens in the body, not what happens with the soul.

Therefore, in order to attain spiritual elevation and attainment of the spiritual world, there is no point in analyzing dreams and there is no significance to the way you sleep. Our sleep is merely a physiological phenomenon, as in all animals.

THE SOUL OF PHARAOH

Q: I understand from your words that all the situations that the soul goes through in the spiritual world, materialize later on in our world. If the soul has already gone through the spiritual state called Pharaoh, will this Pharaoh materialize afterwards in our world? Will it be in a body with a soul in the state of Pharaoh, or within a body that answers to the name Pharaoh with his earthly attributes?

A: You are confused because you are discussing the object from outside, not from within it. The Torah tells us only about the way we can attain the highest spiritual state. It never speaks about history. In the spiritual world, this history is not yet created. It is written by each soul, which goes through the states of "gentile," "Pharaoh," and "Moses" in each person. The Torah is written for each person, and one must only refer to it as personal instructions.

The soul can go through changes only within its existence in the physical body, and that is precisely the reason for its condition. All the parts of the collective soul must complete their corrections, from the lowest state to the highest, while dressed in this world's body.

In other words, a person who lives in our world must experience all the states of elevation in the 613 degrees to the last degree, which is equivalence of form with the Creator.

Q: The Torah speaks of what happens between forces in the Upper Worlds. Everything that happens in our world, in its substance, is no more than a replica or a seal that has been imprinted and sealed. Did Moses and Pharaoh (the humans) have the power, the spiritual degree that the spiritual Moses and Pharaoh had? Was the first temple, or the second, compatible with their spiritual degree?

A: I don't understand what you mean by "compatible." Compatible with what? Do you search for spirituality in those? Do you search for their spiritual attainment? They were not souls with spiritual attainment from below upward, but rather an evolution of the worlds from up downward. Pharaoh, Moses and their like are examples of spiritual situations that a person must experience inwardly.

The Torah speaks of the way each person must rise from the situation it speaks of. We must feel everything that is written there. We will have to experience all the events and the characters in it, and only after that will we be able to actually sense what the Creator has in store for us.

The Torah says that every person will be like Moses, or to be exact, that each of us must be like all the other characters in the Torah, such as Pharaoh, Balaam, etc. But Moses is the goal of the development of the soul and because of that it speaks of him. However, it is also obvious that that such a degree of evolution cannot be attained without the evil inclination of Pharaoh being revealed.

Q: When the soul goes through a certain situation in our world, is it already going through its next situation in the spiritual world? And is it possible that a person is in one situation in this world, and in another in the Upper World?

A: One soul cannot be in several situations at the same time. All our future mental situations, to the last and most complete of them, are but future situations of the soul, which will attain them upon its ascent in each degree.

From below upward: our world is the world of *Assiya*, which resembles the world of *Yetzira*, which in turn resembles the world of *Beria*, which resembles the world of *Atzilut*. And from above downward, the worlds were created and were "copied" one by one, the worlds of BYA and our world.

The Torah speaks of what happens in the world of *Atzilut*. The same thing happens in all the spiritual worlds of BYA, which are beneath the world of *Atzilut* (of a lesser degree), but on a smaller spiritual scale. And so it is in our world, everything happens as it happens in the world of *Atzilut*.

However, this is in another substance, not in the spiritual desire, but in the corporeal one: the desire to delight self alone, which is the substance of our world. That is why we cannot describe what happens correctly.

The link between our world and the other worlds is inconceivable because we have no conception of the spiritual worlds. Only a Kabbalist feels both worlds at the same time, but cannot explain that sensation to one who cannot feel spiritual substance. The wisdom of attaining the Upper World is personal and is therefore designated as "the wisdom of the hidden." Only one who attains it can see the results, and no one else.

The Pharaoh of the world of *Atzilut* is the collective uncorrected will to receive that had been created by the Creator. It is always in the height of the degree of the Creator, but opposite Him. Therefore, the correction of Pharaoh in the world of *Atzilut* means a complete correction of *Malchut*, which is the whole of creation.

Pharaoh in the world of *Beria*, which is below the world of *Atzilut*, symbolizes the corrected Pharaoh, one degree lower than the final one.

Pharaoh in the world of *Yetzira* is two degrees lower, two degrees below the top.

Accordingly, Pharaoh in the world of *Assiya* is three degrees lower - three steps below the final degree.

In our world, meaning in the physical body of Pharaoh, there is nothing of the spiritual situation because our world consists only of matter: our bodies and that which is around them - still, vegetative and animate.

But if the soul of one accompanies his body in our world, that person is called a Kabbalist. If the soul does not accompany him, that person is then still in the stage of preparation in the development of spirituality, prior to the reception of a soul. He then has no connection with the Upper Worlds, whether they are *Assiya*, *Yetzira*, *Beria* or *Atzilut*.

In the corporeal world, in the substance of our world, there is a picture that accompanies the soul, which is an external adaptation of the picture of the world of *Atzilut*. For example: the rulers of the world are an external adaptation of Pharaoh (egoism, a shell).

Moses, the force that aspires for the Creator, stands against Pharaoh. If Moses goes to Pharaoh along with the Creator in his soul, then Pharaoh and the Creator are equal in a man. Then, he has the freedom of choice.

Therefore, everything in our world and in the substance of our world must follow a well-defined formula of equivalence of form with the Upper Worlds. But that happens without man's interference, as an extension from above downward, which brings about historic events in this world.

Some time in this world's history, something should happen that would cause the souls to experience the spiritual worlds by themselves, rising from our world to the world of *Atzilut*.

The state called Pharaoh is one where a person who studies Kabbalah feels one's precise nature to the fullest, as it was first created, and feels how opposite it is to the nature of the Creator. This is the most powerful negative degree, which stands against the complete correction, coming right before the last ascent to the final corrected degree ~ the End of Correction. If a person corrects that state of Pharaoh in oneself, complete correction is then attained.

Everything in our world, in its history, is an example of spiritual situations in substance that each person must go through within self, according to the rule: "Man is a small world." That is what humanity evolves towards throughout its history. Every generation's renewed souls descend into the bodies, moving them toward material progress, but they lead the man in us toward spiritual advancement.

When the soul reaches the full development of the egoistic nature that is needed for its progress, there appears in it the aspiration for spiritual development. A person begins to study Kabbalah, gradually goes through the degrees, from zero (the state of a spiritual embryo) onward and upward to the end of correction. In each degree that person gets greater desires, corrects them and by that attains the light that belongs to that degree by using corrected desire.

The various degrees have different names to the negative and the positive situations that a person goes through in each degree. Only by going from situations of the "left line" (uncorrected) to situations of the "right line" (the force of the Creator) and then to the state of the "middle line" (the correction of the left by the power of the right) - is there an ascent to the next degree.

Man himself, while feeling the desires of his nature, gives himself the name, Gentile. As the book of Genesis writes: the first man, once created, began to name the objects and attributes of the world around him. Along a person's spiritual ascent, he becomes corrected and names the attributes of his inner world. He calls himself Pharaoh, Gentile, Moses and so on.

When a person feels his negative desires to receive, he names them "Nations of the World." The particular situations where his nature is shown have particular names of gentiles. Positive appearances are generally named Israel, from the Hebrew words *Yashar El* (Heb." straight to God") that indicates that a person wants to go directly to the Creator. The state named Israel has some particular manifestations of its own, such as the Children of Israel, Levy, Priest etc.

There is never a withdrawal, only progress, even when a person feels the opposite, as when one falls into desires to enjoy for self alone (uncorrected left line), which already grow to fit the next degree.

CHAPTER 7.
BELIEFS, MYSTICISM
AND THE SUPERNATURAL

HIDDEN EVOLUTION

Q: Is it true that Kabbalists can change everything in a person's life?

A: It is true that Kabbalists can do anything, but they don't. It is not their job to do things instead of us. A person encounters all sorts of difficulties in life: shortage, disease and loss, all in order to develop, and use them to make contact with the spiritual world. If a Kabbalist cancels the difficulty that one is given, he disrupts that person's evolution toward the Upper World.

It is not a good idea to do good for a person before you understand what is actually good for him. It is like giving a child everything he asks for without committing him to anything: you simply ruin him that way.

That is our nature: the fact that things appear 'good' to us is a result of our limited vision, whereas those things are rarely the absolute good.

Q: What is the absolute good?

A: We have only one desire: to feel good, regardless of whether we obtain that good feeling through a better job, a new car, a mate, or successful children. Behind all those changes is the search for satisfaction. We try to attain what appears to bring us that sensation, and regard anything that helps us feel satisfied and good.

When we begin to feel spirituality, it changes our scale of values. We begin to see which are more important and which are less so. We begin to weigh our lives not just according to what we see and know in this life, things that our physical bodies see right now, but also feel ours past and future lives. This way, we begin to see what favors us, and what does not.

Then, we naturally change the evaluation of our environment; we no longer want what we did before: a different job, a different car, or a different mate, but seek something different altogether.

We change in accordance with our ascent in the spiritual world, and begin to understand what is good for us. It is the same as in our world: when a child, we want a toy car. When we grow up, we want a real car.

Our desires change as we grow in spirituality; we want something different from what we wanted when we first came to this world. The earlier objects of our desire seem like toys now compared to the real things that we begin to seek. It is that search that finally leads us to the absolute good.

INCREASING DESIRE

Q: So I cannot ask for whatever I want, or activate a book on Kabbalah to give me what I want? For example, if I want to be healthy, I will not be given health. Instead, if I am ill, my thoughts will tell me this is good.

A: No, not true. One can only ask for that which one really wants. A little boy wants a little toy and his father promises that if he studies well, he will buy him that toy. He studies hoping that he'll receive that little toy. But when he completes his studies, he now wants a bicycle. So what does his father do, buys him a toy or a bicycle? One changes all the time, and receives the things that one currently desires.

But when one begins to study Kabbalah and interferes with reality, one interferes in it with his current desires. A person needs nothing more than an inner desire, a heart's desire, to change a reality one feels is intolerable.

A GREATER RESPONSIBILITY

Q: Does this mean that all Kabbalists feel good?

A: No. The higher a person rises in spirit, the more he includes within him the sufferings of all the people. The higher the Kabbalist climbs, the more responsible he feels, the more his mind is occupied. All souls are linked together. Until they are happy in the highest level, the Kabbalist cannot rest.

A TIME FOR CONTROL

Q: What do contemporary Kabbalists influence, if there are any?

A: There are a great many Kabbalists. There are hidden Kabbalists who have no intention of becoming known, or of teaching others. They exist simply in order to balance this world, in order to perform their unique operations in it.

In order for the world to exist, people have to correct it from below upward, precisely from our world. For that reason, there are Kabbalists in each generation who perform such corrections and deal with tuning the system of the Supreme Leadership from within our world. Because the generations never stop evolving in spirituality, there are currently many people who can and should rise to take control over the leadership, instead of the few discrete Kabbalists.

Q: Are there people who have attained the end of correction?

A: Today, as in the past, there are great Kabbalists who are busy correcting the world. Their goal is to perform the instructions of the Creator on our corporeal level, and for that reason they have a body and a soul. They are known to no one, and should remain that way.

ALL SHALL KNOW ME

Q: What is common to, and what differentiates Kabbalah from, other religions and mystic methods?

A: The wisdom of Kabbalah is related to no other religion or belief. It does not deal with meditations, prophecies, questions of religion, or even one's mental state. The wisdom of Kabbalah is the science of the system of creation and its management.

Kabbalah teaches how anyone can attain the revelation of the system of creation. It is said: "For they shall all know Me, from the least of them unto the greatest of them" (Jeremiah 31, 33). This means that every soul, every person must ultimately attain the complete sensation of the entire creation, and not just the small part we perceive with our five senses.

GRADUAL EVOLUTION

Q: How does the Kabbalah relate to other cultures, including ancient ones?

A: The Kabbalah teaches about the Upper World, the origin of everything in our world. The substance of our world is born from the lowest degree of the Upper World. That substance is organized according to the four degrees of the Upper World and is divided to the four levels: still, vegetative, animate, and speaking.

The still substance was also divided to four levels: solid, liquid, gas and plasma, and so were the other levels. I am speaking of these things only to show that in our world, just as in the spiritual world, everything is built by the four degrees of the expansion of the Light.

Mankind is gradually evolving by the positive/constructive force and by the negative/destructive force. Each phase, or degree, comes as a result of the negation of the previous one. Every form of administration lasts only as long as it takes for the disadvantages to show, and for a strong enough degree to overturn it.

The more the negativity of the present situation is recognized, the nearer the new situation - which does not have the disadvantages of the present situation - becomes. Those disadvantages that appear in each degree and ultimately eliminate it are the reasons for the evolution of mankind.

The law of gradual evolution is a law that works on the whole of nature and is applied in every particle of it. Take the earth, for example. First, it was just a ball of gas. Under the influence of gravity, it then grew denser and the atoms heated until they began to burn. Then, by the effects of constructive and destructive forces the heat decreased and caused the creation of a thin and hard encrustation.

But that was not the end of the battle between the forces. The liquid gas ignited, once more erupted, and broke the crust. Everything went back to the preliminary state until, after the battle of the forces, the positive force overpowered the negative force.

This caused the heat to decrease and the crust to be reformed, but a little thicker this time, so that it would endure a greater pressure from within and for a longer period of time. This process repeated itself several times.

Thus, the eras changed every thirty million years, and each time the crust grew stronger and harder as a result of the strengthening of the positive force, which finally brought the system to complete harmony. Liquids filled the inside of the earth and the crust became dense enough to create conditions for the beginning of organic life.

However, contrary to other levels – still, vegetative and animate– which end their development automatically, under the power of the inner material forces man must undergo further development regarding his relationship with society.

Hence, cultures came and went all over the globe. Kabbalah accepts the fact of their existence and many corresponding assumptions, including the assumption that there is life elsewhere in the universe. We might even discuss the forms of such life...

The wisdom of Kabbalah contains more knowledge than all of science. But since that knowledge is not connected to man's role on earth,

Kabbalah simply refrains from dealing with it, and sees no need to elaborate on it.

When man's soul descends from the Upper World, it dresses in a body of this world for a specific purpose. The soul must go through certain stages of development during its corporeal life. That is why there is no time to waste on idle quests that stray beyond the range of human power, on which Kabbalists do not want to waste their time.

I can only say that by studying the wisdom of Kabbalah you will understand everything. Not only what happens on earth, but in the entire universe. It is because that study teaches you about the spiritual roots, which descend and create everything that happens in our world. But this knowledge will be revealed to you only if you use it for spiritual elevation, and not to satisfy your curiosity.

KABBALAH IS ABOVE OUR WORLD

Q: Does Kabbalah recognize the existence of Karma?

A: Any system that you might learn, other than the wisdom of Kabbalah, whether superstition or religion, will forever remain at the level of our world, confined by its limitations. These systems have nothing to do with spirituality, but merely with psychological processes that occur around our bodies.

In order to come to the Upper World, we must acquire a screen and break the barrier between the two worlds. That impediment can be crossed only by the system of Kabbalah.

Everything people may feel as karma, auras, etc. is a psychological process, though a very subtle one, which happens around the physical body. There is nothing unusual about it, nothing above our nature. In the future, our science will learn how to work with these systems very well.

THE TEACHINGS OF THE EAST

Q: In one of your talks, you said that Kabbalah is the only method that allows us to come out to the spiritual worlds and to perform the correction of the world by ourselves. But there are other systems, such as Buddhism, Yoga, and sophism that speak of various means of enlightenment to develop cosmic awareness and states of nirvana, or Samadhi.

I've read many of your books, and I think most of the Eastern teachings speak about the same thing, only in a different language, which stems from the differences in culture and psychological differences. But many sages from India and China, such as Buddha, Osho and others climbed very high in their spiritual development. How do you relate to those facts? Can you analyze in depth the common elements between the teaching of the East and Kabbalah and the differences between them?

A: I don't know any teachings but those of the Kabbalah. The difference between all the teachings and the Kabbalah, as I understand it from the perspective of the Kabbalah, is that they are built on the nullification of desires, or at least on their complete suppression, whereas Kabbalah states that the Creator can be sensed precisely by expressing the desire for Him (and certainly not by nullifying it), only by inverting the aim of its use.

Perhaps they are very similar on the outside, but there simply is no other method to attain the spiritual world. The sensations of all other methods are built on the suppression of one's desire to enjoy. A person who suppresses his ego feels in that passive state something that seems spiritual.

That is why there appears to be some resemblance in the description of the approach, but in truth, there is an enormous difference in the expression of the ego and its treatment. To a Kabbalist, who is in the spiritual world, the roots and differences between the various beliefs and faiths are very clear. Therefore, I recommend that you make an effort to enter the spiritual world and see for yourself. Until then all methods will seem alike.

Which way should a person choose to advance? That is an individual choice. Kabbalah shows you nothing beforehand, while other teachings may present some magical hints and enticements.

The ultimate choice will depend on the degree of the development of the soul of each person. If it has developed to the point of needing actual correction, that person will choose Kabbalah.

Q: I recommend that you read the book, "Dao and the Tree of Life" by Eric Yudlev. In it, the author analyzes all the eastern teachings and how they relate to Kabbalah.

A: In order to compare two things you need to know both. Perhaps the author knows the system of the Dao, and, like researchers of other teachings, has come to far-fetched assumptions. However, those are not the result of the revelation of the Light of the Creator, because attainment means the revelation of the Upper Light in the "middle line." That can be developed only through Kabbalah.

Q: Are other teachings harmful?

A: Kabbalists forbid nothing. They are certainly not in favor of burning or banning books. They think that the faster people go through the other paths, the faster they will understand that Kabbalah is the only true path. Therefore, the more people are exposed to various beliefs, and compare them to the wisdom of Kabbalah, the better.

KABBALAH IS NOT MYSTICISM

Q: How does the Kabbalah relate to spiritual quests such as mysticism, Eastern methods, and other spiritual systems?

A: It has nothing to do with them. Those are searches that a person makes, but they have nothing to do with Kabbalah.

Q: What is the connection between Kabbalah, fortune telling and magical forces?

A: There is no connection between the wisdom of Kabbalah and magic, fortune telling, charms, or anything people give to one another to provide them with some sort of pseudo protection from Fate. The wisdom of Kabbalah does not deal with those. The wisdom of Kabbalah is a science that develops in man the ability to monitor his own destiny and not be dependent on a special piece of paper, or a magic charm. The Kabbalist, the holy Ari, prohibited the use of charms in his writings because they provide nothing more than psychological support.

If I see that a certain object will save a person who comes to me for help, I tell him to believe in it, because there is magical power in it. But truly, the magic lies in the psychological strength that the object provides for that person. Physicians and psychologists use the power of psychological protection, but it would be a lie to say that that force has anything to do with upper-spiritual forces.

If that psychological protection works for you, use it, but know that it will not correct you. That is why Kabbalah does not use any "magical" psychological forces. That is also the reason why charms are prohibited in the Torah.

FORTUNE TELLERS - SOCIAL ASSISTANCE

Q: Among the 613 Commandments of the Torah, there is commandment No. 301, which states: "There shall not be found among you... ...a soothsayer, or an enchanter, or a sorcerer" (Deuteronomy 18, 10). What if a parent, despite all requests to stop using the services of fortune tellers, continues to do so? Does it mean that the Creator will punish this person? Will the person suffer for daring to doubt the omnipotence of the King of Kings, turning instead to dark powers created by Him? And will this person's children be punished for failing to convince their parent?

A: The prohibition against soothsaying and fortune telling mainly refers to spiritual idolatry, which is non-existent in our world today, since fortune-telling nowadays is purely psychological. In fact, everyone turns to so-called "Kabbalists" and "wizards" to predict the future.

This ban, like many others in the Torah, shows us that what is described here is one's inner state. It is also observed that the religious masses once more fail to observe it in our world.

Q: Do charms and magic work instantly?

A: They work instantly, but in the long run they worsen a person's situation. When we begin to study Kabbalah, we immediately find ourselves under the private guidance of the Creator, and then no fortune teller or magician can do anything to us, since we are on a completely different path. We move to a different level of progress.

None of them can predict anything for us because we are out of the control of the collective law of nature. The Spiritual Force and nature work differently on us. Therefore, I recommend the study of Kabbalah as the only genuine remedy. That is why it is called a "potion of life."

Q: If I feel that something bad is going to happen to me, how should I react?

A: When you are afraid and do not know your future, that makes you search for a contact with the Upper Force, your root. Only through that contact can you be free from torment; no future teller will help you here. Take one of the genuine sources of Kabbalah, the Zohar, the writing of the Ari, start reading and you will see how the point in the heart begins to emerge in you. Through that point you will begin to understand and feel how you should move on afterwards.

If you do not study Kabbalah, I advise you to take any Kabbalistic book nearby, such as Psalms, and begin to search for that contact. As soon as you feel that you have become dependent on an unfamiliar Upper Force, you will feel the need to make contact with It.

It is precisely for that reason that we are given those situations from Above. If we try to find that contact by ourselves, we will see how it can change our situation. Therefore, the best decision is to use your mortal fear to cry to that Force - the Creator - and He will appear before you.

FALSE LINKS TO THE UPPER WORLDS

Q: Is there a connection between dreams and Kabbalah?

A: There is no connection. Dreams are a result of physiological impressions that a person experienced during the day.

Q: How do you relate to mediation?

A: There are no mediations in Kabbalah. There are intents and precise forces of thought that lead the world (actual leading and affecting of the world is possible only through thought).

Q: Does the Kabbalah prohibit the use of charms?

A: Yes. The Torah forbids the use charms. The Ari also prohibited the use of charms because they misled people, although they do help psychologically.

People who believe in them ascribe great forces and consequently affect themselves. But we must differentiate between influence that is purely psychological and a true influence on life.

Q: What do you think about methods such as Reiki?

A: I am not connected with any other methods, and I do not see any of them in Kabbalah. However, I do not deny the fact that they do help people improve their lives physically and psychologically. I do not object to yoga or Reiki – if they help, why not? But I do not see any spirituality in them.

Spirituality is only a collection of psychological phenomena. There is no harm in one person seeing more than others. The Bedouin tribesmen, who live in the desert, can see much farther than ordinary people can. They can look at a cloud and know of something that is going on many miles away from them, just as an animal can feel the death of their mate a few days ahead of time.

Those phenomena are not spiritual, but are natural physiological phenomena of which people remote from nature are simply unaware. Kabbalah, however, speaks of a spiritual body, about what happens with the soul.

Q: What do you think about Tibetan studies?

A: I know that as soon as one climbs a little higher than this world, the whole Tibetan philosophy vanishes without a trace. That is why I was never interested in those studies. If I had encountered them in the course of my studies, I would certainly have studied them.

These studies are built entirely on the destruction of the ego. But egoism (our desire for pleasure) must not be destroyed because it is our very nature.

Tibetan studies lower a person to a vegetative, or even a still level. From this we can understand how destructive such studies are to one's egoism. Those who study these methods feel comfortable because the most comfortable situation is that of a stone, which is still. After all, what else could man want but to rest?

But this way, man will never attain the purpose of creation. If we are to live like a plant or a rock, we might as well not be born at all. Kabbalah maintains that we should take all our egoism, all our nature, and begin to deal with it correctly. Then we will reach the highest situation, not the lowest.

Therefore, when we ascend in spirituality, we see how quickly those methods collapse, as they were created to diminish desires and decrease suffering. Even the experts in those methods, who understand them in depth, recognize Kabbalah as a unique system, a method of study that is second to none.

BECOMING A GREAT EGOIST

Q: Why do we need to increase the desire in the method of Kabbalah?

A: The wisdom of Kabbalah is a science about the universe and the system that controls it; it explains the way everything around us happens. No other system gives us the ability to lead, monitor and control the world, because they are all based on diminishing the ego, the desire to receive.

It takes a great will to receive to lead, because one can lead only if one has enormous desires, corrected, right desires, because our desires are the forces by which we influence the collective system of creation.

All other systems are based on the reduction of man to a lower degree, even as low as a plant. We are told to eat less, breathe less, move less, restrict ourselves, and live in monasteries.

The wisdom of Kabbalah, however, speaks about being a great egoist, about wanting to swallow the entire world, and after that, working with that desire and correcting it. Because of that, the wisdom of Kabbalah develops in you the ability to rule, guide, and lead. Other methods are built on the suppression of desires, and thus depress your ability to lead creation.

WITCHCRAFT AND KABBALAH

Q: I met a woman who calls herself a fan of Kabbalah, but practices witchcraft. She reads Tarot cards, communicates with spirits, treats with oils and herbs and sells charms. How does this sit with Kabbalah? Do her forces come from the Creator?

A: Kabbalah deals solely with the attainment of the purpose of creation. The purpose of creation is adhesion with the Creator. The adhesion is attained by way of equalizing the attributes, called "equivalence of form."

The Kabbalah studies the attribute of the Creator called "benevolence." It is revealed above the barrier, which is the border between our world and the Upper World. It is a psychological barrier, which limits a certain spiritual development of a person. When one reaches that level of development, one begins to feel the Upper World. Attaining such a level is possible only through the study of Kabbalah.

There are no ceremonies in the study of Kabbalah. It deals solely with bringing a person above the barrier. Kabbalah has no dealings below the barrier, in the level of our world. Here there are corporeal forces, animate, and there are good forces and bad forces among them, such as the evil eye, the ability to predict the future, etc...However, all that relates only to the destiny of our world. The soul begins only above the barrier.

Kabbalah forbids fortune-telling or any attempt to find out about the destiny of the physical body. The body is temporary, negligible and thus insignificant. It is not worthy of attention beyond the question of how it serves the soul.

It is quite possible that the fortune-teller is telling the truth, but the prohibition stems from the fact that a person should rise above all that and rely on the Creator, without searching for other forces with which to change the order of situations that are planned by the Creator.

After all, every Force that stems from the Creator is there to bring us closer to Him. The principle law of Kabbalah is called, "There is none else beside Him." It contradicts the existence of witchcraft and any other kind of idolatry because ultimately "the earth shall be full of the knowledge of the Lord" (Isaiah 11, 9), "for they shall all know Me, from the least of them unto the greatest of them" (Jeremiah 31, 33).

MEDITATION

Q: Is prayer also meditation?

A: Acts such as prayer are independent of thoughts, except for the correction of the inner self. A Kabbalistic prayer is a calculated and precise contact between a person and Superior Spiritual Degrees (the Creator). The prayer is a series of corrections that is conducted by a spiritual coupling between the screen of a person and the Light that stems from Superior Degrees.

TAROT CARDS

Q: How does Kabbalah relate to Tarot cards?

A: It is a common mistake for people to think that Kabbalah seemingly deals with fortune-telling, revelations of the past, and the study of the present. Kabbalah, by definition, is the revelation of the Creator to people in this world, today, not after death!!!

Naturally, as a result of the revelation of the Creator, a person understands the entire creation and its management; the reasons for everything that happens and their consequences. But it is only the direct result that stems from the attainment of the Creator. Kabbalah has never dealt with fortune-telling of any kind, and what Kabbalists know of the future, they do not tell, because there is a strict prohibition on that.

If further knowledge beyond that, which man already has, would benefit man, the Creator would have revealed it to us. But knowing beyond what we should know harms us, because it denies us free choice and the possibility for correction. That is why it says unequivocally, "Neither shall ye practice divination nor soothsaying" (Leviticus, 19, 26), and "Thou shalt not suffer a sorceress to live" (Exodus 22, 17).

You can see for yourself how much unnecessary commotion there was at the dawn of the new millennium, as a result of the fortune telling of Nostradamus. In fact, nothing happened and the year went by peacefully, as did all the years before it.

Man yearns to believe in what he knows. He wants to know the future for his own personal benefit. But the Creator reveals everything ~ past, present and future ~ only to the extent that man will stop needing that knowledge and go with "faith above reason." This means that man rejects his personal reasoning and chooses to cleave to the Reason of the Superior, the Creator.

PLEASURE HUNT

Q: The Japanese have the Tea Ceremony, which is meticulously studied in various religious schools, and is very similar to Baal Ha-Sulam's story, "The Dining Table." How do you relate to it?

A: I personally do not know the Tea Ceremony. The Creator created the desire to enjoy. A spark of Light falls into that desire and revives it. The spark also awakens in it the yearning to be filled with the entire Light, not just a small portion of it.

Therefore, all movements that the creation makes, at all its levels, starting from the still, through the vegetative, animate and speaking, beginning in atoms and the combinations of organic molecules, and ending with the movements of the body and mind, are no more than a pleasure hunt.

When we study the connections that form between the host and the guest, we can discover enormous layers of the "desire to receive" in our inner structure. Apart from this relationship, in which the creature attains the giving Creator at all levels, there is no other relationship in the universe. It is revealed in the reciprocal relation between the poles, in electric and magnetic fields, and forms the basis of every connection between components of both the corporeal and the spiritual worlds. It is also the basis for the existence of corporeal and spiritual substance.

CULTS AND CEREMONIES

Q: There are many spiritual groups in the world that practice various ceremonies that are seemingly related to Kabbalah. Do these customs have any bearing on the world?

A: They are not related to Kabbalah whatsoever. There is no point in searching for a link between Kabbalah and various teachings that use Kabbalistic symbols. That link does not exist!

It is hard to imagine how many superstitions, religions, cults, etc., there are in the world. It is amazing how many directions man—or more precisely, man's will to receive, which is constantly searching for the reason for his condition~can invent, and in what versatile ways!

One may believe that one is closer to the truth, to the Source, and to eternity, but it is all an illusion. You see for yourself how many people go to India in order to seek enlightenment, all in order to attain some immediate psychological feeling of internal freedom.

When we truly climb to the spiritual world, we will see that only Kabbalah was given from Above, and all other customs and ceremonies are the fruits of the human mind, which serve our imagination and desire for pleasure. But it is impossible to convince anyone of that, because what Kabbalah teaches you cannot see with your eyes.

ESOTERIC TEACHINGS

Q: Is there anything in esoteric teachings that helps us understand the Kabbalah?

A: On the contrary, when a student with no background in foreign teachings comes to me, it is easier for him to enter the study of Kabbalah.

EVIL EYE

Q: I am in contact with a lot of people, and from the questions that they ask me, I sometimes feel that they are giving me an "evil eye." What can you advise me?

A: In the Zohar, it is said that many physical ailments come from the evil eye. In our world, the evil eye is a bad bio-energetic influence of one person on another.

But in spirituality, the term "evil eye" speaks of man's feelings toward the Creator, because there are only two forces: the Creator and the creature. Man sees that everything is bad, meaning we look at everything that comes to us from the Creator with an "evil eye"- because we disregard the law of creation, and His Leadership, and we get a response that we consider "bad."

But the fact of the matter is, everything that happens to us is a correction. Its true aim is positive, although its external appearance may seem negative to us. We wish for the corrections to appear before us in a positive manner, as something good. But if we pray to feel the Providence of the Creator only as good, then it is an egoistic approach "for me."

Instead, we should pray and ask for the correction of our attributes, so that we can feel the deeds of the Creator positively, as they were sent to us, as "good mercy." This way, we will be corrected before there is a need for the Creator to send us an unpleasant form of correction.

A CURSE

Q: What is a curse?

A: Kabbalah is man's personal way to attain the Creator. Therefore, there is no worse situation than the sensation of detachment from the Creator. Thus, a state of lack of thoughts of the Creator is regarded as a curse.

But evil thoughts (thoughts that oppose the Creator) are not considered a curse, because they still maintain contact with the Creator, a situation that is better than not having any contact with Him.

The purpose of Kabbalah (Heb. Reception), which is only giving, is opposite to those who think only of themselves. As a result of that, all the terms of Kabbalah bear an opposite meaning to the ones we have in this world. We tend to materialize spiritual concepts and relate them to ourselves. Thus, we interpret the curse as something that goes against us and not against the Creator.

Q: Is there a curse in the corporeal world?

A: Perhaps you are asking about the evil eye, and the answer is: yes, it exists. In the physical world there is a possibility to harm a person, and not only in a visible way. It is possible to influence a person in every degree of this world: one's body, his consciousness and subconscious, the inner structures of one's body by a magnetic and bioelectric field, and heat.

A person's fields can also be influenced by fields around another person, for example by rays that are reflected back from the eyes. It is possible to transfer anything from one person to another. It is simply a matter of technique, as is the case in the spiritual world.

A Kabbalist can convey spiritual information and his influence to another person. But unlike that which is possible in this world, there is no way to harm anyone, or even think about it.

SATAN IS WITHIN

Q: Does Satan exist?

A: There is only one Force, and it is called the Creator. It aspires to bring man to the best possible situation. But that power works on man as two opposite forces, because the attributes of the Creator and those of the creature are opposite to one another.

To the extent that we become corrupted, we feel the positive force acting on us as negative. But after we correct ourselves, we feel it as positive. We ourselves determine if the force is negative or positive, depending on our correction, our spirituality.

We call the negative force, "Satan," but whatever we name the forces, they are inside us, not outside.

THE TRUTH BEHIND THE SUPERNATURAL

Q: We know people who claim they can see into the future, heal by touch and leave their astral bodies. How do you relate to that? What can Kabbalah offer me instead?

A: The things you mention are psychological emotions and sensations that belong to this world. There is nothing you have mentioned that is above our world. My advice to you is to read and try to internalize the books of Kabbalah, because as of now, you are showing some resistance to that information.

Do not fear that you might lose your ability to look at things from a critical perspective. On the contrary, only after you understand will you be able to relate critically to the subject matter.

Healing by touch and other such "wonders" have nothing to do with the spiritual world and Kabbalah. These manifestations exist in reality as an influence of one object on another, which is partly in the subconscious. But that is still below the barrier, within our world, which is affected by our corporeal-egoistic nature.

Kabbalah offers you a way to live in the spiritual world while living in ours, where you feel, see and understand the direction of your personal growth and that of the whole of mankind. Then you will see your life ~ past, present and future ~ in a more correct fashion and live more wisely.

SHAMBALAH

Q: I read in a book that in 1924, Mrs. Elena Blavatsky entered the spiritual world in a body of a Romanian youth.

A: The meaning of "entrance to spirituality" is compatibility between inner attributes and desires, when the outside dressing can be anything, or nothing at all. In Kabbalah, a "body" means desires. The only way to enter the spiritual world is to acquire a screen, which endows one with compatibility with the Upper Forces. Only through that screen is it possible to be in a spiritual place, with spiritual forces, to be in equivalence of form with them, in contact with them, and to lead and bestow.

THE PHYSICAL BODY IS MEANINGLESS HERE.

Q: I read that Mrs. Blavatsky, who dressed in the body of that Romanian youth, attained "Shambalah." Shambalah, from the point of view of science (Ernest Moldshaft), is the gene pool of humanity. In it, there are explicit representatives of the spiritual world, including our biblical fathers.

A: Kabbalah is a science of an entirely different world, completely detached from our own. It is not tangential with our world; there are no common traits, whereas you are trying to find that contact to discover a correlation between those two worlds.

I know through my own attainment of the Upper World that there is only one-way: to climb up there and feel ("see").

You think that there is some hole in this world, through which you can enter the spiritual world without having to change your attributes. From the perspective of Kabbalah, this is a good example of what the human imagination can make of the Upper World without the prior knowledge from Above.

You speak of people who are intellectually great, but they are great only intellectually, without any superior spiritual attainment. You must know this: spirituality is higher than our minds and our natures.

Spiritual attributes can only be given from Above, and only if they are used in a special way, conveyed thousands of years ago: the way of Kabbalah. For spiritual attainment, there must be a void in man, called "the vessel of the soul," in which a person can feel the Creator, and only the Creator, through Kabbalistic knowledge. Try it!

MAN IS ALONE WITH HIS PURPOSE

Q: How does Kabbalah relate to aliens?

A: I can only say that there is nothing like man in the entire creation, and it is only man who can raise himself to the highest contact possible with the Creator, and equalize with Him. All other creatures that exist on earth and outside it do not have a godly purpose. All the talks about creatures from another planet are meaningless; we are alone with our purpose!

UFOS

Q: How does Kabbalah relate to the question of UFOs?

A: Regarding UFOs, Kabbalah does not speak of other life forms in other places. There is no other life ~ we are alone! Man would like to discover something in the universe because he needs it as support. However, besides us, there is only the Creator!

Q: I am a UFO researcher and I have found thousands of descriptions of actual facts, but nowhere is there a mention of the Creator. Why not?

A: I am trying to explain to people like you that there is something in nature around us that we need, yet cannot feel. You may have a lot of facts at your disposal, but man wants to touch! I would say that you, like me, are dealing with a mysterious science. The method of Kabbalah can make something mysterious and intangible become real and open.

A Kabbalist has contact with the Creator, and is willing to teach any person who really wants contact with the Creator. It is like dialing a telephone number: all you have to know is how to dial. Kabbalah does not disqualify anything, because the presence of another culture does not bother one who studies Kabbalah in order to discern the existence of the Creator.

I research the Upper World, not something that may exist in our universe. But the Upper World is for some reason hidden from us. When I study Kabbalah, I know that there are no creatures like us, creatures that the Creator assigned with a certain goal.

What does it matter if there is something else on earth, or on another planet, if the Creator wants to contact you, and not them?

AN ECLIPSE OF THE SUN AND A LUNAR ECLIPSE

Q: How should I relate to and prepare for a solar or lunar eclipse?

A: I don't want to disappoint you, but the best advice that I can give you is to simply ignore it. Such events only psychologically affect people, who long for a change for the better.

There will be no change. Nothing will happen because man has arbitrarily set up a calendar based on the movement of the earth around the sun. It is only possible to affect one's destiny through the spiritual world! Study those rules and you will discover the wisdom and power to do anything.

PARAPSYCHOLOGY

Q: What is the connection between parapsychology and Kabbalah?

A: There is no connection between parapsychology and Kabbalah. All of man's experiments with the mind do not reach beyond the borders of regular psychology. There is still more hidden than is revealed in the human body. You can refer to it as "hidden" only because it is still hidden from us.

But just as science and technology in the 19th century did not succeed in finding out much about the laws and forces of nature (they were hidden from us and then were revealed), so in the future, science will disclose many more of today's secrets, and they will no longer be hidden.

Kabbalah is called "the wisdom of the hidden" because it will always remain hidden, except for Kabbalists. It is a science about the Upper World, which cannot be revealed by orthodox scientific methods or technical instruments, but only by attaining the attributes of the Upper World.

We feel the world through our attributes. If we had other attributes, we would have other ways of feeling. As long as we do not acquire attributes and sensors with which to feel the Upper World, we will not be able to feel it. Science and the instruments of our world only expand our sensory organs, but reveal no genuinely new qualities. Behind all the equipment and deductions we remain as we were, with the same five senses.

Therefore, there is not a single physical science that enables us to peek into the Upper World, but only to acquire further information about the expansion of the abilities of our five senses in this world.

ASTROLOGY

Q: How is Kabbalah related to astrology?

A: In the wisdom of Kabbalah, there is the matter of Kabbalistic Astrology, as well as Kabbalistic Geography and Kabbalistic Medicine. Those topics deal with the connection between our universe and the systems in the collective universe, the broader one, which includes the Upper World.

If you're interested in learning why our world is built the way it is, including the earth and stars, the planets and the links among them, know that in actuality everything corresponds to the forces in the Upper World. All the bodies and the forces in our world are but a consequence of the materialization of those Upper Forces.

The reflection of the Upper World in ours creates various fields called Astronomy, Astrology, Psychology, Medicine, etc. That is why the science in our world is to some extent a reflection of the wisdom of Kabbalah in the material foundation of our world.

Q: Why is it that, in our time, there is such an evolution of sciences such as astrology?

A: People have always searched for any possible way to end the misery of mankind and society. Humanity has slowly gained experience, and became convinced that the progress of science and technology, including medical technology, does not deliver us from pain and torment.

People are less interested in knowledge and progress and more concerned with their own personal fate. The human ego, the desire to enjoy for ourselves, continues to grow with each generation and seek fulfillment. It is happening very powerfully in our time, and therefore, along with technology, there are courses in astrology and the supernatural that are opening everywhere around us, even in universities. Books about mysticism abound on the shelves of bookstores; horoscopes, prophecies and clairvoyants are found in every form of the media.

I published my first book on Kabbalah in 1984. At that time, the public was very "earthbound," with its feet firmly on the ground, and thought that progress and a rational attitude would solve the questions of life. It seemed as though the topic of the book went against common sense.

But in retrospect, when I look ten or fifteen years back, I see that everything has changed completely, even among people who are my age. Today, people believe that which they regarded as nonsense only fifteen years ago: the spiritual world, souls, prophesies, the change of fate ~ these are things that excite everyone today.

The Zohar predicted this time as a necessary phase in the collective development of humanity. For that reason, I am delighted with what is happening. However, as in anything else, after the current enthusiasm there will come disappointment, because magic has existed for thousands of years, and if there were anything real to it, people would have long been using those methods for personal profit in a systematic and scientific way.

The Torah says. "...neither shall ye practice divination" (Leviticus 19, 26), meaning, do not perform witchcraft, although it is possible. When one uses witchcraft, it seemingly improves one's situation. A visit to a fortune teller performs only a temporary change. But the change is only on the physical level, and for that you don't have to be a Kabbalist, or have spiritual forces behind you.

The force that exists in our world is enough to slightly change our inner feelings within our physical bodies, because these are only external forces, not spiritual ones.

Nature is set in such a way that it helps us achieve the purpose of creation and spiritual attainment. If we do not approach that goal of our own free will, but search for a way to avoid the torments life presents us, it is as though we do not relate to the force that promotes us. This brings upon us a more intense, acute and painful effect of that force in the next life.

However, the constant pursuit of a way to eliminate the torments and our attempts to overcome them brings us an accumulation of experience, and disappointment with all these methods. Mankind will ultimately arrive at a single system, received from Above, namely the wisdom of Kabbalah.

Q: We can compare our situation in this world to sailing in a small boat that is carried away in a mighty stream. We are unable to do anything about it. How is it possible to escape the drift and the rocks and maintain the right course in order to come to a safe shore in peace, to the inevitable end that we will come to?

A: We can escape disaster only if we add an engine of our own to the boat, called a "screen." The Kabbalah helps us acquire that screen. With it, we can run our lives by ourselves, without the help of fortune tellers and other such counselors. By so doing, we replace the torment- -the cruel pushing force–that keeps pushing us toward the purpose of creation, with the good Force, as we begin to learn to manage our lives and maintain our course.

Everyone will have to go the way that one is ordained to go, but with Kabbalah it will be done in the best possible way.

Q: And what does Kabbalah offer?

A: Take the book of a real Kabbalist, a genuine book, or listen to talks and lessons about Kabbalah, or watch a class. Today, there are many options open for all, man or woman, in some twenty languages. If you use these possibilities and begin to read the right books, the surrounding Light will immediately begin to work on you, and will start to change everything around you: the collective Providence will become private Providence, a beam of Light that points precisely to you. You will gradually feel it, and will acquire an inner strength of your own to change your own destiny.

All that will happen provided you read the books of Kabbalists. That by itself is enough to change the course of your life.

GIMATRIA

Q: How can a Kabbalist convey his situation to another person?

A: A teacher can take the "case" of his own situation, photocopy it, and express it in a form of an accurate mathematical formula, meaning Gimatria, and convey it to the student. The student then takes that formula, finds it within himself and implements it through his own spiritual powers. This way he goes through the same situation as his teacher. Gimatria is a mathematical formula that expresses the sum total of our spiritual experiences.

GRAVES OF RIGHTEOUS PEOPLE

Q: I have a few questions concerning the graves of the Righteous: Does the Kabbalah ascribe any meaning to the graves of the Righteous? How does a prayer at the grave of a Righteous differ from a prayer in a synagogue? What should one pray for at the grave of a Righteous? If I wish to study Kabbalah at the grave of Rashbi or any other Kabbalist, what is the best thing to read?

A: A prayer is a desire for the Creator, for His sake, in one's heart, not on one's lips. A synagogue is an invention of the last millennia of exile, but every person speaks with the Creator in one's heart. That is the meaning of a prayer.

Visiting a synagogue is not a prayer, it is a ritual introduced by our sages for taking care of the people, as are all other commandments, so that they could exist and not perish. From within this framework, a person starts to question one's existence (why one does certain things, etc.), which eventually leads to the question of one's relationship with the Creator.

Hence, it is to preserve the people, the masses, that it becomes necessary to observe the traditions and the daily rituals.

But one should differentiate between a ritual and a personal aspiration for the Creator. That is one's personal work, and it is carried out inside, hence the name "secret." It is concealed from others and to a certain extent even from oneself.

In the frame of this inner work of approaching the Creator, a person realizes that this goal can only be achieved by addressing Him with such a request, knowing that only the Creator can move one towards or away from Himself. This request is a prayer, regardless of where it is offered.

However, if a certain location calls to you, then go there. My advice is to search for such moments while studying. (This does not exclude "the special places," but we'll discuss them some other time with those who can feel the "specialty of places.")

THE WELL OF MIRIAM

Q: Many people ask where the well of Miriam is, and whether one can drink from it. Is this reality or a legend?

A: Any spiritual source spreads through all the spiritual worlds and must materialize (appear in our physical world). There is a certain force called the "*Bina*," the "superior mother," and in the physical world it reveals in fountains and springs.

However, it is forbidden to relate anything spiritual to water. One who drinks from a fountain does not get anything spiritual from it. The question is, who give that person the water? Water, like anything else, can be linked with its spiritual origin with the messenger of a spiritual force (a Kabbalist), and thus convey spiritual energy to a person.

My rav did that many times. He gave a person a peace of bread, or a sip of wine, and in this way conveyed spiritual energy within that corporeal object. After all, there is no other way to convey it to a person who still doesn't have spiritual vessels.

The Ari did the same with his disciple, Chaim Vital, when he let him drink from the water, which is a very natural thing for a Kabbalist. If that disciple had gone to the Sea of Galilee and drunk the water, he would not have attained any spiritual power. The water, in this case, was just a means for the conveyance of a spiritual attribute, and it doesn't really matter from where it was taken.

The force that the Ari gave to his disciple was called 'The Well of Miriam', not the water itself. I, too, received from my rav all sorts of refreshments. A Kabbalist can convey spiritual strength through a corporeal object, as well.

THE WESTERN WALL AND OTHER MIRACLES

Q: I have a picture of the Western Wall taken from the top of the building facing it. This photograph has healing powers. One starts feeling better when it is applied to a hurting spot. Recently, I treated a severe wound on a dog with it. Could you please explain this phenomenon, in light of the Kabbalah?

A: Kabbalah exclusively deals with man's aspiration for the Creator. Degrees, stages, and steps toward Him are felt as something totally new, as new worlds. There are 125 such degrees. They are divided into five parts, or "worlds."

The essence of Kabbalah consists of climbing through all the intermediary states and worlds, and reaching complete unity with the Creator. Man starts to feel the Creator from the very first step toward Him. It is called "the sensation of the Upper World."

Prior to that step, man feels himself, not the Creator. That feeling is called "this world." The first step toward the Creator signifies that man reaches the Upper World.

Each step forward indicates having a more distinct feeling of the Creator. It is felt in a special sensory organ called the "soul." We also call it the "sixth sense," since man isn't born with it, and it is not a natural bodily sense like the other five senses given to us in this world.

The soul is given to us personally by the Creator from above. Those who receive it rush forward to the Creator, and those who don't (for lack of the sixth sense, the soul) cannot even understand what we do, and if they received a religious upbringing, they even oppose Kabbalah.

What you describe is not the subject of Kabbalah. The answer to your question can probably be found in psychology or paranormal sciences. At that level exist the miracles in this world! The spiritual world is full of miracles, but these are obvious only to a Kabbalist, consciously perceived and controlled by someone who acquires the knowledge of Kabbalah.

MIRACLES

Q: How does Kabbalah relate to the term, "miracle"?

A: If the phenomenon exists in creation, in this world or in the spiritual world, the Kabbalah recognizes it and recognizes it as something that exists. If not, it does not exist.

Books of Kabbalah do not describe everything that exists in reality, but then we don't have to know everything! It is enough for us to know only that which is needed for correction and advancement toward the spiritual world. All the degrees along the way are revealed in the process of progressing toward the goal.

An outcome that was not predicted in the present, and that cannot be predicted by the present reality, is called a "miracle." It is something that is not supposed to happen according to the current laws.

An example is the miracle of the exodus from Egypt. We strive to attain spirituality without even knowing what we are doing. In fact, we don't even know what "spirituality" is because we haven't attained it yet. We aspire to something we do not really know.

The truth, we do not aspire to spirituality, because spirituality is only the desire to give, and we, by our nature, cannot want only to give. But through a special spiritual process, which occurs during the study of Kabbalah called, "from not for Her name," we come to "for Her name." At this point, our– aim changes from receiving for ourselves to "giving the Creator."

I would say that any help that comes from Above, any spiritual ascent, any acquisition of a new spiritual attribute, any time a person equalizes self with the Creator, is a miracle. That is how it is sensed in each degree.

THE DISCOVERY OF THE ORIGINS OF TRUTH

Q: I have seen in stores many books about Kabbalah. The writers of those books promise to reveal all the secrets of the Kabbalah. I checked and saw that they often rely on the material that you teach.

A: Influence through the public and revelation as a result of mental distress are the ways of the Creator in our world. Your question testifies to the fact that we live in a time of the dissemination of the wisdom of Kabbalah into the world.

It doesn't matter if the sources are spreading the truth or not– the next stage will show that, among this wealth of information, the true sources will be revealed. Everyone will clearly understand the meaning of the genuine Kabbalah, the one that speaks of the revelation of the Creator in our world, according to one's adherence with the attributes of the Creator. At that time, all those who are not ready for this understanding will step aside, and many who want to advance in the path of truth will appear.

CHAPTER 8.
PRAYER, REQUEST AND AIM

THE MEANING OF PRAYER

Q: What does a prayer mean from the perspective of Kabbalah and for you personally? Do you pray and observe *Mitzvot* like any other rav?

A: Kabbalah answers the question about the meaning of life, not about the meaning of *Mitzvot* and prayers. A prayer is a desire one feels in one's heart; it is what one wishes for.

Perhaps one is dreaming about a vacation or asks for rain - then that is the prayer, what one asks of the Creator. Kabbalah teaches how to tune one's heart for correct desires, for those prayers will lead to the feeling of the spiritual world, the Creator. Everything that leads to a true request for the Creator is called *Mitzva* (commandment).

So you tell me, who else apart from Kabbalists truly observes the commandments and genuinely prays?

METHOD TO A CHOICE

Q: You say that there is a law that rules nature and man harshly, and that the Source of that law is a mighty Force called the Creator. In difficult moments I turn to Him, but I feel that if I want to change something in my life, it means that I disagree with His Actions, that I am not grateful to Him. What is the actual cry of the soul, the one the Creator listens to and answers?

A: You're right. The one law of creation is what we call "the Creator." Unlike ordinary scientists, Kabbalists feel that which we cannot, and study the system of creation, having developed an extra sense. That is why they can also tell that the Force that leads everything is rich with emotions, and not that nature is indifferent, as it sometimes appears to us.

But that power has an unchanging aim: to bring the entire system of creation to perfection. As a result, He acts on anything that is not in that state of perfection, and pushes it toward perfection. That process works equally on all parts of creation, and we feel it as pain and agony.

One can compare this to the pressure that parents put on their child out of the sheer desire for the happiness of the child. But while still growing and developing, the child feels their pressure as pain. As soon as the child attains the proper attributes, the pressure disappears, and the child is happy and grateful.

From His Perspective, everything in reality is already as perfect as can be. Yet, as long as we are not perfect, His Guidance cannot be felt as perfect. The Creator formed our initial corrupted situation deliberately, so as to give us a chance to choose perfection as something desirable and attain it by ourselves. How? Through the method called "the wisdom of Kabbalah."

Nature did not grant us the power to change ourselves. That is why we need not ask Him to change His Guidance, but to change us, so that we can feel His Perfect Guidance. The only form of progress that exists is in turning to the Upper Force for help. When we turn to this Force, we do not break His Law. On the contrary, we perform the one action we can perform.

But the cry must come out of a clear awareness of what it is we're asking for – is it for myself, in order to satisfy my desires in this world, or is it a cry for spiritual ascent? We now pray to Him because we feel bad, out of an egoistic motivation, and wish to feel good.

To answer your question: Do you condemn His Complete Guidance by that cry? Of course you do!

But the question is, what does your heart feel? It doesn't matter if you cry or scream or stay silent. The Creator feels what's in the heart long before we do. When we ask to change us not because we feel bad, but because we suffer from cursing the Creator in our hearts, that is already a request that is not self-oriented, "for me," but is a true prayer for

Him. To such a request the Creator responds at once! After that you can begin to look at a prayer book...

HOW CAN ONE DISCOVER THE CREATOR?

Q: I can't ask for myself, much less know, how to ask for the sake of the Creator! Even my suffering seems to be partial. How can I discover the Creator? By waiting for more suffering?

A: Man will certainly never ask the Creator for correction without feeling the need to do so. We see how people pray to God, asking for various things. But that is not the request for correction we speak of, not the prayer, as we understand it. A prayer is a certain desire for correction of one's properties for reaching the Creator for His Sake.

We arrive at this kind of prayer very slowly, over years. First, we must cultivate it within ourselves. Man originally has the desires of this world, then for the Higher One, for the Creator, directed more and more towards the goal. Man himself constantly changes the definition of the Creator, the goal, and the correction.

Based on the new understanding, man's prayer becomes oriented differently. As soon as man fully understands the goal, it is reached—the prayer bears fruit and man rises to the Creator. Aspire for it.

ASPIRATIONS TO BE LIKE THE CREATOR

Q: What is a prayer?

A: If a person speaks from the heart, then every call to the Creator is new, even though the words are the same. Since the heart has changed, the prayer becomes so new that sometimes the same words seem strange to the supplicant.

We speak not about the Creator but of how we understand His Properties. Hence our notions constantly change. By "our notions," I mean the ideas belonging to those who work on inner corrections and aspire to be like the Creator.

The feelings in our hearts are the prayer. But the most powerful prayer, as Baal HaSulam writes, is the feeling in one's heart during the study, the yearning to understand the material, meaning to match it with one's own properties.

WHAT TO ASK?

Q: A person encounters quite a few obstacles in the course of one's spiritual work. What should one ask for in those situations?

A: Ask for whatever you can ask, anything your mind will let you reach—and the Creator will give you everything, meaning everything that is needed for the attainment of the invocator. Most important, it must be a correct request. One never knows how to act when seeking spiritual truth, but if one wants to grow spiritually, the Creator gives the seeker all that is necessary.

THE HEART IS GRATEFUL

Q: How should I thank the Creator?

A: The heart is grateful in response to the sensation of the fulfillment of the desire to enjoy ~ the essence of creation, its innermost attribute. That response appears naturally in the heart, even before it is conceived by the mind, prior to any conscious analysis of what is happening.

Therefore, there is no place for the question, "How should I thank the Creator?" If there is such a question, then it is alone an expression of gratitude. It is received and accepted by the Creator directly from the bottom of the heart, even before a person processes it mentally.

The question that should be asked is, "How do I come to the state of thanking the Creator?" That state is acquired primarily by experiencing unpleasant situations: lack of faith, lack of confidence, and confusion regarding the Creator. Those feelings are very unpleasant and are typically accompanied by severe descents.

Later on, the sensation of the Creator appears above these as a sensation of wholeness and confidence in the purpose of creation. All the complete and positive feelings are accepted and assessed from within the opposite feelings that preceded them. One who walks shall conquer!

THE AIM OF THE HEART

Q: What is the role of the "aim" in creation?

A: The aim is the one thing that the creature acquires in addition to the desire to delight in the Creator. The Creator made the creature with an inherent desire to delight in Him, in His Light. The creature feels only one thing: the absence or the presence of this pleasure. It doesn't even feel itself, but only the pleasure and its quantity and quality.

The reason is that one can only feel oneself relative to something opposite the self. Therefore, the creature cannot develop from a sensation of pleasure alone. Such a feeling exists in the still, the vegetative and the animate (including the animate human being).

The ability to sense the Creator is what differentiates man from other forms of creation. It would be more correct to say that one who feels the Creator is called "Man." In the language of the Kabbalah, Man is the vessel that feels not only the pleasure, but also the source of the pleasure. It is necessary to develop the will to this extent because the still, the vegetative and the animate are different to one another only in the measure of their will to receive.

The measure of the desire causes changes in its quality. The will to receive (that is, beyond the still) brings life with it. A greater will to enjoy creates animals and brings about movement in order to search for the pleasure, the feeling of the self as an individual entity.

Pleasure is possible only on the border between two opposing sensations. The sensation of oppositeness between creature and Creator creates the aim in man. A creature is a desire to enjoy. Only the aim allows for two situations: the aim "for me," which is the corporeal state; and the aim "for the Creator," which is the spiritual state, because in that man becomes similar to the Creator.

An aim "for the Creator" is the one thing we need to acquire from the Creator, the Light. The aim leads us to the purpose of creation and makes us equal to Him. Because of that, the Kabbalah is the "wisdom of the aim."

THE AIM -- A SPIRITUAL ACT

Q: Does a physical act in this world change anything in the spiritual world?

A: The physical act by itself does not make a difference in the Upper World! It is said that an act with no intent is like a body without a soul, and therefore it is regarded as a "dead" act -- denied of the spiritual intent "for the Creator." But the aim comes gradually, according to one's progress in the study of Kabbalah.

The wisdom of Kabbalah is about intents, about how to turn one's heart to the Upper World. If a person begins studies and cannot add the right intent "for the Creator," that time is called "not for Her name," not for the Creator, meaning that at that time the student's actions are all for self.

But if a person does nothing in order to develop one's aims, then the person is not even working "not for Her name," but is simply performing a lifeless act. However, the person should not stop doing it, because at some point the aim "not for Her name" will come, and "for Her name" will follow. Physical acts are always justified, but you have to aspire not to be limited by them.

THE WORK OF THE HEART

Q: Is every blessing uttered a vessel that is built and rises upward and takes in a certain amount of Light? Does this also happen with a prayer from the bottom of the heart?

A: A person cannot feel one's heart or one's true situation. It is originally concealed from us, and revealed only gradually, according to our ability to correct our original desires. It is very easy to open a prayer book and read from it, but it is very difficult to attain the situation whereby the feelings in one's heart will match the written word; when the heart will recognize and live by the words as the veritable truth.

When we study Kabbalah, we extend illumination from the Upper Light. As a result, we begin to feel worse and our spirits drop. But we must understand that this is a state of correction; otherwise we would not have been shown from Above that we are evil. We still don't feel ourselves as evil, and we are not in a state of the "recognition of evil" within us.

That is why we still think that we are blessing the Creator with a hundred blessings when we pronounce the prayer. Note that it is perfectly alright for now, because otherwise we would stop praying altogether.

But if we begin to study Kabbalah, we will see our true situation, which is characterized by the words "prayer is the work of the heart," meaning that prayer involves working with the desires of the heart and correcting them. At that time we will begin to understand the true meaning of the words we are saying, and we will know what we have to do.

It will be clear that prayer is the work on the screen over our nature. Only the corrected heart, which feels its two extreme situations--the original condition when it was distanced from the Creator, and its present one, when it is filled with the Creator --only such a heart can feel the blessing of the Creator and bless Him.

Q: If prayer is an inner feeling, what are words for?

A: Your sensation during the study--about yourself and the Creator-- is your most honest prayer! That is what the Rav of Kotzk wrote in the book, *Yosher Divrey Emet* (Honesty and Words of Truth). That is why you do not need the proper prayer texts. The most correct thing is how you feel about the Creator.

The texts are needed in order to examine how far off we are from the complete correction. Reading in the prayer book is a study about the link between man and the Creator, the giver of the Torah. A prayer is the work of the heart! You will discern how far the words are from the prayers according to your progress.

Your understanding of the interpretation of the terms of Kabbalah will deepen according to the extent of the new feelings that will arise within you. (For example, you will see that "Pharaoh" is the uncorrected characteristics of man; that "exile" is when one is distanced from the spiritual world; that "freedom" is the liberation from the authority of your own nature, and so on).

You will be able to see that all the prayers in the prayer book and Psalms were written by people who went through those situations, meaning by Kabbalists in high spiritual degrees. That is why we, too, on our own spiritual level can use those prayers as a handy expression of our thoughts and desires.

THE WORK OF THE MIND

Q: What is the reaction of the mind to prayer?

A: A prayer is the work of the heart, but the mind does not always agree with that sensation. For example: a person has to pass a very important and difficult test, and it terrifies him. His whole being may cry, "I don't want that test!" But the mind helps him understand how important it is to pass the test. Therefore, he turns to the Creator with a conscious request to take the test and pass it.

Q: Can we change our feelings with our mind?

A: The mind can help us decide whether or not to make the effort. We can influence it, convince it to obey us. Ultimately, we will make the effort and from Above we will be given new desires and emotions.

Feelings are what I experience in my will. The mind complements, corrects, evaluates and assesses the feelings, and that is why it can change

317

one's attitude toward them. Therefore, all the things that affect the mind ~ friends, group and teacher ~ are what determine one's future. Study the articles of Rav Baruch Ashlag about the group.

Kabbalah teaches how to change the way we relate to our feelings so that "true" and "false" will have the power over us, instead of "bitter" and "sweet."

PLEADING FOR CORRECTION

Q: What inner work is done through prayer?

A: A prayer is the request of the lower one for correction, and ascent of the desire to be corrected from the lower to the Upper *Partzuf* (raising MAN). If the lower one knows what to ask for, knows exactly what it wants, what it wants to be (meaning that inside there is already a sufficiently tormented desire, and only that desire), at that point the Upper One responds and the lower one rises.

This process involves all the worlds, *Partzufim* and *Sefirot* from our world (the situation we are in right now) through the world of *Ein Sof* (infinity; the situation you cannot feel), although you are just as much in it as in our world. This is the total completeness, attainment and satisfaction.

A CONTRADICTORY REQUEST

Q: On the one hand, we want to draw away from our own natures and into ourselves. On the other hand, we ask the Creator to bring us near to Him ~ a move intended to serve our immense desire to enjoy. Is that not hypocrisy?

A: The answer to a plea of the Creator is the answer of man to himself. Others cannot see inside him, and that is why Kabbalah is called "The Wisdom of the Hidden."

The test and the proof that one has been answered by the Creator, has equalized with Him and entered the spiritual world, is only in the actual sensation of the Creator, of the Light, of equality and unity. That sensation is always intimate and personal, and it is impossible to convey it to a person who does not feel it. That is why the saying goes, "Taste and see that the Lord is good."

As long as one has not acquired a screen and has not felt the inner Light of the *Partzuf*, called *Taamim* (flavors), one thinks that one is not drawing away from one's nature, but rather falls deeper in to it.

Because the Light of the Creator influences one to a greater extent, one regards the remaining attributes (that are yet unchanged) as worse. Thus, one thinks that it is not the Light that is stronger, but that he himself is changing for the worse. But while every step of the way seems to indicate one's situation is worsening, he who walks the road will see its end.

MULTIPLE REQUESTS

Q: What request does the Creator answer when He brings one into the spiritual world: a request for Light, or a request to resemble Him?

A: You have to choose within you all the possible requests, and only after that will you understand which request is the one that comes from you, which request is regarded as such by the Creator, and which might evolve to become mutual to the both of you. The understanding of the prayer is the search and analysis of the meaning of the universe.

After all, the universe consists of a single thought, a single aim and a single request. There is nothing more that I can tell you about it, it is the language of the feelings. You have to study that language by yourself.

PREPARING THE HEART

Q: If I spot a negative quality in me, and I suffer from the fact that it is in me, do I have to ask with all my might of the Creator to help me correct it, or is it better to try to ignore that characteristic

because "one is where one's thoughts are," and think only of the greatness of the Creator, about how everything comes from Him, including that characteristic, and try to see His Guidance in everything?

A: "He created me this way, so why should I correct myself?" The Creator created man opposite to Him in order for man to yearn to be like Him, precisely from that opposite situation. That is the purpose of all requests. Therefore, we should praise the Creator, knowing in our hearts that the attribute of the Creator is the most exalted and perfect.

But if all we do is cry for our misfortune without forming any clear decision that we must be like the Creator at least in something, then our pleas are only for ourselves, regardless of the purpose of creation.

However, man cannot determine what his requests of the Creator will be, or praise the Creator independently, because such requests are directly extended from within, from the heart, even before one knows their meaning. Therefore, praying means preparing oneself to justify any feeling, because only through such a preparation will the reaction that follows be determined.

Man's effort is required so that the right attitude to the attributes and characteristics of the Creator will consciously and purposely formulate in him, so that he will want to cleave to the Creator. Man is not the Creator, and cannot change anything within him. All he can do is prepare self to want to change. That is the prayer.

PRAYER - ASCENT TO THE UPPER WORLD

Q: Is there anything in our world that can affect the Upper World, or raise a person to it?

A: Everything begins in the Upper World and then comes down to ours. Our mechanical movements, as well as everything that happens in nature, have no effect on the Upper World, because our world is merely a consequence of it, meaning it follows the commandments of the Guidance that comes from Above.

Anything that happens here in this world is a consequence of forces, commandments and influences that descend from Above.

The only things that rise from our world to the Upper One are the desires of man that come from the bottom of his heart. Only they evoke responses in the Upper World. That is how they influence it.

As a result, they also influence what comes down to us. The desires of a person that come from the bottom of the heart are called "prayer."

All of man's desires, without exception, are divided according to their aim into desires "for myself" and desires "for the Creator." The Creator determines man's desires and we cannot change them, because the Creator wants us to correct them. When speaking about the correction of desires, the idea is not to change the desire itself, or to suppress it, but to change the preliminary aim from "for me" into the desired aim, "for the Creator."

The Superior Management exists for that sole purpose – to constantly fuel us with desires so we can slowly digest them and come to realize that they need to be corrected. All spiritual acts are actually corrections of the intent of our desires. In order to delight in the Creator, in His Light, we should change our aim from "for me" (in order to receive) to "for the Creator" (in order to bestow).

INTENSITY OF THOUGHT

Q: It is very difficult to constantly maintain thoughts about the Creator. You can go on trying for a hundred years...

A: You may feel as though nothing is happening, or that your situation doesn't change. But in reality, if time passes, you have gone through something, because at any given moment there are changes in you.

When the aim is to overcome some part of your preliminary desire to enjoy for yourself, and correct its use, it can only do you good to be immersed in thoughts about the Creator.

Q: It is written: "Know now before Whom you stand" – but when you remember, it happens without your control. Is there a practical way to remember before Whom I stand?

A: You are reminded of the Creator to the extent that you make inner observations, although they are still not in your consciousness. You can speed up the process only through intensity of thought, by reading the essays of Rav Baruch Ashlag and the writings of Baal HaSulam.

However, I would note here that your questions already testify to your progress.

Q: What is "intensity of thought" and how do I acquire it?

A: Intensity of thought and power of thought are actually determined by the time you are connected in your thoughts with the object of contemplation. You acquire that by practice, by trying to keep your thoughts impregnable despite disturbances. You must go through all of this yourself, as there is none as wise as the experienced. Kabbalah is a practical method that a person must experience oneself.

CHAPTER 9.
RAV, DISCIPLE AND GROUP

A GENUINE RAV

Q: What kind of rav is a genuine teacher?

A: A genuine rav is one who distances the disciple away from him and directs him toward the goal – the Creator. He does not make a "Rebbe" (a parish leader) of himself, but rather guides and leads without making a holy man of himself.

In Kotzk, a small town in Poland, there lived a well-known group of Kabbalists, headed by the famous Kabbalist, Rav Menachem Mendel (the Admor from Kotzk). They realized that their teacher would have to be something very special, a person who would lead them without thinking highly of himself, precisely because he felt the Creator and left everything for Him.

QUESTIONS OF THE DISCIPLE

Q: Are there bad questions, or redundant ones?

A: No. Any desire is a sign of a need that craves a satisfaction. However, we do encounter certain difficulties with the answers. Teachers cannot give an answer whenever there is a discrepancy between the sensations of the asking disciple and the answering rav. Generally speaking, there is no such thing as a response – we must answer our own questions.

Q: If the answer does not exist, is a question the expression of an egoistic desire?

A: A response in Kabbalah is the Light that satisfies the desire. It creates in the vessel a sensation that coincides with the desire, which is called an "answer." That is why an answer can only dress in the sensation that is in the desire. Thus, there can be an answer only if there is a question, a desire, that precedes it.

That is why each person feels the question within as a vessel and the answer as a Light. It is impossible to transmit the answer to another person, but only to help one go through the degrees of creation of the need within, the question, and the answer within. That is why Kabbalah is called "the wisdom of the hidden" – only one who is ready to feel knows what it's about. For that person who is not yet ready, it remains hidden.

THE ROLE OF THE RAV

Q: I feel my own nothingness compared to the exaltedness of the rav. But that is how I should feel toward the Creator; whereas I cannot feel Him at all. What should I do?

A: The rav exists only in order to turn your attention to the Creator. It is natural that you still don't have contact with the Creator and your attention is focused on the rav. But that situation will gradually pass.

Soon you will discover a new and developing egoism in you. Then, you will begin to criticize your rav and find more and more flaws in him. I myself went through a similar process with my rav.

That process is guided from Above so that you can examine whether you are acting out of egoism, or solely for the sake of giving. But when you encounter spiritual sensations, you will need your rav more and more. Only then will you work together, just as a child and an adult do in our world.

In fact, everything we feel in the process of correction is crucial for us, especially toward the end of correction. Any feeling, good or bad, can be accepted in a different way, but we must always understand that any feeling is a necessary result of our way.

We must feel what we feel and remember it (without extending it any longer than necessary to understand it), and then move on.

In the beginning of every act and thought there must be an aim: "There is the purpose of creation and I want to attain it, because that is the contact and the equalization with the Creator. It is the reason I do what I do (sleep, eat, drink, work etc.)." Then the rav will not replace the Creator, but will become your guide.

Q: Does disagreeing with the rav indicate a lack of respect?

A: Absolutely not! You can always express disagreement. However, I cannot tolerate objections that stem from the earthly logic of a student who does not read the texts. Read and object; be mad and find!

THE ATTITUDE OF A DISCIPLE TOWARD HIS RAV

Q: In one of your tapes, I heard that there are times when the student might hate his teacher. How can that be? Right now I feel your kindness and your desire to help. Why should that change?

A: Generally speaking, the attitude of a disciple toward the rav is identical to the disciple's relationship towards the Creator. When the disciple doesn't feel the Creator and His Dominion completely, the challenges (trials, unpleasant feelings, disturbances, conflicts about the way, and continuous disappointments) that come from Above lead one to protest to the rav.

The individual actually thinks that the rav is the source of these ordeals. In fact, one becomes so angry with the rav that one believes the rav's passing or disappearance would end all the bad feelings, the void and the obstacles on the way to the Creator. You will learn the rest yourself as you continue along the way.

Q: You write: "Soon you will begin to discover a growing egoism within you. You will begin to criticize your rav and see more and more shortcomings in him..." If that is the case, how should a student work on the ego in order to get through this phase as quickly as possible?

A: Everything is predetermined for us. Inside us there are all the *Reshimot* (reminiscence), the instructions on our gradual ascent, from our world to the purpose of creation. Those *Reshimot* are like a contracted spiral inside us, which opens progressively. Each moment we feel a certain desire, which is an expression of the surfacing *Reshimo*.

When we enter the right group, the right environment and read the right books, we enhance the influence of the Upper Light on ourselves. That Light illuminates the spiral of *Reshimot*, thus accelerating their appearance in us. We always discover the weakest *Reshimo* from the ones we can realize.

Our freedom of choice is only in our choice of environment. All we can do is accelerate our progress. This is only possible with the influence of an appropriate environment. In other words, we are free to choose between accelerating the process and not accelerating it.

If you listen to people who object to Kabbalah, and is urged away from it, you will still come to the purpose, but much later. Baal HaSulam (Rav Yehuda Ashlag) writes in his essay, "The Freedom," that only by choosing our environment (books, friends and teachers) do we express our freedom to choose our way.

The more correct the choice of the environmental factor is, the greater the acceleration. Indeed, we can make the journey last only a few years instead hundreds of years. This is no exaggeration.

Regarding nullification before the rav: when Baal HaSulam was told that unlike other great teachers, his disciples were not the least bit afraid of him, he answered, "They'd be better off fearing the Creator and not me."

And when he was told that he had only five or six disciples after decades of work, he replied, "The Creator doesn't even have that many."

You cannot direct your thoughts and desires by yourself, as you see fit. Their direction is derived from your inner situation and dictated by the *Reshimo* that is currently being activated, which leaves the sensation and experience from your current situation.

Look at yourself from the side – it is worthwhile to examine yourself and remember how you were a month ago, or five years ago, and begin conversing with your past and present images. It helps to better understand the changes that occur in you. It helps you to relate to yourself as a factor of changing emotions, and not as an individual who thinks and feels independently.

You have to examine yourself from the outside and see what the Creator does with you. Follow His Work – it is the exact meaning of the words – "the Work of God," His Work on you.

FREEDOM OF CHOICE

Q: Does a person who has become a Kabbalist have at least the freedom of choice?

A: There are only two possible situations for us:

1. Surrendering to our nature. We might think that in this case we simply become at peace with ourselves. However, as soon as we begin to feel the Upper World, meaning something spiritual outside us, we will discover that our egoism is not us, but a foreign body that has penetrated us and forces us to serve it. We will find then that we have no freedom of choice in such a state.

2. The other is to obey the nature of the Creator. We might think that this situation implies losing our freedom, but what in fact happens is that the Kabbalist exits his own nature and becomes neutral with respect to the one and only factor that ordinarily controls him completely and without cease. Only then can he take on the attributes of the Creator, and activate his freedom of choice.

Q: Since everything is determined Above, where is the freedom of choice?

A: Man's only freedom is his environment, the society that influences him. You can read about it in "The Freedom" by Rav Yehuda Ashlag. Everyone's situation is determined from beginning to end. The only way to go is forward. We should want to do it ourselves, consciously, but if we don't, nature will force us to want to progress. We cannot attain the final situation if we don't learn how to lead creation.

A RAV AND DISCIPLE IN SPIRITUALITY

Q: What does the disciple mean to the rav, and what does the rav mean to the disciple?

A: We think that a rav and his disciple are simply two people, one of them teaching the other, meaning a teacher and a student. But a rav and a disciple are really two degrees: the disciple is at a certain level of attainment, and the rav is on a higher level. The disciple has a connection and a special relation to that teacher. Thanks to that connection, the disciple can gradually resemble the rav and ultimately become a rav on his own.

A disciple is a person who can learn from a higher degree, or "Rav," and be like him. If, for example, you want to learn how to be a construction worker, you'll turn to a builder to teach you. If man's primary desire is to learn to be like someone else, you can call him a disciple, and the person from whom he studies is called a "rav."

These things can change because during the spiritual maturing of man, while in the midst of studies, there are spiritual ups and downs. At one time, the student considers self a disciple, another time a friend, and sometimes even a rav from whom others should learn.

Being a disciple is harder than being a rav because the disciple is at a lower degree. The disciple must realize who the rav is and what should be learned from him. If the information is already known, the student has already grasped the higher degree and has nothing to learn. If the student understands what the rav has that the student lacks, that is fine, for after some time the student will acquire it, too.

To be a disciple means to see external vessels that are in the possession of the rav, realize that one does not have them, and reach the conclusion that those attributes can be acquired only through cleaving to that higher degree.

The disciple needs to cleave in the full sense of the word: physically – to become a part of the body, to be a supporting organ – and spiritually – to try to think, experience, and aspire to live as the rav does.

If the disciple cleaves like that to the rav, then only through the desires and ideas that they have in common can that person attain the inner attainment of the rav.

Q: If "rav" and "disciple" designate spiritual degrees, how are the *Sefirot* of the disciple linked with those of his teacher?

A: When the vessels of bestowal (*GE* – *Galgalta ve Eynaim*) of the student are ready, the rav brings his vessels of reception (*AHP* – *Awzen, Hotem, Peh*) down to him. We can always use the vessels of *AHP* of the rav because it is impossible to use the vessels of reception of the disciple.

Then the disciple builds ten complete *Sefirot* from his own *GE* and the *AHP* of the rav, and begins to attain the Upper Degree through the *AHP* of the rav, provided that his *GE* correspond to their attributes.

In this process, the disciple nullifies his vessels of reception at first, as though he does not exist. Once the *AHP* of the rav links with that of the disciple, he sees how the *AHP* of the Upper One relates to his *GE*, and becomes a disciple. Thus, to be a disciple is a state that one attains after a certain amount of inclusion.

Q: And what happens once the student has become a disciple?

A: After the disciple has grown accustomed to working with his *GE*, he begins to get used to working with his *AHP*. His *AHP* should resemble that of the rav, meaning that he should give to the rav just as the rav gives to him. Then he will climb to the higher degree through the *AHP* of the rav, and ask of him the strength to raise his *AHP* to that degree, and become as great as he is.

As soon as the disciple rises to the degree of the rav, he sees that the rav is above him. And why did he not see it before? Because he was incapable of estimating the rav as higher than his own *GE*. Only once he has corrected his *AHP* to the higher degree is he capable of seeing the rav and appreciating him, and so the process goes, higher and higher.

You have to believe that the teacher exists, and that his *AHP* is always in your *GE*. As soon as your *GE* are fixed, you will feel how he transcends you and how his *AHP* works like an elevator for his disciples. Everyone is linked to the Upper One independently. You only have to nourish the desire to rise.

RAV AND DISCIPLE - PHYSICALLY AND SPIRITUALLY

Q: When a disciple physically helps his rav and serves him, can he acquire spiritual attributes faster than through his studies? If so, how is that possible, if we learn that physical actions bear no spiritual results?!

A: It is indeed possible because both teacher and student are in the same world. The student is only in this world; he has only the attributes of his will to receive for himself, while the rav is in both, maintaining contact with the will to receive of the disciple through his own body.

When the student is in contact with the rav only on the physical level and gives to him on that level, he begins to make contact with him on the spiritual level as well (provided the student really wants that contact), without even noticing it. He begins to subconsciously receive spiritual ideas from his rav that seemingly flow to him from his teacher.

How is that possible? After all, the disciple doesn't have the vessel for it, he doesn't have sensations of loving others and he doesn't have the aim for the Creator in which to receive those ideas. Regarding this question, see "A Speech for the Completion of the Zohar" by Rav Yehuda Ashlag.

By the way, I tried that principle on myself. I received a lot of ideas about spirituality like a child receives the picture of our world, when he doesn't understand the essence of what is going on, the root of the phenomena, and his insights are superficial and external. That situation is possible, and that is how man attains the Upper World.

Generally speaking, it is possible to understand the spiritual world only to the extent we attain it and acquire knowledge about it, and by the strength of our screen. But that relates to ordinary spiritual attainment. To the extent that we have an opportunity to come close to our rav through service and help, we also attain some of the spiritual conceptions of the rav.

In fact, I do not give my students that chance, because the group is large and I should not make any single person more prominent than the others. I do not want to raise just one disciple, but many. Besides, there are other means and ways to acquire the rav's spiritual conceptions. Some of them were used by Rabbi Shimon Bar-Yochai, such as collective meals, sports activities, trips, weddings, and so on.

Q: When the rav attains the end of correction, will the disciple have to remain on earth in order to live and be corrected?

A: If the disciple is linked to his teacher, it does not matter what their situation is. It does not matter if one of them is still dressed in the dresses of this world, or if he has already taken them off, because the inner link, the spiritual one, is already there.

Therefore, do not despair because there are no spaces in the spiritual realm, everything is near, if you are indeed "near" spirituality. Distance is determined by the compatibility between attributes, desires and aspirations – by the compatibility of the screen. That is what you must acquire, as the summit still lies ahead of you.

Q: When I receive the soul that leads me past the barrier, does that mean I don't need my teacher anymore?

A: On the contrary, only after the entrance to the Upper World will you, as a disciple, begin to really understand who your rav is, and begin to make the most of your connection with him. It is then that you will realize how much you need your rav.

Ravs cooperate with us in our spiritual work and bond with us, on the level called "mouth to mouth," but we'll talk some more about it once you cross the barrier.

WORKING WITH A RAV

Q: There is a notion of "work with a rav." How can a group reach a state in which its relations with the rav would turn into "work" and what does this notion actually mean?

A: Baal HaSulam wrote about this type of work in his article, "A Speech for the Completion of the Zohar." He writes there about a disciple and a rav, but a group and a rav relates to a similar situation. If it is a real group, then it is like one student. At first, the "mouth to ear" condition for relations and learning is applied, and afterwards, if the group merits it, "mouth to mouth" is also applied.

SURPASSING THE TEACHER

Q: While reading the materials on the site, I stumbled across something that aroused my interest. It concerns whether a disciple can surpass one's teacher in one's spiritual quest, and the answer was "yes." But how can it be? A teacher is always at a higher level, and what the disciple "imagines" comes from one's egoism, like in a growing child who feels superior in achievement to its parents. But isn't this just self-deception?

A: A disciple can surpass one's teacher. Baal HaSulam discovered that he had "grown out" of his teacher's (The Rabbi from Porsov) spiritual level. Hence he left for the land of Israel.

If teacher and disciple work with full cooperation, they can be either as teacher and disciple, or as two friends. They can switch places. The difference is rather insignificant.

Take for example, the rav that Baal HaSulam began to study Kabbalah with – The Rabbi from Porsov (a small town near Warsaw). My rav told me that once, when Baal HaSulam came to bid farewell to his teacher, before he came to Israel, he clearly saw that he had risen higher than the degree of his teacher in his attainment. He spoke about this with his eldest son, who was fifteen at the time.

Thus, it doesn't matter if you are a teacher or a student. But teachers, just like at school, guide the students, show them how to enter the spiritual world and give them the skills necessary for the spiritual work. A brilliant student can become greater than one's teacher, yet a teacher remains a teacher.

Between a student and a teacher there remains a spiritual contact, through common attributes and vessels. Thus, in the spiritual world, the two individuals are not considered as two separate bodies, but one collective vessel.

That is why, if I give something to a student of mine who rises higher than I, based on all I have offered, that student retains what I gave, and yet that something bonds the student with me as well.

There is common work that takes place even if my student performs it and not I. At the end of correction, all our common efforts will unite into one.

SEARCHING THE WAY TO PEOPLE

Q: Why do you spend so much time on people of my level, which is ZERO? Doesn't it interfere with your spiritual mission? Why, then, didn't all Kabbalists reveal themselves to the masses?

A: First of all, Kabbalists have not revealed themselves publicly mainly because the masses prevented them from doing so, as in the case of Baal HaSulam with his Kabbalistic newspaper (the texts from the book *Matan Torah*). At that time, the majority of people didn't wish to know the reason for their existence.

Secondly, the environment in which Kabbalists lived often threatened them (for example, Ramchal in the 16th century).

Finally, I spend a lot of time publicizing Kabbalah because my great teacher – the last Kabbalist who received this spiritual enlightenment from Above– commanded me to do so. Today, the egoism of the masses has developed and the events of life make one see the futility of such life.

We in our generation are pioneers in the quest for the Higher World from down up, the first ones for whom Kabbalah was given.

Q: Excuse me for offering advice in a field I know nothing about. However, I suggest that if you attract a dozen new students annually, as well as a few thousand supporters worldwide, Wouldn't it be better to focus all efforts and time on the disciples of only the highest quality? If they can change the state of the universe and attract the Light, then perhaps after a while everyone will be rewarded.

A: In the past, Kabbalists used to sit quietly and cultivate their connection with the Creator, but, upon Baal HaSulam's instruction and according to the demands of our time, we will plunge into a third world war unless we succeed in spreading these ideas.

All we think of is how to avoid our petty troubles, but a problem of colossal proportions is approaching. Baal HaSulam writes about this as a very real possibility. I write this because he did so.

Besides, unlike previous generations, when Kabbalists took the correction of the world upon themselves, today we all must attain the Higher World and establish schools for that purpose.

It's not easy, since we use the method designed for those few whose desire for the spiritual has awakened, and not for the unaware masses. As a result, we search for the way to reach people. We try to spread something quite opposite to ideas of this world, though these are most valuable. I seek your advice. But we have to keep doing what we are doing.

A RAV AND A GROUP

Q: What is the connection between the rav and his group of disciples?

A: A group is a spiritual term that is always linked to a rav. We have all decided that we want, to a certain degree, to cleave to the Creator. That small desire of each and every one of us unites to form a collective desire, and that is called a "group." It doesn't matter if one of us is imbued with the idea this very minute, because we constantly change within. If that decision was taken once, it exists forever, because nothing is lost in the spiritual world. We may rise or fall with respect to our decision, but the decision itself remains intact.

A group is like a partnership. You can fall and have nothing left of the previous spiritual situation, but the group will continue to exist, and so will your share in it, regardless of your present state.

If one makes room for the other, then the group exists in a spiritual realm. You've invested your aspirations, your strength and your goal in the group, but how will you be able to receive help from the group when you need it?

You will receive help only if you are able to nullify your ego and submit to the opinion of the group in everything: the goal, the idea, the way to attain the idea, in all the values and the order of importance. Only then will you make your mark on the group and become like it, meaning as you have created it.

Rav Yehuda Ashlag writes about it in his article, "A Speech for the Completion of the Zohar." He says, "Indeed the sufficient attainment of His Exaltedness that is enough to turn the bestowal to reception, as was mentioned above regarding the important personality, is not at all difficult, for everyone knows the greatness of the Creator who creates every thing and ends every thing without beginning or an end, whose sublimity is endless.

But the difficulty is in the fact that the value of the sublimity depends not on the individual, but on the environment. For example: even if we are filled with good qualities, if our environment does not regard us as such, we will always remain low-spirited and will not be able to take pride in our virtues, although we are well aware of their validity.

And to the contrary, if we are without any good qualities and were appreciated by those around us as having a great many fine qualities, we would be filled with pride, for the importance and the glorification is given entirely to the hands of the environment.

And when we see that our environment slights His Work and does not appreciate His Greatness, as it should, we cannot overpower the environment. Consequently, we, too, become unable to attain His Greatness, and we slight His worship as they do.

And since we have no basis for the attainment of His Greatness, it is obvious that we will not be able to work in order to bring contentment to our Maker, rather than for ourselves. That is because we haven't the fuel for the effort, and for "You labored yet did not find, do not believe."

Thus, we have no choice but to either work for ourselves, or not at all, for bringing contentment to our Maker will not serve as fuel for us under these conditions.

Now you can understand the words, "In the multitude of people is the king's glory," for the value of the glory comes from the environment under two conditions:

1. Appreciation from the environment.

2. The size of the environment. Hence, "In the multitude of people is the king's glory."

And because of the great difficulty in this matter, our sages advised us to "Make for yourself a rav and buy for yourself a friend." This means that we should choose for ourselves an important and famous person and make him our rav, from which we can come to the practice of Torah and *Mitzvot* in order to bring contentment to our Maker. For here, there are two easements to our rav:

1. Since we think our rav is an important personality, we can bring him contentment, based on his greatness. That is because the bestowal has not been turned into reception, which is a natural fuel that can pro-

duce further acts of bestowal every time. And after we grow accustomed to giving to our rav, we can transfer this bestowal to the practice of Torah and *Mitzvot* for Her name, meaning toward the Creator, for the habit will have become second nature to us.

2. The equivalence of form with the Creator does not do us any good if it is not forever, meaning until "He who knows all mysteries will testify that he shall not turn back to folly." But since our rav is in this world and within the boundaries of time, the equivalence of form helps even if it is only temporary and afterwards we return to folly. Thus, every time we equalize our form with our rav, we temporarily cleave to him. Thus, we attain his knowledge and thoughts, depending on his attainment, as we have shown in the parable about the organ that was severed from the body and then put back on.

Hence, the disciple can use the rav's attainment of the greatness of the Creator, which turns bestowal into reception and sufficient fuel for great devotion. Then the disciple, too, would be able to practice Torah and *Mitzvot* for Her name with his heart and soul, which is the remedy for the attainment of eternal adhesion with the Creator.

Now you can understand what our sages said: "The practice of Torah is preferred to the study of Torah." As it is said, "Elisha the son of Shaphat is here, who poured water on the hands of Elijah." It does not say "learned," but "poured." That seems perplexing, for how can such simple acts be greater than the study of the wisdom and the knowledge?

However, the above makes it clear that serving the rav in the flesh with great devotion to bring him contentment brings us adhesion with our rav, meaning equivalence of form. And thus we receive the knowledge and thoughts of our teacher, "mouth to mouth," which is the adhesion of one spirit with another.

In this way, we attain our greatness sufficiently to turn bestowal to reception, and become a sufficient fuel for complete devotion, until we attain adhesion with the Creator.

Because studying Torah from our rav must be for ourselves, it does not induce adhesion and is considered "mouth to ear." And the service of the rav induces in the disciple the thoughts of the rav, and the study is only the words of the rav. The service is better than the study, as the thought of the rav is greater than his words, and "mouth to mouth" excels over "mouth to ear."

But all this is true if the service is in order to bring contentment to the rav. If, however, the service is for self, such a service cannot bring us to adhesion with our rav, and then studying with our rav is more important than serving him.

But just as we have said about the attainment of His Greatness (that the environment that does not regard Him highly weakens us and prevents us from attaining His Greatness), this is certainly also true regarding our teacher: The environment that does not regard the rav highly prevents the disciple from attaining the greatness of one's rav, as on should.

Hence our sages said, "Make for yourself a rav and buy for yourself a friend." This means that we should make for ourselves a new environment that would help us attain the greatness of our rav, through the love of friends who value our rav. That is because the words of the friends who praise the rav give each of them the sensation of his greatness. Thus, giving to the rav becomes reception and a fuel that is sufficient to bring us to study Torah and Mitzvot for Her name.

And it is said about that, that the Torah is obtained in 48 virtues, and in the service and precision of our friends. For besides serving the rav, we also need the precision of our friends, meaning their influence to work on us to attain the greatness of our rav, as the attainment of the greatness depends solely on the environment, and a single person cannot in any way have any bearing on it, as we explained above.

Thus, there are two conditions for the attainment of the greatness:

1. That we always listen to and accept the appreciation of the environment as they praise the Creator.

2. That the environment will consist of many people, as it is written: "In the multitude of people is the king's glory."

In order for the first condition to be accepted, each disciple must feel that he is the least powerful among all the friends. Then, the disciple will be able to be influenced by everyone's appreciation of the greatness, for the great cannot receive from the small, much less be impressed with his words. Only the small is impressed with the appreciation of the great.

In order for the second condition to be accepted, every disciple must appraise the virtue of every friend and appreciate that person as though he were the greatest in the generation. Then the environment will have the impact that a great environment should, for the quality is more important than the quantity.

INNER CONNECTION - ONLY ABOVE THE BARRIER

Q: We speak a lot about the work in groups, about connections between the group members, and about the means for cohesion. Should there be some inner bond among the group members and, if possible, how can it be achieved before crossing the barrier? Can one rely on a teacher's help to attain such an inner bond?

A: Unity is achieved only by attaining necessary properties; nothing can ever be gained forcefully or artificially in the inner (spiritual) world. Hence, as we enter the Higher World and attain the Creator's properties, we should unite with our friends (and with our teacher).

Meanwhile, we should perform everything artificially, knowing that none of our "good" relationships are genuine and exist merely for the sake of reaching their true form upon entering the Higher World.

DISTURBANCES

Q: How should I relate to various disturbances?

A: We normally only discuss a person when *Reshimot* (reminiscence) of the Upper World begin to surface in that individual. One begins to feel the point in the heart – the desire for something that is not yet understood, something not from this world, but above it. A yearning arises for the purpose of creation, the discovery of the Creator during the course of one's life in this world.

We want all the worlds, including the one that is concealed from us ~ the Upper World ~ to appear before us. Then we will be able to see the eternal spiritual degree and unite with it, when there is no difference between good and evil, and life and death. Everything will be united in a state of endless wholeness.

That is the purpose all of mankind should reach, as in the verse: "He is One, and His name One."

He~meaning the Creator; His name~meaning creation. The creature gives names according to its feelings about the Creator, if a creature has been fully corrected, it unites with the Creator. That unification is the goal, the final state of the universe. We can reach that goal today.

Any phenomenon that collides with our intention to reach the goal is regarded as a disturbance, an obstacle. Because we believe there is no force other than the Creator, and we advance to the goal according to His Plan, we have to be creative about the disturbances that come to us from that Source, the Creator, which keeps pushing toward the goal.

We must understand that any disturbance is, in fact, not an obstacle on our way to the goal, but we feel it as such, because our attributes are as yet not like the Creator's. In other words, the sensation of an obstacle indicates inner disturbances and lack of correction. The Creator relates to the entire creation with benevolence, without any preconditions. If we cannot feel the providence of the Creator as good, and feel resistant, it is because we have an inner barrier, not an external disturbance.

Thus, there are no obstacles apart from our own corrupted attributes. Outside our souls, there is only the Creator, drawing us toward Him, to the most perfect situation. That is why we need to relate to any disturbance that we feel as a sign from Above, indicating which attribute is next in line to be corrected. And if we can correct it, it will be yet another step toward the goal.

In fact, our freedom of will is expressed in our ability to see in that situation a possibility to face the situation, to turn to the Creator, to ask for help and learn what needs to be corrected and how.

The feeling of disturbances is called "the concealment of the Creator." It is natural that the minute we feel the disturbance, we cannot assess the situation correctly. All we see is that there is a barrier, but we cannot see the source, the reason for the appearance of the barrier. We must relate to those disturbances with the existence of the Creator in mind, understand that it is the Creator who sends us these disturbances, in order to help and show us precisely where we have to concentrate our efforts in order to discover Him.

By sending us the obstacle, the Creator indicates precisely what we have to focus on in our spiritual efforts in order to find Him. In fact, it is intended to help us, because only after a spiritual effort to confront the disturbance can we discover the Creator.

In order to successfully confront a disturbance (we will leave that word, although we see that it is, in fact, help), we must be spiritually prepared. If we are aware that all the disturbances are intended to correct our spiritual state and bring us yet another step closer to the Creator, and if we are basically positive about those disturbances, then when we stumble upon them, we will know how to handle them.

Let's take an example from a frequent situation in a group: I (a student) learn that someone said something bad about me. I am naturally frustrated; I begin to justify and defend myself; and I see that person as an enemy. I even think of taking revenge on him. Thus, instead of relating to that disturbance in a positive manner and working with it, I want to eliminate it, along with the person, who, I think, caused it.

It doesn't matter whether what he said was true or false. I have to learn to understand not the *meaning* of things, but rather the *manner* in which I must relate to what has been sent to me by the Creator, via a third party. I must do this in order to see and correct my flaw, and, in the process, discover the Creator through my spiritual work.

In fact, the Creator made me face that disturbance to help me advance spiritually. Such opportunities can come in the least pleasant form, as a feeling of guilt, or by learning something good that dazzles my mind. In any case, it is not about the phenomenon itself, but about its origin and the One who sent it ~the Creator. Afterwards, when I aim for the Creator, I can begin to wonder why He sent it to me this way and not another?

If I were willing to take anything that comes to me as something that a-priori comes from the Creator, I would take any criticism with love and understanding, because I would know where it comes from, and that the Creator is bringing me closer to Him.

Every time I hear something bad, I am in a debate. Does this news come from the Creator, or is it just that person who brought it to me. I gradually force myself to relate to that spiritual disturbance as something that I can use in order to come closer to the Creator, and feel Him even more.

There is no better feeling than when I cross the barrier and discover the sensation of complete attainment, unification with the Creator. Confronting a disturbance means working on it, accepting it as a message from the Creator to correct the attribute.

The one correct solution, regardless of how I am informed, whether more pleasantly or less, or more justly or less, is to accept it without argument, as something given, as the Will of the Creator. That is why I relate to it as a call to come to the Creator. These are the Creator's instructions to me, as He marks the points that delay my approach to Him.

GROUP WORK

Q: How can I accept the disturbances in the group?

A: Accepting another's opinion means to live in it, to accept his ideas above your own, and agree that everything that happens is for your own good because a friend recommends it.

Here is a question for you: if a friend criticizes you, should he take into account the possible ramifications, your possible reaction to his criticism? Why can't you relate to his criticism in the same way that he criticizes you? Why can't you counter-accuse him? Why do you need to relate to the opinion of a friend as a "voice from Heaven?" Doesn't he stop being your friend then, and become a representative of the Creator?

We are dealing here with the wisdom of the Kabbalah, the only system of attaining the Creator, of entering the spiritual world. We have become a group in order to shorten the way as much as possible. We must treat everything that happens in the group as signs, instructions from the Creator. We have no right to think that what happens between us is merely a number of routine, everyday problems.

It is not that we calculate whether it is more profitable for us to deal with our petty strife or advance together toward the sublime goal. In fact, if the aim and the reason for the formation of the group is the attainment and revelation of the Creator, then everything we get today should be treated as a message that the Creator sends us in order to approach Him.

What this implies is that we have friends who go along with us on our spiritual path, and if they mistreat us, we should not focus on that. Rather, we should try to build a warm and friendly relationship, and correct ourselves according to the problems that arise. By such action, we go "above our own reason" and thus attain the goal.

Based on the purpose of the group, all the disturbances and the friction that arise in the group are in fact thrusts forward, not disturbances. They are a call from the Creator to the group to spiritually advance toward Him. They are His signs as to what the group should focus its effort on.

It is precisely within a group that problems are vital. Only through a correct spiritual response of all the members of the group, with help and mutual understanding, can the group advance spiritually that much faster than would a single individual.

As the group advances, the disappointments and the strife will increase, but they should be handled with the slogan, "the goal above all." We know that everything comes to us from the Creator, and we must constantly increase our spiritual efforts in order to strengthen our faith in this knowledge. We must believe that He sends us pain precisely in the right amounts for each member of the group, and that the group as a whole, can handle what it receives.

Moreover, it is inadvisable to rejoice at the absence of problems. It may well be a sign that the group is not making spiritual progress, and will not be able to handle problems. We should be glad or disappointed not at the presence or the absence of problems, but at our progress toward the goal.

Generally speaking, we should be glad when we are faced with problems, because they testify to yet more of our attributes that need correction. Before we enter the Upper World and the sensation of the Creator, these problems navigate us while the Creator is concealed from us.

He leads us in the spiritual darkness through the problems that He sends, and uses them to indicate precisely where we should concentrate our efforts in our spiritual journeys. If we succeed in correcting these attributes, we will be able to feel the Creator.

Each of us is faced with problems in our daily lives. The difference is in how we relate to those problems. Are we aware that the Creator is the Source, or do we blame our surroundings? Do we treat our problems as ordinary people do, or as something from which we want to benefit, for the purpose of nearing Him, as Kabbalists do?

The minute we are faced with a dispute, we must not abandon the post and immediately accept our friends' position. Rather, we must review and analyze all the circumstances. And most important, we have to stay focused and aware that we are performing spiritual work, and not descend to the level of "keeping score" with friends.

CHAPTER 10.
THE MESSIAH AND THE END OF DAYS

THE LIGHT OF THE MESSIAH

Q: Do you believe that the Messiah will come?

A: The Messiah is a Light that draws one to the center, to the Creator, and to the source that he must return to. Any person has his own private Messiah, meaning a personal Light of correction. But there is also a collective Light of correction, which will bring the whole of mankind to another level of existence, a sublime one.

Nothing external will change in our world when this Light comes. Everything will be the same, but there will be an internal soaring, the whole of mankind will rise and people will feel that they are in a collective, genuine reality. They will no longer feel such things as life and death and time.

The corporeal body will become meaningless, and we will have no feeling of connection with it. People will relate themselves to the soul. It is, in fact, what happens to Kabbalists. For one who feels the Upper Reality, this lower, inferior world, becomes meaningless.

The Messiah is a Light from the Creator that will raise the whole of mankind to spirituality. It is not a person, although there will be people who will guide humanity to spirituality and teach it the spiritual system, but they will only be representatives of the Messiah.

Q: What is the coming of the Messiah and when will it happen?

A: The Messiah is a Light from Above that affects us when we study Kabbalah and corrects us. That collective force is called "Messiah." It is not a single person, but a spiritual force that pulls us from this world to the spiritual world. It allows one to begin to feel this world and the Upper One simultaneously

346

Q: Is the Messiah a person or a force?

A: People are at a degree where they cannot perceive the Messiah as Light, but only as a flesh-and-blood leader. But when Kabbalists speak of the Messiah, they refer to a superior Force of spiritual correction, a Light that gives one a chance to improve one's attributes.

The Messiah will be the pulling, liberating Force from the government of the desires to enjoy for ourselves. When that Light penetrates us, meaning the "receiving nature," it will correct us and turn us from receivers to givers – like the Creator.

However, all the spiritual forces are revealed in corporeal raiment. For example: Rabbi Shimon Bar-Yochai, the Ari and Rav Yehuda Ashlag--all three represent one exalted soul that radiates a great Light of correction. However, it appears in our world as a person, a Kabbalist, a teacher and a writer of books.

Such a thing happens not only with regard to a super-Kabbalist, but also with regard to a redeeming Messiah. He must be a person, a leader, who under the guidance of the Creator and through the Force of the Creator, will be able to direct the entire world to the purpose of creation.

Humanity will have no other way out of the evil and the torment that each person will feel, other than recognizing him as the leader, and following the path that he will show us.

KABBALAH AND THE MESSIAH

Q: How is the circulation of Kabbalah related to the coming of the Messiah?

A: Indeed, the success in the circulation of Kabbalah is evident all over the world. In the Torah it says that in the End of Days, all the peoples will want spirituality: "For they shall all know Me, from the least of them unto the greatest of them" (Jeremiah 31, 33).

The growing interest in spirituality at this time, in addition to its growing commercialism,, testifies to the coming of the days of the Messiah. Soon there will come a day when a spiritual Force will come down to the world and open the eyes of mankind and enable it to see the complete reality.

Q: What should we expect now with the coming of the Messiah, and how should we understand it from the point of view of the Kabbalah?

A: A person acts only according to one's feelings, to what stems from one's inner needs. It cannot be any other way. New *Reshimot*, new data and new instructions that we must implement surface in us each minute. This is how we advance toward our corrected situation, the eternal and optimal situation.

These instructions are inside each and every one of us, just as the knowledge of the mechanisms of the body is imprinted in our genes. All our future situations are imprinted in us and must be implanted one by one, by a predefined order.

This means that our path has already been set. It is so because we were already in a perfect state, one that the Creator had created in the beginning. But afterwards, we drifted from that state to its opposite, to a state of complete imperfection. Our task now is to go back the same path from which we drifted from Above, from the perfect to the imperfect – to rise by ourselves to the preliminary state from which we descended.

Part of that road is taken by man unconsciously, as we do today. That part of it is called "This World," or "Our World." The part of the road that is taken consciously is the part that lies past the barrier, which is the border between this world and the Upper World, or the "Spiritual World."

Man can only imagine what he can sense, and nothing more. He will never be able to feel the higher degree, the degree above his present degree. That is why he can aspire to the final goal of creation to begin with. In every situation, he pictures the final goal by what he can now see as the best situation from his current state.

Everyone knows that different peoples and religions picture the future world in a different way. Much like that, the Messiah is seen as the force that will deliver us from our present state and help us transcend to the best possible situation. We can all picture that state according to our own level of attainment. For each person, the "next world" and the "Messiah" are different things, and they vary from one degree to the next. But they become fully understood only at the final degree of the spiritual ladder.

The method of the Kabbalah speeds up the pace of the surfacing of the situations concealed in us and significantly shortens the whole process. It is much like what happens in a chemical reaction. It is possible to contract the process by a million times. You can save millions of life cycles in just one lifetime and profit millions of times more than everybody else.

This is not only an improvement in quantity, but also in quality. Your toothaches, for example, will not last millions of moments, but only one moment. That is why it is not a good idea to slight Kabbalah studies.

THE MESSIAH IN THE ZOHAR AND IN THE TALMUD

Q: It is said in the Zohar that before the coming of the Messiah, everyone will learn Kabbalah. On the other hand, the Talmud says that "the face of the generation will be as the face of the dog," meaning that everyone will be out for himself. How is it possible to reconcile those two arguments? In order for the Messiah to come, must everyone study Kabbalah?

A: Baal HaSulam writes in his introduction to the Tree of Life that at the end of time, everyone will abandon Kabbalah because they will no longer be able to trade with it as in the market, because there will be no buyers. People will abandon it because they will realize that it cannot give them anything: it cannot fill them with pleasure, cannot grant them respect in the eyes of others, or control over them. Therefore, there will be no limitations before a person who will want to come and study the wisdom of Kabbalah.

The efforts of those who will study it will induce the coming of the Messiah. Here is a quote from the words of Baal HaSulam: "...And behind these words and that truth, we seem to find a profound contradiction from end to end, in the words of our sages, that the Zohar says that 'at the time of the Messiah that wisdom is destined to be revealed even to the young.' And by the above we find that at the time of the Messiah, that whole generation will be at the highest degree until no watch will be needed, and the fountains of truth shall open to water the entire nation. But in *Masechet Suta* it says that at the time of the Messiah, *Hutzpa* (impudence) will soar and authors' wisdom shall go astray and the righteous will be sick. Thus it is explained that there is none so evil as this generation. So how do we reconcile between those two, for certainly they are both the words of the living God?

Hence, we must establish schools and compose books, to hurry the circulation of the wisdom in the nation. And that was not the case before, for fear lest unworthy disciples would mingle with the worthy, as we've explained above at length. That became the primary reason for our many sins to this day, and consequently for the prolonging of the exile.

Our sages said: 'Messiah Son of David doth not come, but in time when the generation is all worthy,' meaning that every one will retire from pursuit of glory and lust, at which time it will be possible to establish schools and prepare them for the coming of the Messiah Son of David. 'Or in time when the generation is all unworthy,' meaning at such a generation when the 'face of the generation is as the face of a dog,' and 'the righteous shall be considered loathsome,' and 'authors' wisdom will go astray' in them.

At such a time it will be possible to remove the careful guard and anyone who will remain in the house of Jacob with his heart pounding to attain the goal and the purpose, 'Holy' be his name, and he shall step forth and learn. For there will no longer be fear lest he might not stand firm and trade the wisdom in the market, for there is no one in the mob who will wish to buy it, and the wisdom will be loathsome in their eyes, so that no glory or desire can be bought in return for it.

Hence, he who wishes to enter may come and enter. And many will roam and the knowledge will increase among the worthy. And by that we will soon be blessed with the coming of the Messiah and the redemption of our souls soon in our days, amen."

WHAT IS THE SENSATION OF TIME?

Q: The end of the world did not come in the year 2000, and you deny any reference to "human time." What, then, is the sensation of time and where does it come from?

A: There is a spiritual time, which is a sequence of situations (you can read about it in the first part of The Study of the Ten Sefirot – Inner Reflection). The sensation of time in our world is a bit like this: we feel that "time stands still," or that the hours rush by and "time flies." But that, too, is still relative, as we now know.

Indeed, time and space do not exist. There is, however, a sensation of "time": it is how we feel the Light in our desires to delight ourselves. That is the picture that the Light creates as it passes by the inner layers of our desire for pleasure.

When we change the "method" of sensing our environment from reception to bestowal, we learn to evaluate time and space entirely differently, and begin to realize that they are only a result of the effect of our evil inclination, of the "shells," or forces opposite to spirituality. We begin to see that the sensation of time and space is only a consequence of our handicaps.

When we begin to see the structure of the Upper Forces and their composition, we develop a completely different relationship with the outer world, and live in completely different dimensions of time and space. Then, our hard times or happy times are expressions of our spiritual situations, a consequence of the spiritual degree we are in, and not of a piece of paper in a calendar.

In the spiritual world, the degrees are called "years," but they are not connected with our calendar. That is why, apart from the changing of the dates in our calendars, nothing happened on that date.

PROPHECIES THAT DID NOT COME TRUE

Q: Contrary to all predictions, nothing happened in 1984, or at the end of the millennium. Are there similar events that await us in the near future?

A: In 1984, as in 2000, many predicted the end of the world. Of course, those were only baseless speculations and human beliefs. In spiritual worlds there isn't a unique root for 1984, or for 2000, because humans invented those dates. But people want change, and some of them also see pretty good business opportunities here.

Humans invented both the calendar and the dates. The millennium was just a date that mankind agreed upon. It went by just like all other dates. People want change because they are unhappy, and their desire for change stems from their will to delight themselves.

Humanity will gradually open its eyes to realize that the solution to its problems, and the way to perfection, wealth, and health, confidence and eternity, is not in the will to enjoy, but outside that will. According to the Zohar, there will indeed be great wars, but they will be internal ones, within each and every one of us.

The millennium has nothing to do with that process, which is why it went by so quietly, compared to the expectations it raised. I wish you the attainment of your own personal calendars, and that you will see all the dates in it, which are the spiritual degrees.

WAR AND REDEMPTION

Q: It says that the Messiah will come after *Gog u Magog*. What does this mean? Do we really have to wait for him, and if so, how do we prepare for his coming?

A: The Messiah is a Superior Force that shows man the worlds around him. The preparation for his coming is in the desire to live in both worlds, in ours and in the Upper One, develop awareness and recognition, want to attain correction, and equalize with the Creator.

The popular interpretation of the Messiah is that of a man-redeemer, who, when he comes, will bring us personal gain: monetary, health, power and control. There is no one who needs the Messiah in his actual form as the corrector of man. Messiah is a force that pulls one from our world to the spiritual world, the force that brings us to spirituality.

Q: What is the war of *Gog u Magog*?

A: The war of *Gog u Magog* is a spiritual term that relates to Kabbalah. It is not spoken of anywhere but in Kabbalah. *Gog u Magog* happens at a spiritual degree and not as it does in our world, where the wars and torments happen before our eyes.

SPIRITUALITY AND THE TEMPLE

Q: During the days following Pesach (Passover) we mourn for 24,000 of Rav Akiva's disciples who lost their lives in an epidemic. What does this tragedy tell us from a perspective of Kabbalah?

A: All of Rav Akiva's disciples were great Torah sages and were to become Kabbalists. But instead of cultivating love, they devolved to irrationally hate each other. Such negative feelings in the midst of these sages led to the downfall of the entire people and, as a result, to a generally low level of the Jewish people. Their enemies gained strength from Above, attacked, conquered, destroyed and dispersed them.

Our condition is totally dependent on our spiritual level. It determines our strength and our destiny. If we want to feel better, we must ascend to a higher spiritual level. Hence it is said, "A generation in which the Temple is not built is as the generation in which it was ruined."

If we could climb to a spiritual degree where the Temple could exist, in which people live in love, then the Temple would have to be rebuilt. The Higher Governing Force would instill the necessary desires in people and create general events that would lead to it.

However, the level of our people has hardly improved since the ruin of the Temple. The change can come only through the studying of Kabbalah, because it reveals to us the evil that reigns in us.

THE THIRD TEMPLE - FIRST IN OUR HEARTS, THEN IN STONE

Q: Do we have to look for the Ark? Rebuild one? How can we live without the Temple? The time has come.

A: What will you get if you find the ark, or build a new one? And if you do build the Temple, what will you do in it and with it? Will you display it to tourists? It may become good business, but nothing more than that.

We need to first reach the spiritual level of this Temple. The first Temple was of Light of *Hochma* (wisdom), the second Temple was the Light of Hassadim (mercy), but the third Temple has to be of Light of *Yechida*, the highest of all.

The Temple is built or destroyed according to how people in it match its spiritual level. Hence, in order to build the Temple we first need to reach the state of the end of correction. This is what you have to worry about both for yourself and for others.

THE ERA OF THE "SECRETS OF THE TORAH"

Q: Sooner or later the six thousand years will pass, the arguments will subside, the days of the Messiah will come and we will all unite

with the Creator. What will we do afterwards? What will we create? Will we have to raise the animals, the plants and the rocks to a higher level?

A: It is interesting to see how much a person wants to know of what awaits him beyond the highest degree, when he doesn't even know what the lowest degree is like! The difference between the degrees, as between the worlds, is enormous. The number of degrees is 125. By completing his ascent, a creature only corrects himself, his own vessel. After the correction he is ready to perform his real task, unification with the Creator.

But what the soul does in the spiritual summit is not even conceived by our imagination - those are the "secrets of Torah." The secrets are called "*Maase Merkava*," and "*Maase Bereshit*. Those secrets cannot be disclosed because people in lower degrees (even one degree below the top) cannot understand what goes on there... therefore, let us dare to climb the first ones first!

CHAPTER 11.
CONCEPTS IN KABBALAH

WHO IS GOD?

Q: Tell me, is God a personality? (I admit I don't know the definition of personality).

A: By "God," we usually refer to a higher power in general, the design of creation as it is expressed in any level. It must be noted that any definition of something higher than you, the Creator, God, etc., has to do with the feeling inside the creature, since he cannot possibly feel anything outside himself.

Therefore, these definitions are always subjective.

FUNDAMENTAL CONCEPTS: A FRAMEWORK

Q: Everyone ascribes a meaning to his own to life and death, to Light, to the soul etc. How does Kabbalah interpret them?

A: Let me clarify a few concepts:

Time: In spirituality, time does not exist! Creation is eternal.

Creator: The desire to delight the creature.

Creature, soul: The desire to delight in the Creator, in the sensation of the Creator, in the Light.

Life: The fulfillment of the soul by the Light, the sensation of the Creator.

Death: The exit of the Light, the disappearance of the sensation of the Creator from the soul (as a result of the disappearance of the intent "for the Creator").

The reception of a soul: An acquisition of desire (to enjoy "for the Creator"), with which it is possible to sense the Creator.

Screen: The desire to enjoy with the intent "for the Creator"; the holy vessel, the spiritual vessel, the corrected vessel; the vessel of the soul, which can feel the Creator.

Kabbalah (Heb. Reception): The science that explains how to gradually receive a complete soul, meaning complete adhesion with the Creator.

Our world: A state lower than spiritual death, below the sensation of the Creator. Located under the left side of the impure worlds of ABYA (*Atzilut, Beria, Yetzira, Assiya*).

The birth of the soul, acquisition of life: A passage from the sensation of our world, to the sensation of the Creator.

Reincarnation, cycles of life and death: The constant entrance and exit of Light in the vessel of the soul, which continues throughout the correction in the worlds of *BYA*.

WHAT IS LIGHT?

Q: Are the Light of the Creator, which Kabbalah speaks of, and the Light that is referred to in the first day of the creation of the world, the same?

A: There is only one Light and that does not change. But it is accepted in various forms due to differing states of the vessels (the creature, the soul) – depending on the vessel's ability to receive. From this we learn that we have no concept of the Light that is outside the vessel, because we cannot define something that is out of our sensation.

Light is the sensation of the Creator by the creature; what stems from the Creator; something that we feel as "good," whereas we feel its absence as "bad."

The Light that is spoken of in the first day of the creation of the world is the uppermost Light, which includes everything in it. The rest of the Lights are but derivatives of it, particular manifestations of it.

WHAT IS SPIRITUAL?

Q: How do you discern between corporeal and spiritual?

A: Spiritual is that which is above our world. That which is absolutely not "for me," but only "for the Creator," when the outcome of the act is not related in any way to the one who performs it, even indirectly.

The soul is linked with the Creator, senses it and is filled by it, at least in the smallest amount. It is anything that is out of and above time, space and motion, that is not in any way linked with the sensation of the animate body, but is felt in some inner space in man's senses - intended for the Creator only - and revealed only when man is in control of the "spiritual" bearer.

Q: I read that the spiritual is the "nature of the giver," which is outside our world. Why can we not say that the spiritual is a part of our world?

A: How could the spiritual be a component of our world? The spiritual is "in it," but it does not appear in it directly, but rather by "clothing."

Our world is a state where the will to receive enjoys only a very small Light called "minute Light," and we can enjoy it even when the aim of the desire is "for me."

The Creator does this purposely. We can enjoy that tiny Light, although we have not yet acquired a spiritual intent to give to the Creator, and do not have a screen.

The will to enjoy that is found within us is the smallest of the created desires. It is separated from all other desires of the soul, so that we may practice on it: once "for me" and once "for the Creator," and finally attain admittance to the spiritual world.

Rav Baruch Ashlag compared it to how children were taught to write in the old days: pen and paper were too expensive, so the child would be given a piece of chalk and board to write on, so that they would not waste precious paper, until they learned to write correctly.

Q: Is there a spiritual evil, such as shells or the evil inclination?

A: The shells and the evil inclination are impure forces that are above our world. They do not exist in a normal person and appear only when a genuine desire for the Creator begins to emerge in man. In order to intensify that desire, negative forces are incited. By resisting them, man grows and intensifies his desire for the Creator. They were created specifically for that – to interrupt and produce doubts.

Although the shells and the evil inclination do not exist in our world, we still do not call them "spiritual." They exist inside a person and not outside him and serve as a means and aid on his path to the Creator – a "help against him."

WHAT IS *GIMATRIA*?

Q: What is *Gimatria* and how does it work?

A: In order to describe various situations of the soul, we tend to use a name that is specifically adapted to its spiritual level, instead of using many technical details. All the vessels (souls) consist of ten *Sefirot*, just like one's body consists of an equal number of parts – 613.

The Light that fills the souls is what differentiates them from one another. The purpose of the name is to express attributes of the soul that is filled with Light. The sum of the Lights, or better put, the ten Lights that fill the ten *Sefirot* of the soul, are called *Gimatria*. That is why it is no more and no less than a recording of the spiritual situation of the soul and its fulfillment with Light by the Creator.

That Light depends on the screen: the attribute of the soul to give vs. its will to receive. The screen can only be acquired by the method of correction called Kabbalah.

WHAT IS REPENTANCE?

Q: Baal HaSulam writes that one acquires desires to give by repentance, and then becomes qualified to receive pleasure from the Creator. What, then, is repentance for a Kabbalist?

A: To repent means to return to the previous situation, but with a changed self. Otherwise, if the preliminary situation had not changed, and if we had not changed, it would have been the same situation.

Repentance is the return of the soul to the Creator, the place where it came from to this world. In the beginning, the Creator created a desire to receive. That desire was created without intent and was therefore called an "embryo."

By a gradual intensification of the aim "for me," the desire to receive moves farther and farther from the Creator until it is completely opposite to Him. The state where all the desires aim "for me" is called "our world," or "this world."

In that situation, the desire feels nothing but itself, and that sensation is called "body" (a person in this world).

If the desire changes its intent from "for me" to "for the Creator," then the change in the intent causes the desire to return to its preliminary situation, and it becomes like an embryo in the Creator. Each situation in the spiritual realm is measured against the Creator, and determined in relation to Him.

The more the attributes of the creature equalize with those of the Creator, the nearer the creature is regarded to the Creator, and vice versa.

With the aim, "for the Creator," the desire changes its quality and is turned from a "receiver" into a "giver." In this way, it equalizes with the Creator. The creature feels himself not as before – a point, or an embryo – but as something complete and whole and equal to the Creator.

In its equivalence with the Creator, the will to enjoy senses everything the Creator senses: unbounded pleasure, eternity and perfection. That is the purpose of creation.

WHAT IS LIFE AND DEATH?

Q: Is there really such a thing as death?

A: The sensation of death or life begins with the admittance to the spiritual world, and not when a physical body is born or dies. "Death" is an exit of Light, when the sensation of the Creator is gone from the vessel, the soul. Our present state is considered worse than death because we don't feel the Creator whatsoever. We do not even feel that we are denied of any Light, any sensation of the Creator. Feeling the Creator means receiving a soul.

The word, Kabbalah, is derived from the word, Lekabel (to receive). Kabbalah is the science that teaches how to receive a soul and, through it, to attain eternal life. "Death" means distancing from the Creator to its opposite pole (opposite attributes). The condition for the reception of a soul is the existence of a vessel, and a vessel is the aim "for the Creator."

A person can attain the first spiritual degree only after he has attained the understanding that death is detachment from the Creator and life is attachment to Him. The rest is in the hands of the spiritual mechanism. But in order to attain such an understanding, it is necessary to receive help from the Creator – the miracle of the exodus from Egypt! That is the only way God can help. And when He does, then mankind will really be saved!

Q: What is the meaning of the words of the Zohar, when it says that "only the chosen will attain life in the next world"? What about the rest of humanity?

A: Creation is eternal. Time and motion do not exist. We only speak of inner sensations of the creature. The changing inner situations evoke the sensation of time and motion. The Zohar speaks of spiritual degrees and of situations of the eternal soul, about measures of its fulfillment with the Light of the Creator. But the sensation of the animate life can accompany a soul if a person receives it.

Otherwise it is as it says: "...so that man hath no pre-eminence above a beast" (Ecclesiastes 3, 19).

Q: What does man ultimately risk?

A: A person risks the thing that is most precious to him: what he feels, what he possesses, his very life. There is no total absence! But everything he has vanishes. As a matter of fact, there is no risk in anything because everything is in the hands of the benevolent Creator.

But we feel it like that unless we attain spiritual faith: the Light of mercy.

WHAT ARE DELIGHT AND PLEASURE?

Q: Is the word, "pleasure," that Kabbalists use in their books really about delight and pleasure as we understand it, or does it have a different meaning altogether, and they only call it that for convenience?

A: The purpose of creation is to delight the creatures. The complete Creator can only delight the creatures with completeness. The Creator cannot create an incomplete creation. By "complete" we mean that only He fills the entire reality, which is also why He is the only One. Because of that there is a desire to be filled with Him. That desire is satisfied entirely, unreservedly. That is why His state is called "*Ein Sof*" (infinite).

But the Creator creates that situation for the creature to feel himself complete in his own right. For that to happen, the creature must attain a sensation of appreciation. He can only acquire that out of the sensation of the oppositeness of form and incompleteness. That is the purpose of his being distanced from the Creator to a state called "this world," where the creature feels corporeal animate pleasure – our current situation – instead of feeling the Creator.

The more the creature becomes aware of his incomplete situation – which is possible only by studying Kabbalah – the more he becomes aware of the perfection that is the Creator. He begins to realize that perfection is adhesion with the Creator, equivalence with His attributes, being filled with Him.

During the study one realizes that to be complete means to be as close as possible to the Creator, as similar as possible to His attributes; to equalize with His form. As a matter of fact, that is already the situation, but he cannot feel it as such, and therefore he cannot regard it as such.

As a person comes to understand himself and the Creator, he begins to feel the completeness as though he is returning to it. The sensation of fulfillment in these situations is called "pleasure," and the desire to feel the Creator as supreme completeness is called "vessel."

WHAT IS THE FEELING OF COMPLETENESS?

Q: What is completeness, and how can we feel it?

A: It is only possible to understand and appreciate completeness when one feels the Creator, because only He is perfect. Furthermore, the power to correct is also given by the Creator. Therefore, the purpose of the study, in the beginning, is to attain the sensation of the Creator. Then everything becomes clear.

Before that, we cannot understand what completeness is, and the Creator chooses to be shown to man precisely in his most incomplete attributes.

WHAT ARE THE ACTIONS OF THE SCREEN?

Q: How does the screen create new spiritual objects?

A: Spiritual objects are things that the Kabbalist creates over his screen. They are the result of the impact of the Light on the screen of the Kabbalist. As a result, a new picture of the spiritual world is created in the Kabbalist's mind.

Spirituality is only born after a spiritual coupling whose power determines the depth of the spiritual picture. If the Light does not hit the screen, nothing new is born, and all that a person gets is the picture of this world.

In other words, to beget a new spiritual object means to build from our substance (the desire) the image of the Creator, through the screen. In fact, the screen is a sculpturing tool in the hands of the Kabbalist.

A person observes himself from the side (restricts his desires, and erects a screen made of the intent "not to receive for himself"). He uses the screen to cut off desires that he cannot simulate to the Creator (the "stony heart").

Desires in which he can resemble the Creator he brings to equivalence of form with the attributes of the Creator, to the extent that his screen can bear it. Thus, the higher his degree is, the more a person resembles the Creator. He studies the attributes of the Creator (the upper nine *Sefirot*) and adopts them.

FROM THE CREATOR TO THE CREATURE

Q: How many worlds separate the soul from the Light?

A: Here is what happens from above downward:

1. The four phases of "direct Light."
2. The birth of the world of "*Ein Sof*" (infinity).
3. The first restriction of *Malchut*.
4. The birth of the world of *Adam Kadmon* (AK).
5. The second restriction.
6. The breaking of the screen of *Malchut*.
7. The creation of the worlds: *Atzilut, Beria, Yetzira, Assiya*.
8. The creation of the soul of the First Man (*Adam ha Rishon*).
9. The breaking of the soul into pieces.
10. The descent of the pieces to our world.
11. The development of the souls by descending to our world, to our present state.

As you can see, the way down here is very long, but we can already come to certain conclusions about the nature of creation, the attributes of the Light and the vessel.

MALCHUT AND THE WORLD OF "EIN SOF"

Q: What and where is the world of "*Ein Sof*"?

A: We must refrain from interpreting "*Ein Sof*" (infinity) as a term of time or place. "*Ein Sof*" is something endless, unlimited by action or attributes; hence the name "*Ein Sof*."

Spirituality has no time or space. Therefore, these two limitations of our world do not apply to the spiritual world. For that reason we cannot imagine spirituality for what it is. We cannot imagine a cup, that, although filled to the rim, it is still in a state of endless filling (naturally, everything is measured according to the cup itself, because we measure everything with regards to the receiver).

Malchut, the soul, corrects itself through the worlds. The worlds are degrees of concealment or manifestation of Light. Time and again, the soul receives desires (which are the vessels) and Light (the power to correct the desire) from the degrees.

By using that desire and the Light of correction, the soul, by correcting itself, seemingly rises to the same degree from which it received the power and desire to correct. All and all there are five worlds, within which there are five *Partzufim*, with five inner *Sefirot*. Together they make up 125 degrees. But there are still an enormous number of transitory situations.

Q: You write that a "world" is also every phase of *Malchut*, of the souls, the collective vessel. Is *Malchut* a *Sefira* or a world?

A: *Malchut* is the tenth *Sefira*, the last one after the nine *Sefirot* of direct Light that extend from the Creator. *Malchut* receives the Light from all other nine *Sefirot* and divides in ten parts. Those ten parts of *Malchut* are the worlds and everything in them.

Q: Is creation *Malchut*? And what are all the Upper *Sefirot*?

A: All nine other *Sefirot* before *Malchut* (also called the "Upper Nine") are attributes of the Light. *Malchut* must resemble those nine *Sefirot*. The extent of resemblance between *Malchut* and the nine *Sefirot*, which are the attributes of the Creator, depends on the power of the screen in *Malchut*. But the resemblance of *Malchut* to the nine *Sefirot* exists even with the smallest screen.

Therefore, even a minimal screen should make *Malchut* resemble all nine other *Sefirot*. Thus, any spiritual attainment is comprised of a whole picture (which includes all the *Sefirot*). A picture with a minimal screen can be comprised of a small number of shades or details, but it still makes for a relative picture of all nine *Sefirot*.

Just as, when we are born, we perceive with all five senses, regardless of whether we are adults or children, the power (depth) of the attainment depends on the power of the screen.

THE EVOLUTION OF MALCHUT

Q: The world, in and of itself, is something limiting, inhibitory. How then does *Malchut* of the infinite evolve through the souls?

A: The term, "world," means concealment, hiding, limitation of the extension of the Light. But every situation of *Malchut*, of the collective soul, is also called a "world."

The world of *Ein Sof* is a state of unbounded fulfillment of the collective soul and not of an individual creature/soul. Everything that fills the collective soul is called "Light" or "Creator." But in order to be filled with the intent "for the Creator," and thus equalize with Him, *Malchut*, the soul, gradually corrects her intent from "for me" to "for the Creator"; it empties itself in the first restriction, hides under five covers, worlds, and gradually, in accordance with the acquisition of the screen (the aim 'for the Creator').

Then, it exposes itself to the Light, the Creator, like a bride before the groom. Her degrees of correction, her exposure, her fulfillment with

Light, are five worlds with five *Partzufim* in each world and five degrees in each *Partzuf*, all and all, 125 degrees.

It is also possible to divide the spiritual distance to 613 degrees (*Mitzvot*), and it can be divided in 6,000 degrees – three groups of 2,000 in each. But the distance itself, the extent of the correction of *Malchut*, remains the same. It is only a more convenient way to describe the degrees – the extent of correction~ in a convenient way.

THE LIGHTS OF *MALCHUT*

Q: Which Light fills *Malchut* - is it one Light or five Lights?

A: *Malchut* (the soul) is divided in five parts (from fine to coarse): *Keter, Hochma, Bina, Zeir Anpin,* and *Malchut*, in ascending order of the power of the will to receive. The strongest desire takes the last part – the *Malchut* of *Malchut*. These desires receive with five pleasures – Lights that fill them respectively: *Yechida, Haya, Neshama, Ruach, Nefesh*.

Malchut is divided into five parts in a reversed order, from coarse to fine: still, vegetative and animate, speaking and Godly. Hence, the strongest will to receive (the *Malchut* of *Malchut*) is called still, and is filled by the dimmest Light, in the level of still, the Light of *Nefesh* (*Nefesh* of *Nefesh*).

In the spiritual worlds is a law called "the opposite value of Lights and vessels": the coarser the desire that aspires to receive greater pleasures, the more Light it extends. But the Light goes not into the coarse desire, but into the finest one, into the desire to give without any reward, because the Light and the finest desire to give are in equivalence of form.

It is also customary to say, "The Lights enter the *Partzuf* gradually." But any change in the Light means a change in the vessel, and therefore, in the entire *Partzuf*. Everything is new each time, all five *Sefirot* and all five Lights.

WHAT ARE *SEFIROT*?

Q: What do the *Sefirot* in the books of Kabbalah describe?

A: *Sefirot* are attributes that are given to the creature, the lower one, through which to feel the Upper One, the Creator. That is why the *Sefirot* express supremacy, the attributes of the Creator, attributes that the Creator wants the creatures to attain in order that they feel Him.

Just as we capture a person by his mind, which is his essence (whereas the body is only an outer clothing), so is spirituality grasped through its clothing, because the essence is in the interior attributes behind the clothing. Externality is only needed for the purpose of acquaintance, and not in and of itself.

A person attains the Creator through the *Sefirot*, meaning through His outer appearances. Similarly, we know a person for certain only after we know all his attributes and reactions in varying situations. Through the *Sefirot* we will ultimately come to know reality, which is all a dressing for the Creator, just as the body is a dressing for the soul.

The Creator works within a person's soul. Therefore, he who learns to attain the Creator knows Him and attains Him by His actions in his own soul, meaning by the action of the Light on his own point of *Malchut*. That point is not empty, although it is felt that way, but rather filled with goodness. However, in order to feel it, we need to experience every emotion, and only then does a person learn to feel the Light as it enters a specific point in the soul.

Completeness is a pleasure that is sensed only after there is a hunger for something and a shortage of it, to the extent of the incompleteness that was felt prior to the reception of the delight.

It is impossible to sense continuous pleasure in this world, because nature has it that hunger and satisfaction do not come together. Precisely that attribute is given to the soul in order to feel hungry, in order to crave pleasure, so that a person will learn that although he is able to satisfy the hunger, he will never get his fill.

But the Creator wants to delight us, which is why He sends us a special fulfillment. The souls try not to spoil that satisfaction by crossing the line. It is only in this way that they arrive at completeness. The hunger and desire do not go away~on the contrary. As a result, the souls extend more fulfillment from a wholeness that does not fade, an eternal wholeness.

We know that we enjoy eating because of the prior hunger, the sensation of shortage. As the shortage disappears, so does the pleasure. The Creator gave the souls a great "trick" that prevents them from being satiated, despite the reception of pleasure. The fuller they feel, the hungrier they grow. That is the perfection of the action of the Creator.

DIRECTIONS OF DEVELOPMENT

Q: When you said that everything moves from up downward, from the root to *Malchut*, I understood that it is *Malchut* that is in all the other attributes and the whole flow is going upward. But from what I read, it seems that the flow should be toward the middle, inside, to the root phase, which is within man. Does "up" mean "inside?"

A: In the spiritual world, there is no volume or place. It is like describing our feelings: we say "deep emotion," "high note," "great joy," etc. Creation can be described as spreading from the Creator, from above downward; from the Upper One, from the exalted attributes, to the lower one, the lower attributes.

But we can also look at the development of creation from within, from the Creator outward to a point that draws farther from Him, like moving from the innermost, the most personal and hidden, to something external and less important.

We can also speak about the development of creation as though the Creator surrounds it, "wrapping" it with His goal and controlling it from all sides. Creation is within, like an egg inside a brooding hen.

There are other descriptions of just one thing: the relationship between the creation and Creator. The actual words are merely tools that we use, depending on which attributes, characteristics, qualities and interrelations we are talking about.

WHAT IS A SPIRITUAL VESSEL?

Q: If a vessel is designed to receive Light, what is the meaning of a "giving vessel," and how can the "will to receive" give?

A: The Creator created a desire to delight, meaning a desire to feel pleasure. Real pleasure lasts as long as the desire lasts–it is insatiable. But when the desire to enjoy receives – it feels shame. That is why one cannot attain eternal delight by receiving, because receiving restricts the Light and even extinguishes it, thus nullifying itself.

For that reason, the only way to take pleasure is to enjoy not the pleasure itself, but the contact with the giver of the pleasure. If the pleasure of the giver is what you get from Him, then your pleasure will not disappear and will not diminish your desire for pleasure.

On the contrary! The more you receive, the more you give and enjoy. That process lasts indefinitely.

However, the pleasure that we derive from feeling the one who gives is infinitely greater than the pleasure we receive when taking for ourselves. This is because the first kind of taking ties us with the Complete Giver, the Eternal One.

Thus, a mere desire to receive is not considered a vessel yet, because it is unsuitable for reception. Only if there is a screen over the desire to enjoy (a screen is the intent "for the Creator," meaning a willingness to take pleasure only to the extent that it delights the Upper One), does the desire become worthy of reception, and can then be called "a vessel."

From this, we can understand that all we really have to do is acquire a screen! When the will to enjoy receives, and feels the giver, it feels both pleasure and shame, because by receiving we become opposite to the Creator. The presence of the giver makes the receiver feel shame, and that shame stops us from enjoyment. When we receive, we feel we must give something back to the giver, to equalize with the giver so as not to feel as if we are only receiving.

The sensation of shame is also called the "fire of hell." There is nothing worse than the sensation of shame because it completely and directly destroys the one thing that we possess: our ego.

The Creator purposely paired receiving with shame. He could have avoided it, but the phenomenon of shame was created specifically for us so we could learn to receive from Him, to delight without shame.

That is why we, as creatures, (the will to enjoy) immediately felt ourselves to be receiving from the Creator and decided and acted out a restriction (limitation of the Light) of the receiving of the Light. That act is called "the first restriction."

A giving vessel is one that still cannot receive for the Creator, but can only refrain from receiving, because if it would receive, it would be for itself.

The creature can exist without receiving Light because the sensation of shame extinguishes its pleasure at reception, and turns the pleasure of reception into torment.

Then, when we feel the desire of the Creator to please us, we decide that despite the sensation of shame, we will accept the pleasure because that is what the Creator wants. Therefore, by doing so, we can bring pleasure to the Creator for His Sake, not for himself. The act remains as before, and we still receive, just as we did when we felt shame, but the intent of the reception has now changed.

The decision has been taken only out of the desire to delight the Creator, and despite the sensation of shame, but we as creatures discover that by acting for the Creator, we do not feel ourselves as receivers, but as givers, equal to the Creator, and we both give to one another and express love for each other.

As creatures, through our equivalence of form with the Creator, we feel ourselves as the Creator: total wholeness, eternity, unending love and pleasure.

But the decision to restrict the reception of Light (the first restriction), to receive Light only with the aim "for the Creator," will come only if we feel the Creator, the giver, because only the sensation of the Creator can awaken such a resolution in us.

The question arises: if the presence of the Creator can evoke such a sensation in us, how can we say that the decision was really "for the Creator"? After all, the first restriction was a consequence of the shame, and the reception of the Light was seemingly a result of the pressure of the giver.

Therefore, in order to take an independent decision to receive "for the Creator" and in order to resemble He who created the creature in order to delight him, the Creator has to be concealed, so that His Presence would not be compulsive, like placing a knife on one's neck.

That is why there must be a situation where we creatures feel that we are the only ones here. Then, all the decisions will be our own.

THE LIGHT OF CORRECTION AND THE LIGHT OF FULFILLMENT

Q: I read about the screen and now I am confused. You always said that the Light cannot come into an uncorrected vessel; that there has to be a screen first, meaning that I should develop in me a desire to receive Light "for the Creator" and not for myself. Only then, you say, is it possible to receive the Light. But the book says that in order to build a screen there must first be Light in the vessel because the vessel cannot build the screen by itself.

A: There is Light that fills the desire to enjoy, meaning the vessel, and there is a Light that corrects it. It is the Light that gives the vessel the intent "for the Creator" and builds the screen over the desire. These two Lights act completely differently on the vessel: the Light that corrects is called "the Light of correction of creation," while the Light that fills it is called "the Light of the purpose of creation."

The Light of correction can enter the vessel even before there is a screen; it is specifically for the purpose of building a screen. It gives the creature a feeling that the Creator is supreme and mighty, and from that feeling the creature subdues its nature in order to draw near the Creator. That is how the vessel acquires a screen.

Then, by the power of one's strength and by one's intent "for the Creator," there is *Zivug de Hakaa* (spiritual mating) and the vessel is filled with Light.

TWO SCREENS

Q: Despite all the explanations, there is something I still don't understand: is the vessel a desire, or an aim?

A: A vessel is a desire that receives Light, the response from the Creator. It is the intent not to act "for me," but for interests beyond my own. That is why we don't consider the mere desire to be a vessel, but rather the screen, the altruistic aim to bestow, the returning Light.

Q: Is there something that does not let the Light inside the vessel, but only creates an opening, without which the Light cannot enter?

A: The Light is the Creator. We always speak from the perspective of the vessel, the creature. Any other perspective that is not from the sensation of the vessel is unfounded. In the state of *Ein Sof* (infinite), after the vessel receives the Light for itself (in order to receive), it decides never to do it again. It decides to restrict the reception of Light in its own desire to receive for itself.

That is called the "first restriction." From that state down to this world, all the vessels wish not to receive Light in order to receive. In other words, the law of the first restriction is kept in all the degrees. The power to keep the restriction is called a "screen," because it protects the desire from using the Light for self-profit. But other than that, there is another screen - not just for maintaining the restriction, but also for receiving the Light for the Creator.

SPIRITUALITY AND THE LOVE OF MAN

Q: What is the love of man in the spiritual sense?

A: A true act of love is when I do something good for someone I love only because I want to delight that person, even without their knowing that I'm the one who did this good thing, and even if I do not derive any direct pleasure from it. Love would be my only motivation to act.

The Torah explains that a true act of altruism (love of man) is when one party does not know about the other party, whether or not the party is giving. Otherwise there is pleasure derived from it.

If the Creator knows about a person's act, this is already a reward. But for true giving, there need not be any kind of reward. We always speak from the perspective of the person with real feelings and not of abstract creatures. One must come to that sensation of genuine giving step by step, meaning one must attain the spiritual level of giving, while in the meantime performing it only mechanically.

But all the while, we should be aware that such existence is only mechanical, in the degree of this world, our temporary place.

WHAT IS *BINA*?

Q: The term "*Bina*" is derived from the Hebrew word for understanding. Does that mean that *Bina* is one of the rational attributes?

A: In the spiritual world, there is no such term as ratio (mind). The mind is in constant pursuit of pleasure "for me," under accepted conventions. *Bina*, however, is the state where the soul wants nothing for itself.

WHAT ARE 6,000 YEARS?

Q: What are the 6,000 years that are mentioned in the books of Kabbalah?

A: The books of Kabbalah speak about 6,000 years, which are – in the language of the branches – 6,000 degrees that each soul must climb.

They have nothing to do with a calendar that you hang on the wall. There are the souls of the righteous that have attained the end of correction - the seventh millennium - many centuries ago.

Rav Baruch Ashlag compared birth and death in our world to the changing of one's clothing. That changing is gradual from generation to generation, each time in more developed bodies with more developed minds and desires. There is no connection between the degrees in the spiritual world and the changing of the bodies.

For some creatures, a thousand years of life will not be enough for them to enter the spiritual world, while others complete their corrections within a single lifetime.

WHAT IS A JEW?

Q: What is a Jew?

A: Abraham, our father, who went from Mesopotamia to the land of Israel, is called the first Hebrew (and the first Jew), because he was the first to cross from idolatry to the land of Israel (land - *Eretz* and Israel - from the words, *Yashar El*, meaning "directly to the Creator"). He went over from a state of worshiping idols to recognition of the existence of a higher power that controls everything, and identified himself with that power of his own free will. That is why he was designated Hebrew (*Ivri* - from the word Over) and Jew.

The terms "Jew" and "Gentile" are completely different in spirituality from the meanings we are familiar with. Anyone who did not exit this world to the spiritual world is called a "gentile," and a person who crosses over to the spiritual world, is called a "Hebrew," or "Jew" (from the Hebrew word *Yehudi* - *Yechudi*, meaning unique and unified), because that person unites with the Creator.

SPIRITUAL DIVISIONS

Q: Why is everything in our world divided into seven, ten or twelve?

A: Creation – a desire for pleasure – divided itself to the nine attributes that it received from Him: the upper nine *Sefirot*, and *Malchut*, the tenth *Sefira*. Thus, everything in reality is initially divided by ten. Then there are other divisions: a *Partzuf* divides to the three *Sefirot* of the *Rosh* (head), and the seven *Sefirot* of the *Guf* (body).

Then there is a division to twelve, which stems from the number of *Partzufim* (faces) in the world of *Atzilut*. In the wisdom of Kabbalah you will find the explanations of every division and the interrelations between them.

THE *SEFIROT YESOD* AND *ZEIR ANPIN*

Q: Why is *Zeir Anpin* divided by six parts instead of the ordinary five? What is the purpose of *Yesod*?

A: *Zeir Anpin* has to be in contact with *Malchut*, in order to convey the Light to her. For that to happen, he must build a special *Sefira* to serve as a bridge between *Malchut* and him, meaning that it will possess similar attributes. For that purpose *Zeir Anpin* consists of:

1. *Hesed – Keter*
2. *Gevura – Hochma*
3. *Tifferet – Bina*
4. *Netzah – Zeir Anpin* of *Zeir Anpin*
5. *Hod – Malchut* of *Zeir Anpin*
6. *Yesod* – the sum total of all the previous *Sefirot* (like a salad made of five original components that when put together, form a new attribute).

After *Yesod* comes the collective *Malchut* – the creature, the soul, the part that must unite with the Creator (*Zeir Anpin*) through equivalence of form. *Malchut* is the creature and *Zeir Anpin* is the Creator. *Zeir Anpin* is the one to which all prayers to be raised and corrected turn, and he, at the request of *Malchut* (MAN), builds a bond with her – contact and coupling – through his *Sefira* of *Yesod*.

WHAT IS A SOUL?

Q: What is that spiritual object called a "soul"?

A: The Zohar writes about the relationships between all five *Partzufim* of the world of *Atzilut*, which is the world that governs reality. It says: "Therefore shall a man leave his father and his mother" (Genesis 2, 24), meaning the soul will become independent from its mother and father, attain completeness and independent coupling with *Malchut*, to unite with the Creator, and create new *Partzufim* – corrected souls.

A soul is the *Partzuf* of *Malchut* of the world of *Atzilut*. *Zeir Anpin*, the Creator, is her husband. The *Partzuf* of *Abba ve Ima* – *Hochma* and *Bina* – provide the soul with everything it needs.

WHAT IS AN AWAKENING FROM BELOW?

Q: What is an awakening from below? Is there anyone who can act independently beside the Creator?

A: In the Kabbalah, everything is described from the perspective of the emotions of the attaining Kabbalist and the way the Creator is revealed to that person. Even when we speak of the Creator, and seemingly only about Him, regardless of ourselves, we still rely on our own understanding of Him.

Our desire for a spiritual ascent stems either from Above (the Creator), or below (from us). Of course, it is only the Light that rocks and awakens us, as vessels. But then, either we clearly feel that the Creator is the One awakening us from Above, or we do not feel the influence of the Creator, but only the side effects of that influence: ours inner will, meaning that there is suddenly an aspiration for the Creator, because the Creator has secretly awakened us.

THE SPIRITUAL FORCE CALLED "MESSIAH"

Q: What is the Messiah from the perspective of a Kabbalist?

A: The term, "Messiah," comes from the Hebrew word "pulling." This refers to the pulling of people up from the ignominious worldliness to a higher level. Messiah is a spiritual force, the Upper Light; the Upper Spiritual Force that descends to our world and corrects mankind, raising us to a higher level of consciousness. It is quite possible that along with it will also be certain people, leaders, who will teach others to come out to the spiritual world, but in principle, it is a spiritual force, not a flesh-and- blood personality.

WHAT IS CONFIDENCE?

Q: What is confidence and how can we attain it?

A: Confidence is the ability to suffer, to be constantly nourished by the goal. The attainment of confidence depends only on the attainment of surrounding Light. That Light is ready and waiting to fill the soul when it completes its correction. Therefore, now, when that Light shines upon the soul, it gives it the sensation of protection and confidence.

Only a direct and concrete feeling of the Creator gives man confidence and the ability to endure all the degrees of correction. It is done by the Creator purposely so that man will not be able to overcome even the lightest spiritual obstacle by himself, but will need the Creator every step of the way.

In our world, we can exist without the sensation of the Creator. But in the spiritual realm, we cannot. The extent of the sensation of the Creator is the extent of the actual confidence of man, and I would add, our ability to defend against disturbances.

WHO IS A FRIEND?

Q: Whom can I regard as my friend?

A: The word, "friend" (*Haver*) stems from the word, "connection" (*Hibur*), unification. The connection is only possible if there is a resemblance in attributes, thoughts and actions. Thus, according to the equivalence of attributes, a friend can be nearer or farther. Your "friend" (*Reacha*) stems from the root *Re'a*, which means "near."

WHAT IS HUMBLENESS?

Q: What is humbleness from the perspective of the Creator?

A: Humbleness is the most important trait. There is a special chapter in the Zohar called "The Book of Humbleness" (*Safra de Tzniuta*). This is the book of those who have a screen. Through the screen, we become like the Creator, precisely in the attribute of humbleness! This happens because we suppress our own nature and place the Creator above ourselves.

Humbleness demands of man to be aware of the lowness of our own nature, and to aspire to acquire the nature of the Creator – the attribute of giving, bestowing. Humbleness is the ability to activate our own nature to enjoy with the intent not for ourselves.

RIGHTEOUS AND EVIL

Q: Can you please explain who is righteous and who is evil?

A: Any spiritual degree is divided in two parts: righteous and evil. If a person justifies the Creator that person is regarded as righteous, while one who condemns Him is regarded evil.

A person who is in the world of *Assiya* is regarded as evil, but in the world of *Yetzira*, that person is regarded as evil *and* righteous. In the world of *Beria*, the same person is righteous. Before one enters the spiritual worlds, one does not fall into any of the above categories, because from a spiritual perspective one does not exist. Read a lot of the texts of Baal HaSulam and Rav Baruch Ashlag, and learn the right definitions from them. That will prevent you from being confused by your previous knowledge.

WHO IS RIGHTEOUS?

Q: Who is righteous and what is the meaning of the saying, "the righteous inherit the land" (Isaiah 60, 21)?

A: A righteous person is someone who has attained a spiritual degree called "righteous." This person has attained the screen that stands and prevents all pleasures from entering and filling the will to receive. That is why the righteous can always justify the Creator.

As for "the righteous that inherit the land" – in each new degree, the righteous inherits, or "receives" new desires (desire – *Ratzon* – stems from the word land – *Eretz*) and places over them a new screen, called "receiving for the Creator."

GOOD AND BAD

Q: Is it true that the human and corporeal conceptions of good and bad correspond to spiritual laws? If not, then what is the source of the good deeds in our world?

A: The corporeal meaning of good and bad does not correspond to spiritual laws at all. It does not mean that it is opposite, that bad in our world is good in spirituality. That is not so! But it is true is that the good deeds of man in our world do not promote us to spirituality.

The Temple is a result of upper laws. It is the source of the goodness in this world. But it is conditioned. I'm sure you've heard that the Creator is considered to be all goodness and benevolence, that He creates everything, and only good.

So where is that good? What do we see around us? The answer is that the connection between this world and the spiritual worlds is indirect. Otherwise, everyone would willingly come to the Creator and would not need the correction from Above.

POWER OF LIGHT

Q: What is the function of evil in our world?

A: Evil does not really exist in our world. It all depends on the intensity of the Light: when Light shines a little stronger, we feel it as good, as rest. That is the Light of which people speak who have experienced clinical death. A smaller amount of Light is sensed by us as states of depression, disaster and disease.

It all depends on the power of illumination that shines over each person individually. "Bad" is actually the lack of Light.

WHAT IS PUNISHMENT?

Q: What is the system of reward and punishment in Kabbalah?

A: There is no punishment in spirituality, only correction, which brings us to the attainment of perfection. In our present level of development, we normally picture the reward as receiving what we want. Therefore, the reward depends on the degree of each person's soul.

One must reach a state where the reward will be in doing something for the Creator. Then the effort to add to the intent "for the Creator" is considered work that merits a reward. However, the work itself is actually the reward. Its cause – the will to receive – and the effect – the reward – become one. Time and pain vanish, to be replaced with a sensation of total completeness.

WHAT IS SIN?

Q: Ejaculation is a sin, and so is getting drunk. Is every act performed in order to please yourself a sin?

A: First, let me stress that anything that happens in our world has no bearing on the Upper World, because a person does not evoke any spiritual act by his physical actions.

When a person enters the Upper World, having acquired a screen, the person performs spiritual acts, using all of the 613 desires with the aim "for the Creator," from the weakest desire, the first degree in the spiritual world, to the strongest, the highest desire of the spiritual world.

There are two types of pleasure:
1. The Light of wisdom - felt in the desire for pleasure.
2. The Light of mercy - felt in the desire to delight.

Both types can be received either with the intent "for me," or with the intent "for the Creator."

There are four actions that can be performed, depending on the measurement of the correction:

1. Receive pleasure for myself.
2. Give pleasure (delight) for myself.
3. Give pleasure (delight) for the Creator.
4. Receive pleasure for the Creator.

Ejaculation, in the Kabbalistic sense of the word, is an act of reception of pleasure, meaning Light of Wisdom, inside the uncorrected (lacking a screen) *Malchut*, while using the intent "for me."

A correct use of the Light of Wisdom is attained only through a correct mating between a "man" and a "woman": the mating between the desire to give and the will to receive, between *Zeir Anpin* and *Malchut* of *Atzilut*. The souls compel them to mate by raising desire for correction, called MAN.

Only at the end of correction, when there is a screen over all the desires, will it be possible to receive without limits. That is why in the holiday of Purim there is a *Mitzva* to drink until you cannot tell between good and bad, because it symbolizes the end of correction.

But there is a difference in severity between ejaculation and intoxication until one cannot tell good from bad, until the ability to correct is lost.

In the case of intoxication, a person descends from the level of "man" to that of a "beast," where one is not considered a sinner, but simply detaches from consciousness, from correction. But the act of ejaculation without a screen is a sin. You might say that the intoxication in and of itself is not a sin, but the sin is the deviation from the purpose of creation caused by the intoxication.

Through the correspondence between root and branch, ejaculating semen instead of mating with the corrected female and multiplying is an act that goes directly against correction, and the intoxication goes only indirectly against correction. I would also add that spiritual ejaculation is a sin regarding both the first and second restrictions.

END OF THE WORLD

Q: What is the end of the world in Kabbalah?

A: The end of the world refers to the end of the situation we are currently in, which is the worst and lowest of all. The end of that situation is considered a passage, after which a person begins to identify self with one's soul, to be in the spiritual world. That ends the question of whether to live in this body or outside it. One stops feeling under the authority of one's own body, and that is called "the end of the world." From now on, one feels only the life of the soul.

WHAT IS HELL?

Q: Are we in hell?

A: Hell is the sensation of shame – the only sensation that our ego cannot tolerate whatsoever, because it humiliates it and completely revokes it. The sensation of hell places the creature in a lower status than the "One and Only," the Creator, Who exists outside him.

It shows us that we are the lowest and the meanest of entities. The ego cannot tolerate this to such an extent that it is willing to give up its own attribute. That is the reason that hell is felt precisely by those who are called "evil," meaning those who call themselves evil, because they want to become righteous, they want to justify the actions of the Creator on them.

WHAT IS PARADISE?

Q: Please describe paradise.

A: Paradise is a perfect state, one that man attains after having finished correcting his will to receive and attaining complete adhesion with the Creator. Adhesion means equivalence of all man's attributes with those of the Creator, the attainment of complete awareness and the sensation of eternity and perfection.

We are compelled to attain it, and we can do it in this very life. The completion of the 6,000 years, the end of correction will force us to come to it.

HAPPINESS

Q: What is happiness?

A: Happiness is the sensation of the fulfillment of the internal capabilities of man. It is fully clarified only when we realize precisely what and how we should fulfill, what are goal is, how eternal it is and independent, and to what extent it is the one meaningful thing in the world that is now being realized.

In other words, happiness is the sensation of nearing the Creator, because that is the purpose of creation – a sensation of advancement toward a never-ending wholeness.

FEELING THE PASSAGE

Q: Does one feel the process of crossing the barrier? If so, is this feeling continuous or temporary? I mean, can we tell ourselves with certainty that we are already THERE?

A: A person goes through all the processes both before and after crossing the barrier in full consciousness, but the crossing itself is impossible to predict in advance. Crossing the barrier occurs only in a one-way direction, to the spiritual world but not back to ours. It means attaining "*Lishma*," the intention "for the sake of the Creator," and consequently, complete unity with Him, like a fetus inside its mother's womb, hence being filled with such a sensation, we certainly realize we are THERE.

"THE TREE OF LIFE" AND "THE INNER REFLECTION"

Q: Could you please explain the titles of two books: "The Tree of Life" and "The Inner Reflection"?

Does "The Tree of Life" mean life in its general sense organic life, the force giving and supporting life, or life as being opposed to death, as not being?

How can one briefly characterize the process of "The Inner Reflection"? What or who is the object of this reflection (watching, observing, contemplating)?

A: "The Tree of Life" means the correction of altruistic desires (above the *Chazeh*) and working with egoistic desires (below the *Chazeh*) with the intention to give in the entire *Partzuf Adam*.

"The Inner Reflection" is the attainment of the inner Light, which fills the *Partzuf* from *Rosh* to *Tabur*. This attainment gives man the feeling of unity with the Creator, of knowing Him and therefore all the wisdom and understanding of the reasons and the origins of the universe.

CHAPTER 12.
REFLECTIONS AND THOUGHTS

DOES THE CREATOR EXIST?

Q: Before one begins to study Kabbalah, one must answer the question, "Does the Creator exist?" Otherwise, how is it possible to search for contact and unification with something that does not exist?

A: Does the Creator exist? The Kabbalah is studied precisely in order to find out, meaning to feel and see the Creator. You, too, will find Him, notice Him, see and feel Him. Only then will you be able to say whether or not the Creator exists. It is only possible according to the measure of equivalence of form with the Creator. If you could feel the Creator right now, you'd be a Kabbalist.

DOES THE CREATOR HAVE A BODY?

Q: Prophets who can contact the Creator say that He doesn't have a body, or size or image. Thus, they shatter all the common concepts about the Creator. Yet, idioms such as "the hand of the Creator," "under the foot of the Creator" are abundant. How do you explain it?

A: Not only does the Creator not have a body, but we creatures, too, have no body. The creature is not a corporeal, physical, biological body, but pure desire. The desire to be filled with the Light of the Creator exists in each of us, and it is called a "soul."

The soul is divided into parts named after parts of the body, but there is no connection between those parts of the soul that are called by names of organs of our corporeal body. Kabbalists have found a way to express in the words of this world, concepts in the spiritual world. These could not otherwise be expressed except by making use of the language of the branches.

Kabbalists take words from this world and use them to depict spiritual powers, which are the roots of those objects.

PHARAOH AND THE CREATOR ARE EQUAL

Q: Who is the Creator really, if Pharaoh had priests capable of doing what Moses did and even more? If I possess the same powers and I have everything – then how can I know that your God is better?

A: There is only one power: the Creator. He influences man in a variety of ways, using contradicting forces. Thus He forms man, affecting him in various ways, generating various reactions. In these ways, we develop an attitude to the Light and to the darkness, and an understanding of giving and receiving and so on.

The created desire in its entirety, which is equal to the Creator's greatness, is called "Pharaoh." A born man receives only a small desire, and little by little discovers his Pharaoh, rising spiritually to the extent that he can overcome him.

The difference between the Creator and Pharaoh is not in the power, but in the goal. If it is "for myself," then it is Pharaoh; if it is for the Creator, then it is the end of correction.

WHAT SHOULD I REMEMBER?

Q: What is the most important thing that a person should keep in mind throughout one's life?

A: That there is only the Creator, and that there is no other. Read, "There is None Else But Him."

THE ORIGIN OF SIN

Q: Researchers found that genes determine character. Therefore, how can a person be blamed for one's sins; after all, they are committed without any freedom of choice?

A: One's character is predetermined by nature, and it certainly has no relevance to the essence of man. It is the same for animals; they all have their unique predetermined characteristics. Anyone who works with animals knows that they have just as complex a character as humans.

The character is fixed and cannot be changed. It can be less or more conspicuous, depending on the circumstances, but it never changes.

However, the origin of sin is not found in the character, but in the lack of knowledge of the truth. If one would know, one would not sin!

Generally speaking, "sin" does not exist in the corporeal meaning we ascribe to this term. Man always works by the situation he is in: if the Creator is concealed, man only performs actions that are dictated by his nature - that is the only thing that motivates him. However, if we could see the Creator, to the extent that we could see Him and His Power, we would correct our actions, meaning that we would act out of a new motivation. That is why the revelation of the Creator is the one remedy for sin. That remedy can only be attained through the wisdom of Kabbalah – the method that reveals the Creator to man, for only then can we see how to operate correctly.

Before the revelation of the Creator, all of man's actions are called sins and the punishment for them is the sensation that the act is negative and the recognition of the negativity of the act. Those sensations and recognitions help man exit his situation.

Cam we talk about freedom of choice with animals? And what about humans? If we knew all the components that comprise one's mood, character, health, environment, the way it works on each person, etc, we could accurately predict one's reactions in every situation. Where is our freedom of choice? Why does it exist, and why is it not sought in animals?

Freedom of choice becomes possible only if a person has the ability to work against one's own nature. For that, we must be completely freed from ourselves. We must be able to observe ourselves from outside ourselves, and from that perspective decide and execute.

What does it mean to be "outside one's own nature?" In spirituality, besides man, there is only the Creator. To the extent that we acquire the attributes of the Creator in addition to our own, we are freed from our own nature, and from the nature of the Creator.

Then, we become independent and free to choose whether to remain as we are, or to be like the Creator. There is no third possibility. From this we learn that in order to have freedom of choice a person must be a Kabbalist and attain the attributes of the Creator.

I OR HE

Q: What's greater than I?

A: Nothing, if that is how you feel it. But if you feel the Creator, your "I" disappears. There is nothing except these two.

LEARN FROM SIN

Q: Is there a correction for a person who has been a sinner all one's life?

A: There cannot be a correction if there is no sin. Therefore, each must go through a spiritual phase of a sinner, an evil. Only after that comes the corrected spiritual phase of "righteousness." I wish for you to first attain the phase of "complete evil" and then go through all the degrees of correction.

The progress and elevation to a higher essence is gradual and built through falling in each degree: first becoming "evil," and then correcting your sin and becoming "righteous," and so on. That means that it is impossible to advance without mistakes.

On the contrary, each progress incorporates within it a new sin, a new recognition of evil and its correction, and then again sin, recognition, and correction. There is no other way for us to learn, because man learns only through himself.

We must experience each mistake, be tormented by it and correct it by ourselves. From the moment we begin to study Kabbalah, we will have time to correct. We can do more in one lifetime of study than in hundreds of lifetimes if we do not study Kabbalah.

WAR IN THE SPIRITUAL WORLD

Q: You once mentioned a war or a battle in the spiritual world, but never explained what you meant. Can you explain it now?

A: The laws of nature and the entire creation are clearly divided between positive attributes (those of the Creator) and negative attributes (forces that object the Creator). The Creator arranged it this way on purpose.

The bad powers help to select the good powers. We need the bad in order to choose the good.

We seem to be between these two systems of good and bad. If we use them correctly, we will develop to the level of absolute equivalence with the Creator. We gradually absorb within us bad powers, study them, discern them as harmful, disqualify them and prefer the acquisition of the powers of the Creator to them.

These two systems - of good powers and bad powers - are not fixed, but change both synchronically and a synchronically, according to certain rules such as: weekday, holiday, *Shabbat* (Saturday) and many others.

In addition, the Creator cannot be imagined as frozen or as a dry law that doesn't change. Generally speaking, everything is in motion, and the attainment of that literally grips the soul. Thus, sometimes you see that the devil wins, and sometimes the good is triumphant.

THE RIGHTEOUS ARE THE FIRST TO FALL

Q: When a whole people degrade, sinking deeper into egoism, the first ones to fall are the best. Why is that so?

A: Because they live among us only to convey the Light of the Upper World to us, and if we don't deserve it, then there is no reason for their existence in this world. So they go.

WHEN THINGS CLOSE IN

Q: What do I do when everyone around me pushes me into the corner... What do they all want from me?

A: It is wonderful when you feel your present situation as intolerable, because now you are willing to leave it! The Creator Himself puts you in those circumstances because He wants to bring you closer to Him. All you have to do is shout, "What do you (the Creator) want from me?" And address that shout to Him, because He is the source of everything.

But in order to direct the cry correctly, to be aimed at the Source of life, at the Creator, and not at blind faith, you need Kabbalah. Otherwise your cry is like a cry in the desert. One feels this world just as a desert. It offers nothing to satisfy our petty desires.

Your cry should be accompanied by a longing for the Creator, and not just a desire for everything to be right again. This world was created precisely for pain! If you want out of that situation, get out of this world. That is what Kabbalah offers you. Read constantly, and you will get it.

SUICIDE

Q: Why is suicide considered so terrible in Judaism? If one sees no point in living, why cannot that person choose death? After all, it is known that man cannot tolerate pain, so how does suicide sit with the purpose of creation?

A: If a desperate person separates from life only in order to avoid pain, it shows that the most important thing for that person is not life, but pleasure! Without pleasure, life becomes a burden that any person would love to get rid of. It follows that we are nothing but a desire to enjoy.

One should always be aware that whatever the torments arise, they are given by the Creator for the purpose of correction, for advancement. Suicide is one's total refusal of the offer of the Creator to advance, a rejection of the means for correction.

We must remember that the only place for advancement is this world, and only in this body. That fact might sometimes be hard to accept, but it is nonetheless true.

OBTAIN THE PICTURE OF REALITY

Q: If we feel bad about ourselves and want to be rid of our troubles, can we begin to study Kabbalah?

A: We can never see with the senses of this world what is in store for us. We cannot see where our troubles come from; they only appear before us as a fact of life, as a reality that we are born into. In order to succeed in seeing how that picture is formed, we must study the wisdom of Kabbalah.

With this wisdom, we learn exactly how the picture of reality is built. There is no special wisdom that we need to acquire; mere interest is enough. But here is where our problem lies: we are not interested!

If we haven't sufficient interest in understanding what happens with us, the collective force of reality comes and acts upon us. It forces us, in order to escape the torments, to open the books, or at least take some interest in the fact that we belong to a collective reality through which we should influence this world.

THE SYSTEM OF THE UNIVERSE

Q: What do you mean when you say, "control nature?" Has man ever done that consciously?

A: Leading means knowing the system and knowing how to affect it in the desired way. By intervening with the system, we evoke movement and change in it. Naturally, we assume that it is always we who perform the actions, but the question is how well do we know the system we are trying to influence? Often enough, we want to do something a certain way, because we want to attain the best result for ourselves, but instead, we get a bad outcome. This is because we only know a part of the system, and we see that we did not calculate the outcome of our action correctly.

In fact, man always stands opposite the collective system of the universe, and deals solely with affecting it.

INSTINCT

Q: Why doesn't man receive this knowledge naturally, like animals?

A: It's true that animals know how to sustain themselves correctly and naturally. They receive this information as instincts, because they all exist in a certain and fixed level of development, as it says, "A day old calf is called an ox." This is all they need.

The developing man, however, does not receive the inborn attributes of animals naturally. That difference is so apparent, that it is amazing to see the difference between the correct and meaningful movements of a calf, and those of a human infant. You can read more about it in the essay: "The Essence of Religion and Its Purpose."

AFFECTING NATURE

Q: What is the connection between ordinary science and Kabbalah? Is the objective of that science to help man better utilize the corporeal laws of nature, as with physics and chemistry, or perhaps even discover new laws?

A: Neither! Kabbalah teaches man to aim his thoughts and desires correctly in order to best relate to his environment. It tells him how much his thoughts, and specifically the way he relates to what happens around him, affect more than his physical acts. The stronger the means and the force, the deeper they are hidden.

We begin to discover that nature feels how we relate to it. For example: a plant feels if a person next to him is good or bad. If an animal wants to eat it, the plant does not react because it was created for just that purpose, it is inherent in it. But if a person thinks negatively about it, although the plant might be treated well with water and care, it still withers.

Scientists have recently begun to see that the result of an accurate experiment depends on the person who performs that experiment, meaning, the results of a concrete physical experiment depend on who performs it. We all press the same button, but we will get different reactions.

Q: So what is the right way to affect nature?

A: An act by which a person can affect the world, apart from a physical act, is called an "aim." If we learn to think correctly, we can instruct nature to perform useful acts through our thoughts. But in order to know how to influence the world, the entire reality, there is a great deal to learn. And just as in any other science, not everyone is willing to study that much in order to succeed.

People are unhappy in our world, although they all want the opposite. But in order to be happy, one has to know what to do in order to feel good. We should know that our very existence affects our world in one way or another. Therefore, the more we do, the more we should learn about the effect of our actions.

Q: Will a person who has not yet learned how to influence the world correctly suffer during one's studies?

A: When we begin to study Kabbalah, our approach to nature changes entirely, because nature relates to man according to his aims and not his actions. Therefore the most important thing is to try and aim right.

AN ANSWER FOR A SCIENTIST

Q: I am a scientist. You say that Kabbalah is a science. Is it possible to come to the spiritual world using scientific tools?

A: It is an honor for me to discover the scientist in you, because the wisdom of Kabbalah is a science, and that makes it easier for us to understand each another. Anything that a person discovers in this world through scientific methods is not spiritual because, by definition, spiritual is something that one can feel only in spiritual attributes of giving, called a "screen." That screen is a vessel for the understanding of the other world, and that understanding can only be acquired through the wisdom of Kabbalah.

Our body has impressive secret abilities, sophisticated ones, but they are all corporeal! We can develop those abilities by training. Animals have those abilities as well; these are throughout our world, but we cannot actually feel them.

Only when we acquire a screen do we begin to feel spirituality, but those sensations cannot be conveyed to one who does not have a screen. I would not want you to regard my answer as mere excuses, as they don't actually answer the question, but regrettably, it is impossible to convey the idea in such a dialog (without knowledge of terms and definitions in Kabbalah), regardless of the education level of the listener.

IS MAN'S ORIGIN FROM THE APE?

Q: At what stage in creation did the ape evolve to become a man?

A: The Kabbalah calls the phenomenon you are referring to "*Malchut* of the upper becomes the *Keter* of the lower." This is a passage from one level of creation to the next, but not from one nature to the next. It is a mistake to think that it is possible to switch between levels of the screen in the same manner, or between the four parts of the will to receive in creation: still, vegetative, animate and speaking.

Such passages are impossible! The spiritual genes are eternal! That is why there cannot be a development from a rock to a plant, and from an ape to man. But it is certainly possible for a person to develop spiritually, meaning rise spiritually from a level of "still" to the level of "vegetative," to the level of "animate" and to the level of "speaking," called "man."

This only refers to the manners and the abilities to use the desire, and the implementation of the coarseness, referring to a change in quantity, but not in quality. The Creator created the collective desire in a strict formation, and man utilizes it gradually, according to the level of his adaptation to the screen.

Q: How is that metamorphosis done? If possible, please explain the feeling it creates in the heart, rather than how it is done technically.

A: A new situation cannot materialize before we begin to find the previous insufferable, and want wholeheartedly to replace it with a new one. In fact, there is a detachment between man's present and future situations. That detachment stems from the fact that an act "above reason," meaning against the mind, is needed to cross over. Just as a seed must rot completely in the ground before a new bud grows, so must our desires. The present desire must "rot" entirely and then we must reject it. Only then can we even contemplate the possibility of something new materializing.

Q: Is it true that our responses and character belong to our world and do not change when we become Kabbalists?

A: It's true. The Zohar says that the character is a collection of natural habits that relate to the "animate body," or corporeal desires that do not change, precisely because they belong to our world, and everything in our world is considered dead and unchanging compared to the spiritual world.

That is why in Kabbalah, birth is the reception of the first, minimal, screen, immediately after we cross the barrier from the sensation of this world only to the sensation of the spiritual world. This is called "the crossing of the Red Sea." That concludes the first phase of our development, after which we enter the spiritual world.

Q: Can a person become a Kabbalist and an altruist in spirituality, and yet remain an egoist in our world?

A: You contradict the definition of the term, "spirituality." Spirituality can be attained only by attributes that are adapted for spirituality. Such attributes as bestowal and giving are called "for the Creator." All other intentions, such as "for other people," "for mankind," etc. are actually "for myself." These aims come from the desire to be rewarded indirectly, or they stem from desires for control, power, respect, and so on.

Only if we attain complete detachment from our own nature, and that is possible only if our intentions are "for the Creator," do we become liberated from our desires. Then, we see that through the intent "for the Creator" we begin to love all mankind and actually wish it well.

We come to that precisely because we attain the attribute of the Creator. We begin to love people as much as the Creator does, but only from the attributes of the Creator, and not from within our own attributes.

Perhaps you have a different definition of egoism and spirituality. Perhaps spirituality is, for example, something fragile, noble, lyric and pleasant, detached from the world, and so on.

But all these definitions of spirituality are completely different from ours because they are felt and surface in another substance, different from our own nature. That is why they are sensed completely differently from the way we are accustomed to sensing them. Here is precisely where Kabbalah becomes the wisdom of the hidden.

Regrettably, only those who attain spirituality can understand Kabbalists. But that is precisely the source of the dispute between Kabbalists and other people, between the Creator and the corrupted creatures, and between those who object to Kabbalah and those who attain it. A Kabbalist's spirituality is different – while we value everything in our world as good or bad based on whether it favors us or not, to a Kabbalist the world seems completely different, because they are above it.

A Kabbalist sees everything that extends to our world, including the source of agony and the reasons for everything that happens in the world. He sees what disrupts the happiness and completeness of the world. You can read by yourself and see how sharply great Kabbalists write about the cause of humanity's suffering, which can be traced, in fact, to the lack of the desire to study Kabbalah. Only the study of the Kabbalah extends the Light that brings happiness and bliss to our world!

I recommend that you read the "Introduction to The Book of Zohar" by Baal HaSulam.

THE PASSING OF A KABBALIST

Q: When a Kabbalist dies, who takes his place?

A: You will not be able to understand the meaning of the connection of a Kabbalist with eternity, with the Creator, and with his dimension of existence, but I will try to answer you just the same. The Creator is the one who places the Kabbalist in this world, and when there is a need, He replaces him and puts another in his place. The Creator does not do this because the previous Kabbalist didn't do enough, or grew old, but because each soul performs only the task it is assigned, and cannot perform other tasks.

The Creator places the force and then replaces it, but does not change it, because each soul can perform only a specific assignment, and from there it moves on to another act, a more sublime one. You cannot see it, but Kabbalists can.

And what will become of my disciples? When I am gone, they will receive the necessary guidance from other leaders. As a whole, death in this world should be met with joy, not with grief, but that is another topic altogether.

Q: I am surprised to find that great Kabbalists can be victims of murder and persecution. I always thought that Kabbalah renders unlimited powers and control in the world, whereas now I think that Kabbalah has nothing to do with this world. Why is a Kabbalist who rises in the spiritual world not immune to the torments of this world?

A: You are beginning to think correctly! There is no connection between the corporeal (animate) world and the spiritual world, as we imagine it to be. The body of a Kabbalist is no different from that of any other person. There are no such links between the body and the soul, where the soul influences the protein, corporeal substance of the body. The Creator does not change the law of creation especially for Kabbalists, and all the physical, natural laws apply also to Kabbalists. The Kabbalist cannot fly in the air like a sorcerer, or perform other unnatural operations, and he can get sick, like any other person.

The world gets it wrong because it doesn't feel what a soul really is, and so it searches for spirituality in matter, or searches for connection with the matter. A Kabbalist need not do anything external, because spirituality is in a different dimension. The link with spirituality happens through inner contact. Nothing in our world is directly connected with the Upper One.

The characteristics of this world are no more than signs that there is no spirituality in them! Man finds spirituality through his soul, which is a part of the Upper World. If he feels it, he finds a link (spiritual coupling) with the Upper World, with the Creator.

IS ALL OF NATURE INSIDE ME?

Q: I was always amazed by the versatility of the types of birds, plants, fish, etc. Finally, in one of your lectures, I received understanding. It is all a result of the reciprocal penetration between the *Sefirot* and the cooperation between them in the spiritual world. My question is: Does man include everything within him, and how is it reflected in me? Is it in the versatility of my emotions?

A: What happens in one body, in one soul in the spiritual world, is divided into many bodies within our own. For example, inside man there is a Pharaoh, Moses, birds, fish, everything around us and anything we can possibly imagine is within us. They exist in us in the form of spiritual forces, desires.

Each of these inner attributes also exists outside us, as a separate body, a different species and a different attribute. In fact, it would be more correct to say that I am the one who divides, through my emotions, the force that surrounds me into bodies, attributes and various forces. This is what we call "our world." But the spiritual commandment of "Love thy neighbor as thyself," for example, is obvious, because both the other and I are one spiritual body.

That is why the good attitude of one particle of the collective body toward another is obvious. And so it is with all other things that are separated in our world. All our problems stem from the fact that we feel the various parts of the universe as disconnected and independent of one another. But since inside each person there are all the forces and the attributes of our world, it is said in the Torah that he who corrects himself, corrects the entire world.

It is more accurate to say that when we correct ourselves and begin to relate to the whole world as we do to our own body, we thus correct within and outside ourselves.

WHERE IS THE SOUL?

Q: If science can clone people, where then is the Creator, and where is the soul?

A: Kabbalists hid the wisdom of Kabbalah for hundreds of years, and in fact, they only permitted it in our time, when the souls are ripe enough for that study. In the past, many people wanted to misuse it, but there aren't such people anymore; people are too immersed in fulfilling their petty desires to take pleasure in such things.

The prohibition against disclosing such sublime knowledge in public was applied to other sciences, as well. Both Aristotle and Plato mention in their writings the prohibition against teaching and disclosing scientific knowledge for people to trade for money or other pleasures. They saw in the knowledge itself a power that was not to be conveyed to people for use against others. The few that were of high enough standards to keep this knowledge secret were accepted as disciples.

Unfortunately, that rule has been broken for hundreds of years, and we suffer the consequences. We did not gain a thing from our technological progress because it is not in accordance with our moral development. Therefore, all we get from it is pain.

You want to know where is the soul in a cloned person. Let me ask you this: Where is the soul in a non-cloned person? Where is it in a person who's had an implant operation? What is a soul, anyway? Does it exist in an ordinary person, in an animal, in a wild, savage person? How developed should the body be before it is worthy of being clothed with a soul? Why doesn't a cloned person deserve to have a soul?

The soul is a special sensory organ that I like to call "the sixth sense." In that sense, we feel the Upper World, something we cannot feel with our natural senses. It is the reality beyond this world. That sense can be developed only through the system of Kabbalah. It is called Kabbalah (Heb. "reception") because it is a system that enables one to receive a supreme sensation, attainment, and everything that is beyond ordinary sensation.

LIFE IS A GAME AND WE ARE ALL TOYS

Q: How do you relate to computerized robots and their reactions to humans?

A: Believe me, I don't have any! Of course, they are only mechanical toys without any egoistic desire. However, they can be programmed to simulate desires, and then they'll have demands according to the program. It will fool us if we wish to be fooled, and if the toys are sophisticated enough (which will certainly happen in the future), it will be hard to distinguish between programmed and natural behavior.

The point is that it makes no difference whether it's the object's own desire or it was installed in it. Watch how education and advertising imprint desires in us that become our own! What else, besides these acquired desires, do we have?

So the important thing is not how these toys are made, but one's attitude towards them and whether or not we project ourselves on them, thus animating them. These developments occur so that we will mature and realize who we are, and ultimately correct ourselves reaching the Creator's level.

HUMAN ROBOTS IN KABBALAH

Q: How can you compare a living human with a mechanism, programmed by nature? In this science of yours, everything boils down to a predetermined behavior. But then, even you speak about feelings, so where is the logic?

A: You probably read about modern programmable toys. Some of them even look like real animals! They are equipped with very sophisticated programs of behavior, including seemingly spontaneous acts, and can be self-taught. In time, the program develops and a person gets the impression that the toy grows up, recognizes its name, and needs to be fed (recharged) when it expresses a desire for food.

Since people attach feelings even to their computers, they start relating to such toys in a special way. They project their emotions on it. The toy recognizes only its owner's voice and obeys only its owners' commands. By tuning the toy to one's needs, a person acquires a better friend than a computer, and not worse than a dog or a human.

People are growing lonelier today. They are often single and childless. This is caused by the development of our egoism. Therefore, such robots will fill a growing part of our void. It all means that real feeling, as all of us will soon discover, is possible only toward the Source, the Creator.

We will feel toward everything else the way we do to those toys. But through the Creator, we humans will grasp the entire world and learn to love all people as we love the Creator.

Q: Will they clone people to harm mankind in the future?

A: You don't have to be a prophet to say the simple truth: everything we do before we see the entire system of creation is only to harm us. It is only the wisdom of Kabbalah that enables us to see it.

VEGETARIANISM

Q: I have recently stopped eating meat and fish because I think that living creatures (those with a nervous system and a sensation of pain) shouldn't have to suffer just to serve as my food. But Judaism permits eating fish and animals, and does not see anything negative in it (at least it does not forbid it). Is there a profound meaning to eating meat that is hidden from me?

A: The whole of nature, including all the Upper and lower worlds, was created for man, and rise along with man. That is why we must use everything for ourselves: extinguish pests, grow and slaughter domestic animals, sow and reap, cultivate the good and extinguish the bad. This is how nature becomes included within man. Then, if man rises, he raises nature along with himself.

The purpose of creation is that man will enjoy his surroundings in the most correct way. He cannot act as he pleases: isolation, denial of pleasure, fasting and restrictions are against the practice that the Torah preaches.

If you continue to study correctly, you will understand what you must do (although there is not a single word about vegetarianism). Such is the virtue of Kabbalah: the very study builds in the student the right outlook on life.

KEEPING FIT

Q: If someone does things to strengthen to become more fit for the spiritual work, do these acts become spiritual acts, if that is the purpose of keeping fit?

A: During the twelve years that I served as personal secretary and assistant to Rav Baruch Ashlag, I regularly went swimming with him, or on walks in the park or went with him to a gymnasium. He was between the ages of 75 and 86 at the time! He made great efforts to keep physically fit so that he could lead and accompany dozens of young students. Moreover, we took voice lessons so that he could talk for hours nonstop, without fatigue or hoarseness. Something that is needed for the spiritual work is indeed considered a part of it.

I hope that you can clearly discern your true motivation for your choice of physical activity, so as not to portray the desired as the actual. You can do what you like in your physical activities, but whatever you do, refrain from any kind of meditations and thoughts.

THE CORPOREAL DEVELOPMENT AND ITS PURPOSE

Q: Does one's physical activity reduce the quality of the spiritual Light?

A: There is no direct and solid correlation between the spiritual Lights and the corporeal bodies and forces, though it becomes clear only above the barrier. The essence of man's physical activity lies in the detailed analysis of one's approach toward the Creator and his connection with Him. The connection is only possible through corporeal dresses.

Even at the end of correction we will still need the ties and dresses of our world, in order to feel the perfection at its fullest.

FASHION AND DRESS - FROM A SHELL AND FROM HOLINESS

Q: What is the root of fashion, jewelry and cosmetics?

A: Like all our actions, man's desire to have an attractive appearance is dictated by the inner urge. Kabbalah states that all clothing is, in fact, corrections. This alludes to *Adam* who, upon sinning, discovered his nakedness and the lack of correction in his egoism, whereas previously he had felt no shame before the Creator, since his egoism had been concealed from him.

In our world, the urge to be covered stems from a different form of egoism, since it comes not from the feeling of the Creator but from our aspirations to power and fame. As a result, dress and jewelry do not come from the desire to be corrected, but contrary to that, as with all shells that aspire for the external and add more outside covers.

Those who seek the innermost revelation are ready to give up everything external, pay no heed to medals or citations, and can walk around in rags. It happens because they increasingly discover their inner depths. Hence, what was felt as the inner yesterday, becomes external and destined to be shed today.

ART AND SPIRITUALITY

Q: It is hard to believe that the greatest artists are ordinary people. I think they were "marked" by the Creator and have attained divine goodness.

A: There are many people in our world who have special talents – for better or for worse–beginning with the most wicked, scientists, musicians and politicians, and ending with philosophers, religious figures and scholars. However, that fact does not testify to their attainment of the Upper World. It can be proven easily that, despite their genius, they remain in their uncorrected desires, and in that area, they are often less evolved than ordinary people.

Those people have a mission of their own, which is sometimes corporeal and not spiritual. The fact that we feel their creation and achievements as something sublime stems from the fact that we can only appreciate that kind of human attainment and production in our uncorrected attributes.

A Kabbalist is a person, who, in all his senses, openly and vividly, lives in the palace of the Creator, just as we live in our world. He can study the acts of the Creator and move and thrive in spiritual worlds.

If you acquire spiritual attributes, you will feel the Creator and notice the change in your priorities. But before that happens, do not fear that as you grow, you will stop admiring art. Just like a child that has grown, you will learn and attain the meaning of true wholeness through your new spiritual attributes.

THE ATTITUDE OF KABBALAH TO ART IS RELATIVE

Q: How do you relate to art?

A: One's attitude towards everything in the world has to be constructive. Everything was designed for us as a basis for correction. Once, as Rabash and I were passing by a stadium, he pointed out that we should respect this place since it brings pleasure to a lot of people.

You may draw your own conclusions, but this was said by a man who had entered the Higher World. In regard to art, I can refer you to the words of the late Chief Rabbi of Israel, Rav A.Y. Kook. Unlike his opposition, he was a prominent Kabbalist, hence a Zionist, and approved of establishing the first Israeli Academy of Arts "Betzalel"

The Kabbalists' attitude to the world is somewhat different from that of the orthodox public; hence the saying, "The rule of Torah is opposite to the rule of the masses."

LITERATURE AND KABBALAH

Q: What do you think of literature in general, and books in particular?

A: All the books, except Kabbalah books, were written by people who perceive only our world. Therefore, they are either incorrect or at best, correct in a very narrow sense. It is not recommended to live by them, just as you cannot build man's education on imaginary disciplines.

Lately, we see how many rules, disciplines and suggestions come and go and how quickly they replace one another, because they lose their validity.

Kabbalists, on the other hand, write their books from their perception of the connection between the spiritual root in the Upper World and its physical branch in our material world. Therefore, Kabbalists cannot err in their advice.

It is a completely different matter that their advice is hard to follow, but this is the only advice that produces a happy result, starting from "how to choose the right spouse" to "how to feel another reality."

Because everything that happens in our world is a consequence of operations performed in the spiritual roots, we cannot understand what happens correctly as long as we remain within the boundaries of the knowledge of this world, since the majority of creation is out of reach for the researcher in our world.

How can you advise without seeing the root of events? The problem is that genuine Kabbalists are not interested in giving tips about improving our corporeal life; this is not their task. Their task is to raise mankind to the Upper World, reach spiritual attainment and live in the spiritual world in our own right.

I certainly do not favor burning books, although many mistakes and dead-ends can be avoided. Man naturally learns only by his own mistakes.

FANTASY

Q: What is fantasy in Kabbalah?

A: Fantasy is a combination of knowledge that stems from the inner Light and a certain speculation that stems from the surrounding Light. Only a Kabbalist can fantasize because pictures of creation can only be formed from a Light and a vessel.

KABBALISTIC MUSIC

Q: The songs of Rav Baruch Ashlag have really inspired me. Can you explain the place of this music in the study of Kabbalah?

A: The songs and the melodies are also Kabbalah, but in a different language--one we can all understand. It permeates us even when we still understand nothing, and begins to "act" on us from within. I recommend that you listen to the music more frequently, even in situations that are unsuitable, or when you are not in the mood for music. You can even listen to it while driving.

This music will accelerate the process of changing your situations and lead to faster advancement. We are interested in spreading knowledge about Kabbalah and allow you to copy it in any form you choose. Just, please do not alter it.

INFLUENCE

Q: How can people who did not receive such an outlook from childhood be taught to think the way that Kabbalah teaches?

A: We must simply and clearly explain to everybody that man should know how to conduct himself in this world. After all, everyone wants to be happy and fortunate, and they don't turn to scientists for that, but to fortune tellers and Kabbalists.

That means that people believe there is a way to influence our future and our luck. If you look at the instructions written in a Kabbalistic prayer book, you will understand what can be done with the upper *Sefirot*, which we can use to lead the world.

That system of affecting the world is called "aims." However, those are special aims, which can only be acquired through Kabbalah.

THERE IS NO COERCION IN SPIRITUALITY

Q: I read the Torah, the Zohar and your books. I feel that I'm beginning to understand that these books plant seeds in me. I want to extend that Light to others. But these days, people do not relate to Torah and Kabbalah. How can I persuade them that this is the only real Torah?

A: The Kabbalah strictly forbids any persuasion. It permits only demonstration, guiding and explaining. The extent depends on one's desire to listen. There cannot be any coercion; otherwise you are performing the most anti-spiritual act there is!

Coercion has no room in the spiritual world. Even in the corporeal world, the origin of coercion is not in purity, in holiness, but stems from the shells (Klipot).

Beginning students are overwhelmed with emotions and want to share those feelings with others and excite them, as well. But the expression of emotions must be passive only. It can be done by distributing flyers, books and tapes, not by coercion. Otherwise you will only harm yourself.

SHARING EMOTIONS

Q: Is it good to share what I feel with others?

A: You must not share your relationship with the Creator, or describe how you feel about Him with anyone. But that does not apply to the knowledge you have acquired in the wisdom of Kabbalah.

When you disclose your feelings before an uncorrected person (not the knowledge, which can be conveyed), you allow, even if against your will, that person's uncorrected thoughts and aims to penetrate your soul. The other person is not aware of it and wishes you no harm. However, his lack of correction is joined with yours and harms both of you.

CHILDREN LEARNING KABBALAH

Q: Is Kabbalah a way to look on life that does not require studying in school or in university?

A: You can begin to teach the wisdom of Kabbalah to little children at school because it relates to them, as well. They, too, live in both worlds, and they, too, like adults, still can't feel the wisdom, for it has not yet been revealed to them.

Great Kabbalists had hoped to come to teach the wisdom of Kabbalah at very early ages. For example, the GRA (Vilna Gaon) said that if it were possible, he would start teaching children as early as nine years of age, or even six, which Kabbalists regard as special ages.

NAMING CHILDREN

Q: Is it good to give a child a second name? Can this be done when a child is not a baby anymore?

A: Give one name of a deceased close relative of yours if the name had an upper root of a middle line from the Torah, or any other name from there. That is quite sufficient.

I don't advise giving children random names designating objects of nature and the like as is fashionable today. One's name should correspond the name of a sacred *Partzuf*.

FAMILY DISINTEGRATION

Q: What will the future connection between men and women be like, and what is the future of the family? Can Kabbalah and spiritual evolution improve it?

A: One of the consequences of human development is the disintegration of the basic family unit. Soon, the term "family" will cease to exist. As mankind evolves, the ego evolves, and we can no longer be together with others.

Once, there were towns and villages populated by large families. In the generations that followed, the basic family unit was still observed by man's animate nature, but today even that is gone. We are alone with ourselves; nothing ties people together anymore.

That is why families disintegrate. There is an ongoing process called "the recognition of evil," whereby ordinary, non-spiritual contact gives no reward. The basic family unit disintegrates because it is unreal.

However, genuine contact should start from within, and that is possible through only the Kabbalah. Kabbalah allows you to find your true mate, create the genuine spiritual contact with him/her. Because everything is included within it, everything else will be corrected on the human-biological level.

The amazing quality of Kabbalah lies in its ability to revive humanity. Everything we see in the development of our world comes from that "spiritual gene" in us. Humanity should come to a situation of complete fragmentation, after which a process of correction will begin.

If we want to picture the future family, it is possible only to the extent that a man, with his spiritual masculine gene, and a woman, with her feminine spiritual gene, bond in so well that they will be connected like the male and female in spirituality.

Those who have learned the wisdom of Kabbalah know that there is a *Partzuf* called ZON, which is *Zeir Anpin* and *Nukva*, the ideal image of man and woman in our world, the spiritual masculine and feminine origin. The same bond should exist between biological men and women. Otherwise, there will be no connection at all.

That is the situation our world is headed for. Therefore, the unification of all parts of creation, including the feminine and masculine, will take place as all other corrections, through the wisdom of Kabbalah.

Q: You mentioned that there were women prophets. What possibilities await those who come to the world in the body of a woman? Do they only perform assisting roles? Are there any exceptions?

A: This is a very delicate question. Are all the people, all nations and all types of personalities capable of attaining the purpose of creation? Or is there perhaps a difference between sexes, age, nationality, etc.?

The Creator formed His creation with still, vegetative, animate, and speaking. The lowest form is the still, and the speaking (Man) is the highest. Also, each degree is naturally divided by two genders.

Man is different from nature because he has a task he must perform: attaining the purpose of creation by himself. All other parts of creation depend on attaining their purpose of creation, their perfection and eternity, through man.

Thus, everyone ultimately attains the purpose of creation. People are also divided by degrees, and inner and outer parts. As I have previously mentioned, the feminine and masculine part of creation stand in contrast to one another.

Before our time, studying Kabbalah was the privilege of a chosen few. But from our time onwards – as was written by all the great Kabbalists of the past and as Rav Yehuda Ashlag, the greatest Kabbalist of our time, writes, everyone can study Kabbalah, including women. There are no exceptions.

Women usually aspire to play masculine parts, but how is the part of a woman expressed in creation? The difference between the sexes in this world stems from a difference in the spiritual root. Therefore, the method of the study and the application of the knowledge of the wisdom of Kabbalah are different between men and women. It is for this reason that they need to study separately.

SPIRITUAL DEVELOPMENT

Q: If the meaning of life lies in spiritual elevation, what is the meaning of the lives of billions of people who do not have even one of the 600,000 souls?

A: The meaning of life of every creation, even vermin, lies in nearing the ultimate state of perfection. But the attainment of that situation does not depend on the level of still, the vegetative and the animate of nature, only on that of the speaking level, man.

Everything has a soul. Every person on earth has an animate soul, similar to that of any other animal. In addition, everyone has an embryo of a spiritual soul. People can develop that spiritual soul and become eternal. Otherwise, they remain like any other beast.

The number 600,000 is the number of sparks of the collective soul, named "*Adam*," that broke into tiny pieces, and then continued to develop. Therefore, you needn't worry--there will be enough for everybody, because the most important thing is that there will be someone who will want to receive them and rise.

CORRECTION THROUGH ILLNESS

Q: Who are the mentally ill, and what is their part in the world?

A: Mental illness is one of the many corrections that souls must go through. However, not all souls experience that situation; in fact, there is a reciprocal connection among them. Some of them perform this correction for all other souls, just as in our world, a person has need of every trade, but doesn't have to learn all the trades in order to enjoy their benefits.

There is an extensive system of interrelations and reciprocal connections between people that stems from what occurs on the spiritual level. That phenomenon is called "the inclusion of the souls." It is a reciprocal bonding and connection between souls.

Q: What makes people who believe in the existence of the Creator relate to mentally ill people or autistics as "men of God," as if these are people through whom the Creator speaks? Is there any truth to that?

A: The mentally ill do not attain the Creator. They are miserable people who cannot even attain this world, much less the spiritual world. At some point we will find out why the Creator needs them and for what.

Some do, indeed, regard mentally ill people as spiritual, higher, as "men of God." Those who think that actually yearn for the "switching off" of the mind and skepticism; they actually want fanaticism.

But the path to the Creator does not go "below reason," without testing the validity of the path. In this way, there is no attainment of the Creator.

The path to the Creator is built in such a way that each lower degree cannot grasp the reason of the Upper Degree, or understand it. That is why we need the help of the Creator. Only when He is revealed, and one can feel Him, can he act against his mind, and thus rise.

When one negates one's present mind, one receives the next, higher spiritual degree, one that has greater wisdom. That is why Kabbalists go against the mind and above it, and thus become wiser, whereas those who go against the mind and below it grow more foolish and more extreme.

When a person rises, the mind grows. That is why Kabbalists respect the wiser, whereas the masses respect the ignorant. That is why all religions, which go below reason, bow their heads before torments, without exception. They are unaware that the Creator is the One who sends those torments precisely in order to get us going, and not for us to blindly obey and place the torment as a goal. That is how the forces of impurity speak in man, they call upon him to suffer and respect the situation.

Now you can see how different the divine Kabbalah is from man-made religions.

Q: What is insanity? Why are the insane punished?

A: Insanity is a hindrance to health to the point where one's self-awareness and freedom of choice are denied, and the person becomes totally captive by the will of nature – the Will of the Creator. No one has complete and objective freedom of choice, though we think that there are many degrees of freedom in the choice of every act. But if we examine the behavior of normal people from the side, it will not be clear to us in what way they are normal.

The correction in the existence of mentally ill people is that within the collective soul, *Malchut*, called "The First Man," there is a part that must be corrected in such unconscious states. That part of *Malchut* exists in all of us.

In our world, each trait of the collective soul appears in separate individuals, but in the collective soul of The First Man, all the parts merge and complement one another. That is why the mentally ill correct something for us, and we correct something for them.

Q: Is there a connection between one's illnesses and one's spiritual world?

A: Yes, certainly. One's illnesses, as with every other kind of suffering, is one of the ways to reveal our nothingness, and consequently push us toward the question, "Why am I alive, why do I suffer so, and how can I change it?"

The Upper Light that descends on us heals us from spiritual, as well as from physical, illnesses.

I cannot say, however, that Kabbalists are healthier than others. A Kabbalist who rises in the spiritual degrees begins to include within souls of other people in order to correct them, raise and thus save them. Then, the Kabbalist seemingly collects their illnesses. But that relates only to special Kabbalists.

FROM SUFFERING TO THE GOAL OF CREATION

Q: The vessel is forced to develop only by suffering and by the "point in the heart." Therefore, starting from Phase 1 and until the end of correction, everyone is destined to develop. Suffering is sent to achieve the purpose of creation, finally providing the vessel, which is by now anguished by thousands of descents into this pathetic little world, with a happy end – eternal and perfect delight. One may believe that, too, but please explain why is this not fanaticism.

A: If you believe that everything will happen as you pictured, then you are right. But suffering pushes us to understand, grow wiser, achieve, wish, love, aspire. The suffering we get is not for the pleasures, but is rather strictly selective, in order for us to sense the Creator and become like Him. The purpose is not to be beaten and then be given pleasure for relaxation.

Troubles force us to develop and arrive at the right suffering – the one that brings delight, pains of love felt as Light and pleasure, not fading but ever-growing. We are so tired of corporeal suffering and wish for nothing more than rest and relaxation. We cannot swallow something different and complete with our exhausted soul.

I understand you, but... save yourself! The question, "What is the meaning of life?" is the necessary precondition to the development of which I speak. Develop it correctly, don't let it quiet down and it will lead you to the Creator – and the answer to your question.

THE CONNECTION BETWEEN OUR WORLD AND THE SPIRITUAL WORLD

Q: There are many questions about the connection between the spiritual world and our own. You say different things in different places. If there is no connection between the two worlds, then how is spirituality connected with externally observed Mitzvot?

A: You are, indeed, quite right. Only the Mitzvot performed inside connect man with the Creator. However, observing Mitzvot externally also becomes a means for connection. Everything comes through the soul. A Mitzva is a spiritual act of giving to the Creator, which likens man to Him. External action has no such effect.

The Creator doesn't put on Tefillin made of animal skin. His action is the Light of Gar de Hochma in Gadlut of Zeir Anpin, which is defined as Tefillin. That is what one must attain.

WHAT IS YOUR SCHOOL OF JUDAISM?

Q: Which school of Judaism do you belong to?

A: I belong to the only ancient ever-existing school, which was started by Abraham, the very first Jew. Upon the destruction of the Temples, as a result of a spiritual downfall, various "schools" of Judaism emerged because, as Rav Yehuda Ashlag writes in his Introduction to The Study of the Ten *Sefirot* (item.1), an iron wall has been erected between us and the science of Kabbalah. Since then "schools," "currents," and "parties" emerged.

Kabbalists never related themselves to anything, since their course has always been directed towards uniting with the Creator, and there is only one method to achieve that goal – Kabbalah. We are not connected with any "schools" or "streams" that were formed to reflect a character, a way of life, or a relation to Zionism.

These worldly relations produce various communities, sects, parties, call it what you will. Since we do not take into account anything material, believing that man should confine himself to his aspirations to the Creator, there is no basis for defining any other "schools" beside the one we mentioned and to which we belong.

WHY ONLY JEWS AND MEN?

Q: The things you say are so right. But I cannot understand this nationalistic differentiation. Why are most of your disciples Jewish and why aren't there women among them (in the photo), if this science really brings truth?

A: Jews are obliged to correct themselves and pass this method on to the world. Non-Jews are not forbidden from it, if they like it, but it is only an obligation for the Jews.

Women receive the Light through men. The duty to correct themselves and the world lies solely on men. The wife's role is to help. Our world is designed in the likeness of the Upper World. Learn from it.

HOW CAN ONE FEEL RESPONSIBLE?

Q: Can one say that the Jewish people are the *Keter* of the nations of the world?

A: The Jews are the GE (*Galgalta ve Eynaim*) of the collective soul of *Adam*. They must be the first to receive the Torah. They must learn how to correct man's nature, and then, as Rav Elazar (the son of Rabbi Shimon, the author of Zohar) said, they must pass this knowledge of man's correction to the rest of the world.

Therefore, if the world is bad, the Jews are the ones to blame! So instead of "pride," let us feel "responsible."

POINTING AT THE PROBLEM

Q: Why do you believe you have the right to blame Israel for its misfortunes?

A: If we look at ourselves, we'll come to the conclusion that we are innocent. As the poetess asks in her poem, "Why does the whole world blame us...?" As Jews, we love to count those prominent representatives our people gave to the world and the things we contributed. Yet somehow, the world pays no attention to our credits; on the contrary, it hates us and regards us as superfluous.

This is clearly a paradox: we are the smallest nation, which has contributed to the world more than any other nation, without even a land of our own. We are still trying to prove to the world that we can be useful, that we are just like the others, hoping to get our own place in this world. But no one ever considered us to be like the others! Let us stop rationalizing the irrational. This is not about religion.

The solution to our eternal problem can only be found in the Higher World. That is why the Torah was given to us. If we use it correctly, to seek the Creator, then the world will live in peace.

There is no other way to stop terror. Our stubbornness will lead to disasters. I do not blame anyone. I am just pointing out the problem and its solution.

EXPECTING GOOD THINGS - WASTE OF TIME

Q: You write: "If we use it correctly, for seeking the Creator, then the world will live in peace. There is no other way to stop terror. Our stubbornness will lead to disasters."

This world deserves no peace, and we will probably fail to complete our "mission." So let us just wait for the end of the 6000 years and then the Creator Himself will correct everything, and peace and good will prevail. We don't have to wait too long... In regards to terror: we will have to fight the Arabs, the whole world, and the Creator... And you, Rav Laitman, stop being a local Cassandra (the role won't pay off), since it doesn't help anyone, only irritates!

A: You have just described how I look in the eyes of society; there is nothing I can do about it. It will only get worse, I know. Everyone will be against Kabbalah, curse it as they now curse the Jews. Then this circle will get smaller. So much the worse for the world, since it will receive even less Light. But perhaps there is a chance, because Kabbalah was given from Above!

THE CRITICAL MASS

Q: More and more people discover Kabbalah, including those who join in through your disciples. Nonetheless, Jewish affairs are only getting worse. I wonder what critical mass of people studying Kabbalah is needed to stabilize the world?

A: Up to 10% of our people.

WHY DID PROPHECIES STOP?

Q: In biblical times we had many prophets. Then at some point they disappeared. Why?

A: Because Rav Akiva's disciples' spiritual downfall from the level of "Love thy neighbor as thyself" caused the entire Jewish people to fall and led to the ruin of the Temple. From that moment on, the connection between the spiritual world and ours ceased to exist and, as Baal HaSulam says, "an iron wall has been erected between Israel and Kabbalah."

However, all this describes falling from the level of the 2nd Temple (*Mochin de Neshama*). Before that, there was the ruin of the 1st Temple, a fall from the level of *Mochin de Haya*. At that time, all prophets vanished, since a prophet's level is *Haya* if he says "I saw," and *Neshama* if he says, "I heard."

In addition, to be able to interpret a prophecy, one must be on a certain level of spiritual attainment. A prophet is not a fortune teller who tells you your future. Rather, he explains to you what essential corrections you can make, even without seeing them. And if you can't make any corrections, then a prophet will not appear. That is why they disappeared.

LIBERALISM

Q: Can one consider liberalism among Jews and non-Jews as a subconscious, and hence distorted, attempt to fulfill the principal commandment of the Torah – "Love thy neighbor..."?

A: Kabbalah sets the general principle of correct human behavior: whatever the circumstances, first establish a connection with the Creator, and then start researching the current event.

If all of our actions stem from the purpose of creation and we do not lie to ourselves, then they can be called adequate.

LOVE

Q: What is love?

A: Love is a consequence of equivalence of inner traits, meaning attributes. In Kabbalah there is only one law: the law of equivalence of form, attributes and desires. If two spiritual objects are equal in attributes, they unite. That does not mean that from two they have now become one, but that they *are* as one. Everything that happens to one, enriches the other, is immediately felt in him.

That mutual feeling, that two separate objects equally feel in the senses between them, that there is absolute equality between them (be it two people, or the Creator and a person) – is called "love." Love is the sensation of equivalence of spiritual attributes. Distancing in attributes and desires distances people from one another, even to the extent of hate.

The nearness of desires, thoughts and attributes (which is actually the same, because the attributes determine the thoughts and the desires), makes them draw near, love and understand one another.

Kabbalah states that the greatest pleasure in the world is the sensation of equivalence of form with the Creator.

A LIMITED ABILITY TO ACT

Q: Does the ability to lead the world necessarily demand purification?

A: Yes. To the extent that we purify, we merit the right to determine our own destiny. Otherwise, we might harm ourselves and others.

For example, nature doesn't give its powers to an infant, for fear he might harm himself. Nature determines that the powers that a person receives be proportional to one's knowledge of how to use them.

The rule that applies in the wisdom of Kabbalah is that a person will never be allowed into the spiritual world and perform a spiritual act that pertains to a greater measure of correction than one's own for fear of harming self or others. That is why the spiritual forces that correct a person place one at a certain degree, and only in that measure is one included in the system of the leadership. Hence, there is nothing to be afraid of, because man cannot do anything of his own choice, but only out of his degree.

THE COLLECTIVE

Q: Can I help others by the study of Kabbalah?

A: Certainly. All problems and troubles stem from a shortage of the Upper Light. The wisdom of Kabbalah gives us the ability to extend that Light and be filled with it. By that wisdom, we can attain the structure of the soul of man and all other souls and bond with them, because we are all parts of one collective soul called *Adam ha Rishon*, or the "First Man."

Therefore, to the extent of correction that a Kabbalist attains, he must correct his individual part that is in the other souls. And so we all must correct. That is why the *Mitzva* of "Love thy neighbor as thyself" is the basis for progress. No elevation is attained without bonding with other souls and the collective correction with them.

Therefore, a collective study in a group is the most practical measure for spiritual advancement.

CONDITIONAL FAMILY

Q: Which is more important, to study the wisdom of Kabbalah, or to be nice to others?

A: Treating others nicely is not real if it is not based on spiritual attainment. We see how in our days the family disappears, and in five or six years, the concept of the family will cease to exist. Even today in many families in Europe, husbands and wives work in different cities and meet only on weekends.

The will to receive (egoism) will grow to such an extent that even a tiny unit such as a family will no longer be able to exist. That disintegration will continue until humanity comes to realize that it must live by equivalence of form with the Upper System, and that this is the only way for it to ever be happy.

Only then will it understand and be able to actually do something good for itself. Then, too, the family will return to being a family, but only through the wisdom of Kabbalah.

Man and woman in our world are a consequence of the spiritual structure called *ZON de Atzilut* (*Zeir Anpin* and *Nukva* of the world of *Atzilut*). A family can exist correctly only if it functions similarly to that spiritual structure.

People will be so immersed in their own pains that they will resolve to build their relationships on spiritual foundations. Such a spiritual attainment will show man the perfection of it, in order for him to be able to do the same in our world. Until then, there will not be any affection among people.

THE COLLECTIVE EGOISM OF SOCIETY

Q: Is it not enough to not steal and curse and be kind to one another?

A: Certainly not. That is not what the Creator demands of us. The spiritual attributes that we must attain are quite different from what is considered as good in our society. We have created definitions for acceptable behavior, such as how not to annoy one another. We call it "a civilized society."

In truth, it is only a modified use of collective egoism and has nothing to do with the spiritual attributes that we must attain.

We have to develop within us spiritual attributes through the influence of the Upper Light, which shines and affects us only by studying the books of Kabbalah. This is because, when the author wrote them, he had attained a certain spiritual degree and was in contact with that Light.

A NEW APPROACH TO WELFARE

Q: The question," How can I help the world?" bothers me all the time. Should I use Kabbalah for that?

A: How do you intend to help the world? Even if you can help all the poor and homeless people on earth, what can you really influence? Mankind is beginning to understand that this is the wrong approach.

We cannot correct anything with a direct approach, but only through the Upper World. If we try to do something directly, we are manipulated from Above in such a way that we feel more pain and uselessness and misery.

The contradiction is that the harder we try to do good to our world, the worse it turns out to be. The world is now far from creating new Hitlers and concentration camps. Therefore, we have to stop trying to improve the world that way, because everything we do is turned to evil!

If we become ill, there are doctors to help us. The doctor has permission to cure. It is a spiritual law. We do have to build welfare systems in the world, but we cannot correct the world this way. The correction of the world can only be accomplished from Above, where it is controlled.

THE ONLY PEACE

Q: To what extent can the study of Kabbalah change the world around us?

A: It says: "Bear in mind, that everything has internality and externality. Israel, the descendants of Abraham, Isaac and Jacob, is generally considered the internality of the world, and the seventy nations are considered its externality. Within Israel also, there is internality, which are the wholehearted worshipers of the Lord, and externality, those who do not devote themselves entirely to the work of God. And among the nations of the world, as well, there are internal parts, which are the Righteous of the Nations, and external parts, which are the rude and the destructive among them." (Introduction to The Book of Zohar, item 66)

Is it not enough to observe the practical Mitzvot in order to change the situation? No, it is not enough! Especially today! Moreover, it is written in that Introduction that he who does not study Kabbalah makes the externality of the world overcome the internality. This means the worst, the most harmful and destructive among the nations of the world, rise over the internality of the nations of the world, the righteous nations, and bring worldwide wars and destruction.

It does not mean that everyone must immediately immerse themselves in systematic Kabbalah studies. It is enough if we overcome our inner inhibitions and begin to take an interest in this wisdom, in a very simple way.

Believe me, after only a few days, you will feel stronger and more confident than ever before. It is as though you connect to a new source of power that immediately begins to charge you. Your enemies will begin to feel your strength and will immediately withdraw. They will subconsciously understand that that is a power they cannot deal with.

But as long as we remain inactive, we bring about the negative forces that "land" on our heads in order to force us to act. All the destructors in the world raise their heads, aching to destroy Israel. We have already seen it happen, and today we are witnessing one of the peaks of that process.

We can change all that. Our personal situations, how the world relates to us, and the situation of the entire nation all depend on the study of the wisdom of Kabbalah. The power we derive from the study of the Kabbalah works on the people of Israel and the nations of the world alike. It will help everyone to begin to prefer internality to externality.

Spiritual and physical redemption are linked together. A spiritual redemption will bring the whole world to genuine happiness, freedom from terror, disease and death, and unity with the Upper Power.

DETAILED TABLE OF CONTENTS

OUR OTHER BOOKS

A Guide to the Hidden Wisdom of Kabbalah (with ten complete Kabbalah lessons): provides the reader with a solid foundation for understanding the role of Kabbalah in our world. The content was designed to allow individuals all over the world to begin traversing the initial stages of spiritual ascent toward the apprehension of the upper realms.

Attaining the Worlds Beyond: is a first step toward discovering the ultimate fulfillment of spiritual ascent in our lifetime. This book reaches out to all those who are searching for answers, who are seeking a logical and reliable way to understand the world's phenomena. This magnificent introduction to the wisdom of Kabbalah provides a new kind of awareness that enlightens the mind, invigorates the heart, and moves the reader to the depths of their soul.

The Science of Kabbalah: is the first in a series of texts that Rav Michael Laitman, Kabbalist and scientist, designed to introduce readers to the special language and terminology of the Kabbalah. Here, Rav Laitman reveals authentic Kabbalah in a manner that is both rational and mature. Readers are gradually led to an understanding of the logical design of the universe and the life whose home it is.

The Science of Kabbalah, a revolutionary work that is unmatched in its clarity, depth, and appeal to the intellect, will enable readers to approach the more technical works of Baal HaSulam (Rav Yehuda Ashlag), such as *Talmud Eser Sefirot* and *Zohar*.

Although scientists and philosophers will delight in its illumination, laymen will also enjoy the satisfying answers to the riddles of life that only authentic Kabbalah provides. Now, travel through the pages and prepare for an astonishing journey into the Upper Worlds.

Introduction to the Book of Zohar: is the second in a series written by Kabbalist and scientist Rav Michael Laitman, which will prepare readers to understand the hidden message of "*The Zohar*". Among the many helpful topics dealt with in this companion text to *The Science of Kabbalah*, readers are introduced to the "language of roots and branches", without which the stories in *The Zohar* are mere fable and legend. *Introduction to the Book of Zohar* will certainly furnish readers with the necessary tools to understand authentic Kabbalah as it was originally meant to be, as a means to attain the Upper Worlds.

Kabbalah for Beginners: By reading this book you will be able to take your first step in understanding the roots of human behaviour and the laws of nature. The contents present the essential principals of the Kabbalistic approach and describe the wisdom of Kabbalah and the way it works. *Kabbalah for Beginners* is intended for those searching for a sensible and reliable method of studying the phenomenon of this world for those seeking to understand the reason for suffering and pleasure, for those seeking answers to the major questions in life. Kabbalah is an accurate method to investigate and define man's position in the universe. The wisdom of Kabbalah tells us why man exists, why he is born, why he lives, what the purpose of his life is, where he comes from, and where he is going after he completes his life in this world.

The Path of Kabbalah: "Thou shalt not make unto thee a graven image, nor any manner of likeness" (Exodus 20:3). This commandment from the Bible is the basis of the Kabbalistic wisdom, for Kabbalists know that the only true reality is that of His Essence, the Upper Force. When we accept this concept, we can become truly open to the prospect of freedom for every person, for every nation, and for the entire world.

While the structure of reality and how we perceive it are at the surface of this book, it is the underlying story of the human soul that truly captivates us: this is about you and me, and all of us. It is about the way we were, the way we are, and the way we will be.

ABOUT BNEI BARUCH

B nei Baruch is a non-profit group centered in Israel that is spreading the wisdom of Kabbalah to accelerate the spirituality of mankind. Kabbalist Michael Laitman PhD, who was the disciple and personal assistant to Kabbalist, Rav Baruch Ashlag, the son of Kabbalist Rav Yehuda Ashlag (author of the Sulam Commentary on the Zohar), follows in the footsteps of his mentor in guiding the group.

Rav Laitman's scientific method provides individuals of all faiths, religions and cultures the precise tools necessary for embarking on a highly efficient path of self-discovery and spiritual ascent. The focus is primarily on inner processes that individuals undergo at their own pace. Bnei Baruch welcomes people of all ages and lifestyles to engage in this rewarding process.

In recent years, an awakening of a massive worldwide quest for the answers to life's questions has been underway. Society has lost its ability to see reality for what it is and in its place easily formed viewpoints and opinions have appeared.

Bnei Baruch reaches out to all those who seek awareness beyond the standard view. It offers practical guidance and a reliable method for understanding the world's phenomena. The group's unique method not only helps overcome the trials and tribulations of everyday life, but initiates a process in which individuals extend themselves beyond the standard boundaries and limitations of today's world.

Kabbalist Rav Yehuda Ashlag left a study method for this generation, which essentially 'trains' individuals to behave as if they have already achieved the perfection of the Upper Worlds, here in our world.

In the words of Rav Yehuda Ashlag, *"This method is a practical way to apprehend the Upper World and the source of our existence while still living in this world. A Kabbalist is a researcher who studies his nature using this proven, time-tested and accurate method. Through this method, one attains perfection, and takes control over one's life. In this way, one realizes one's true purpose in life. Just as a person cannot function properly in this world having no knowledge of it, so also one's soul cannot function properly in the Upper World having no knowledge of it. The wisdom of Kabbalah provides this knowledge."*

The goal-orientated nature of these studies enables a person to apply this knowledge on both an individual and collective basis in order to enhance and promote the spirituality of humankind, and indeed the entire world.

HOW TO CONTACT BNEI BARUCH

Bnei Baruch
1057 Steeles Avenue West, Suite 532
Toronto, ON, M2R 3X1
Canada

E-mail: info@kabbalah.info

Web site: www.kabbalah.info

Toll free in Canada and USA:
1-866-LAITMAN
Fax: 1-905 886 9697